Ezekiel

Kieth Bernard Kuschel

SAINT LOUIS

The interior illustrations were originally executed by James Tissot (1836–1902). The illustration on page 216 is by Gustave Doré (1832–83). All other maps and illustrations were done by Northwestern Publishing House artist Matthew Schaser.

Commentary and pictures are reprinted from EZEKIEL (The People's Bible Series), Copyright © 1986 by Northwestern Publishing House. Used by permission.

Scripture is taken from The Holy Bible: NEW INTERNATIONAL VERSION®. Copyright © 1973, 1978, 1984 by the International Bible Society. Used by permission of Zondervan Publishing House. All rights reserved.

The "NIV" and "New International Version" trademarks are registered in the United States Patent and Trademark Office by International Bible Society. Use of either trademark requires the permission of International Bible Society.

1 2 3 4 5 6 7 8 9 10   03 02 01 00 99 98 97 96 95 94

CONTENTS

ILLUSTRATIONS

Ezekiel

PREFACE

The People's Bible Commentary is just what the name implies—a Bible and commentary for the people. It includes the complete text of the Holy Scriptures in the popular New International Version. The commentary following the Scripture sections contains personal applications as well as historical background and explanations of the text.

The authors of *The People's Bible Commentary* are men of scholarship and practical insight, gained from years of experience in the teaching and preaching ministries. They have tried to avoid the technical jargon which limits so many commentary series to professional Bible scholars.

The most important feature of these books is that they are Christ-centered. Speaking of the Old Testament Scriptures, Jesus himself declared, "These are the Scriptures that testify about me" (John 5:39). Each volume of *The People's Bible Commentary* directs our attention to Jesus Christ. He is the center of the entire Bible. He is our only Savior.

We dedicate these volumes to the glory of God and to the good of his people.

The Publishers

INTRODUCTION

Historical Background

This book of prophecy can be precisely dated, not just as a whole, but also in its parts, because the prophet has dated fourteen events for us. On the basis of this chronology we can get a very good idea of the events which were occurring in the world of Ezekiel.

It had been one hundred years since the Assyrians had carried off the northern ten tribes of Israel and destroyed the capital city of Samaria. The date for this event was 722 B.C. In 612 B.C. the Babylonians had taken over the role of world dominator from the Assyrians. In 605 Nebuchadnezzar (ruled 604-562) had given legitimacy to Babylon's claim of being world ruler by defeating the only possible opposition, Pharaoh Necho of Egypt. The decisive battle took place at Carchemish. Since this battleground was in Syria, Nebuchadnezzar used the opportunity to seize control of the entire area, including the kingdom of Judah. On this occasion he took some captives, including Daniel, from Jerusalem back to Babylonia with him.

The year 597 B.C. saw Nebuchadnezzar return to Judah to put down a rebellion in Jerusalem. This was one of many attempts by the "postage stamp" nation of Judah to throw off the domination of the world powers. Often these attempts were made by trying to play off Egypt against the northern power. The result was usually the same — the dominant world power moved in and crushed Judah. This time Nebuchadnezzar took Jehoiachin, the king of Judah, and the upper crust of society back with him to Babylon to

1

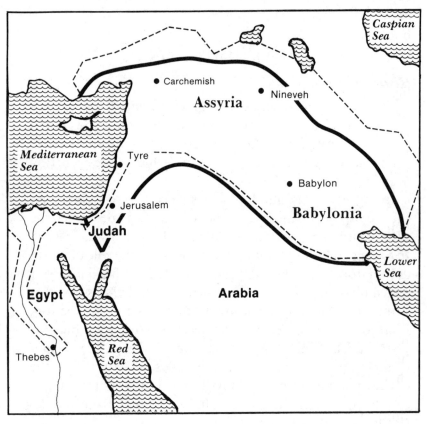

Assyrian empire
11th - 7th century B.C. ----------

Babylonian empire
6th - 5th century B.C. ━━━━━

Assyrian and Babylonian empires

try to insure no future recurrence of such a rebellion. This capture of Jehoiachin is the reference point in Ezekiel 1:2 and in the other chronological references throughout the book. Ezekiel was included in the group of people who were taken captive in 597.

Later King Zedekiah of Judah attempted another rebellion. This time the Babylonians destroyed all of Jerusalem, including the temple. The rest of the people of Judah were carried off into captivity (586). The work and prophecies of Ezekiel, then, were all in the context of exile, from the fifth year (1:2) to the twenty-seventh year (29:17) of the exile of Jehoiachin.

A look at a map of the Assyrian and Babylonian empires helps in understanding this history.

Ezekiel's Mission

Since Ezekiel was an exile, all of his work was among the exiles. Yet, his work can be divided into two distinct segments because of the tremendous event which occurred, not in Babylonia, but back home in Judah. Previous to 586 B.C., his major role was to try to dispel the false hopes of the exiles that the temple and the city of Jerusalem would be preserved from destruction. His message was a prophecy of destruction. The meaning behind the message was punishment, punishment from God for their rebellion against him. Ezekiel's purpose was to warn in order to achieve repentance. He wanted to warn the exiles in order to prevent a similar rebellion against the Lord while in Babylonia. Ezekiel wanted to teach them to obey the Lord and submit to his will, even while he was displaying his anger and allowing the destruction of the temple and the city of Jerusalem.

After the fall of Jerusalem, when the tendency of the exiles was to despair over their future as a particular nation,

3

Ezekiel's role changed. He became a messenger of destruction, not a destruction impending against God's people, but against the other nations who had been enemies of Judah and of the Lord. The meaning behind this message was deliverance, deliverance from exile because of the changing roles of the other nations. Ezekiel's purpose now was consolation and encouragement. He wanted to console the people and encourage their faith so they wouldn't turn their backs on the temple and their homeland, even though the temple had been destroyed and their land had been devastated.

Most of the exiles had become quite comfortable in Babylon. They had started businesses, were prospering, and generally had a good situation for their health and education. It would have been very easy for them to totally repress any thoughts of the temple and their homeland, especially after both were destroyed. It was Ezekiel's work, which for a period of twenty-two years maintained a nucleus of people who still wanted to serve the Lord in their homeland and in a restored temple. It was this work which helped to produce people who later under Ezra and Nehemiah were willing to return to Judah and Jerusalem.

We shall take a more detailed look at Ezekiel's life in the discussion of Ezekiel 1:1-3.

Literary Style

The book of Ezekiel is a mixture of poetic, artistic description and detailed prose. The writer, too, is a mixture of personalities. Sometimes he is a stern preacher of punishment to the impenitent. Sometimes a gentle confessor and counselor to a despairing people.

The outstanding characteristic of Ezekiel's prophecy is the living pictures it paints. Points are made not with direct statements, but with symbolic actions. Many of these actions were not actually carried out in Ezekiel's real-life existence, but are only described in his vision. In other biblical literature we find parallels in Jesus' parables or in the vision granted to Peter in Acts 10. Many of the symbols, actions and pictures used by Ezekiel appear again in the New Testament book of Revelation.

Theme and Outline

The book's theme is summarized in a phrase used several times in Ezekiel (for example, 6:7): "*You will know that I am the LORD.*" Through his powerful judgments and tender mercies God makes himself known.

The book of Ezekiel falls into three major divisions with numerous details under those divisions:

> I. Threats of Judgment on God's Impenitent People (1-24)
>   A. God Sends a Spokesman to His Rebellious People (1-3)
>   B. The Siege of Jerusalem Symbolized (4,5)
>   C. Discussion of Cause and Effect (6,7)
>   D. The Glory of the Lord Departs (8-11)
>   E. Predictions of Captivity (12-19)
>   F. Warnings Prior to the Fall of the City (20-24)
> II. Prophecies Against Hostile Nations (25-32)
>   A. A Prophecy Against Ammon (25:1-7)
>   B. A Prophecy Against Moab (25:8-11)
>   C. A Prophecy Against Edom (25:12-14)
>   D. A Prophecy Against Philistia (25:15-17)
>   E. A Prophecy Against Tyre (26-28:19)
>   F. A Prophecy Against Sidon (28:20-26)
>   G. A Prophecy Against Egypt (29-32)

PART I

THREATS OF JUDGMENT ON GOD'S IMPENITENT PEOPLE
EZEKIEL 1 — 24

God Sends a Spokesman to His Rebellious People
The Living Creatures and the Glory of the Lord

1 **In the thirtieth year, in the fourth month on the fifth day, while I was among the exiles by the Kebar River, the heavens were opened and I saw visions of God.**

²On the fifth of the month — it was the fifth year of the exile of King Jehoiachin — ³the word of the LORD came to Ezekiel the priest, the son of Buzi, by the Kebar River in the land of the Babylonians. There the hand of the LORD was upon him.

Since the reference to the thirtieth year has no cross reference to the other dates in the book, it is most likely a statement of the age of Ezekiel at this time. According to Numbers 4:3, thirty was the age at which Israel's priests began their duties. It happens to correspond to the age Jesus began his public ministry and is close to the age pastors of our church body finish their seminary training. Perhaps the thought passed through Ezekiel's mind: "If I were back in Jerusalem, I'd be starting my life's work as a priest." But he was in exile a thousand miles from Jerusalem, and God had a different commission for him.

The Babylonian King Nebuchadnezzar first attempted to stop recurrences of rebellion by taking the leaders of the society back to Babylon with him. The Babylonians realized the priests were leaders in Judah's society. Because Ezekiel was a priest, he was taken captive with the group in 597 B.C. Ordinarily Ezekiel would have been in Jerusalem beginning his life's work of carrying out priestly functions at the temple. Now, because he had been deported from his homeland, he had been picked by the Lord to be a spokesman of the word of the Lord — in other words, a prophet.

During his exile Ezekiel lived at Tel Abib (3:15) near the Kebar River. He possibly owned the house which became a gathering center for the exiled elders (8:1; 20:1). Ezekiel was married, but his wife died (24:15ff). His work lasted twenty-two years, from 592 to 570 B.C. The Kebar River was a major irrigation canal, a fact which indicates that some of the exiles were engaged in agriculture.

Although God doesn't actually have a hand, "the hand of the LORD was upon him" shows the Lord was giving Ezekiel the power to do things which on his own he couldn't do, in this case seeing and proclaiming heavenly truths.

Three phrases in this section all emphasize the same thing: Ezekiel did not take the initiative. He did not seek some special visions or receive them as a result of some self-induced altered state of mind. Rather, the Lord took the initiative: "the heavens were opened" by the Lord; "the Word of the LORD came"; "the hand of the LORD" acted. This is always true. Revelations from God are not products of our own efforts, activity, meditation, investigation, or self-instruction. It is not a person's special talents, or charisma, or scholarship which makes a person a spokesman for God.

The "LORD" is said to have called Ezekiel. The divine name, spelled with all capitals in most translations, is God's

Old Testament Savior name. This name describes him as the God of the covenant, the God who bound himself by solemn contract to ancient Israel. It was this God of free and faithful grace who revealed himself in writing. It is he who gives his Word to men. He opens the heavens for people, if he chooses to. And he places his hand upon people when he wants them to do something for him.

This chapter gives us an opportunity to practice the Lutheran principle of letting Scripture interpret itself. In order to do this, we must go to verse 28 before we approach the rest of the chapter. After the intriguing description of his vision, Ezekiel himself tells us what it was a vision of — the appearance of the likeness of the glory of the Lord. All the details of the vision must be understood in light of the explanation given to us by the prophet himself.

⁴I looked, and I saw a windstorm coming out of the north — an immense cloud with flashing lightning and surrounded by brilliant light.

Wind, cloud, lightning and bright light had been parts of visions of and revelations from the Lord in the past. God had appeared to Israel on Sinai in a dense cloud, with thunder and lightning. He had led Israel through the wilderness by means of a pillar of fire and cloud. Moses had even described the Lord as a "consuming fire" (Deuteronomy 4:24).

It was from the north that the Babylonians — and before them the Assyrians — had invaded the land of Israel. They had brought destruction on Jerusalem and would continue to do so for a time. Here, however, we have the statement by God "I am behind it all." The brilliant glow of God's brightness indicates God was working through the cloud of fiery judgment from the north. The north was not the home of the gods of Babylon, who didn't really exist. The Lord, who is everywhere and rules everything, was at home in the north also. The fiery storm cloud said, "The Lord controlled nature, not Marduk, the lord of the storms, or Shamash, the god of light." The Lord is in control of all things at all times. He is behind the storm clouds of life to discipline, direct and strengthen us.

The center of the fire looked like glowing metal, 5and in the fire was what looked like four living creatures. In appearance their form was that of a man, 6but each of them had four faces and four wings. 7Their legs were straight; their feet were like those of a calf and gleamed like burnished bronze. 8Under their wings on their four sides they had the hands of a man. All four of them had faces and wings, 9and their wings touched one another. Each one went straight ahead; they did not turn as they moved.

10Their faces looked like this: Each of the four had the face of a man, and on the right side each had the face of a lion, and on the left the face of an ox; each also had the face of an eagle. 11Such were their faces. Their wings were spread out upward; each had two wings, one touching the wing of another creature on either side, and two wings covering its body. 12Each one went straight ahead. Wherever the spirit would go, they would go, without turning as they went. 13The appearance of the living creatures was like burning coals of fire or like torches. Fire moved back and forth among the creatures; it was bright, and lightning flashed out of it. 14The creatures sped back and forth like flashes of lightning.

Later in the book (10:15) Ezekiel will tell us what these four living creatures were. They were cherubim. The next question of course is, "What are cherubim?" Cherubim are mentioned for the first time in Scripture when God drove Adam and Eve out of the Garden of Eden (Genesis 3:24). Those particular cherubim were to keep humans away from the tree of life. At the time of Moses, two golden representations of cherubim were attached to the mercy seat, the cover above the ark of the covenant in the Old Testament tabernacle (Exodus 25:17-19). Since the mercy seat represented the presence of God, they were located there to guard the presence of the Lord. Representations of cherubim were also woven or embroidered on the inner curtain and the veil of the tabernacle. Years later, when King Solomon built the temple in Jerusalem, he placed two representations of cherubim, made of olive wood and overlaid with gold, in the Most Holy Place of the temple, the symbolic location of God's presence among his people. The cherubim, then, are celestial, spiritual beings belonging to the general classification of creatures which we call angels. The Bible mentions them most often in connection with God's holiness, the characteristic which separates him from sinful men.

Like the rest of the angels, cherubim are messengers of the Lord who do his will. Their four faces, each looking in a different direction, remind us that God rules over all four corners of the world. At times God acts independently and at times through his angels. The wings remind us the Lord's messengers move swiftly to where they are to carry out God's will. Combine this thought with the meaning of the four faces and we learn that no matter where the Lord wants to exercise his rule, he can do so immediately, also through his cherubim.

Of course, the four corners of the world included Babylon and the Jewish exiles. Part human and part animal creatures did not determine the course of human events, as the Babylonian religion insisted. Whatever happens to individuals and nations is the result of the Lord's directions, often implemented through his angelic messengers, the cherubim.

These creatures are able to carry out God's will perfectly because they have the combined intelligence and power of representatives of four different classes of living creatures: man, wild animal (lion), domestic animal (calf, ox), and flying animal (eagle). They have the capacity for service of a calf or ox, straining stiff-legged under a burden with hardened, bronzelike hoofs firmly dug into the soil. They have the manual and intellectual talents of man. They have the regal strength of a lion, and the independence, swiftness and eyesight of an eagle. The cherubim go straight ahead with undivided attention. They aren't distracted to this side or that as they carry out God's will. Since they exist for the sole purpose of serving God, their spirits always lead them in the direction God has prescribed.

The burning coals, torches, fire and lightning remind us of God's holiness and purity, just as they had on Mt. Sinai (Exodus 19). The movement of the fire points to the ceaseless activity of the Lord.

[15]As I looked at the living creatures, I saw a wheel on the ground beside each creature with its four faces. [16]This was the appearance and structure of the wheels: They sparkled like chrysolite, and all four looked alike. Each appeared to be made like a wheel intersecting a wheel. [17]As they moved, they would go in any one of the four directions the creatures faced; the wheels did not turn about as the creatures went. [18]Their rims were high and awesome, and all four rims were full of eyes all around.

[19]When the living creatures moved, the wheels beside them moved; and when the living creatures rose from the ground, the wheels also rose. [20]Wherever the spirit would go, they would go, and the wheels would rise along with them, because the spirit of the living creatures was in the wheels. [21]When the creatures moved, they also moved; when the creatures stood still, they also stood still; and when the creatures rose from the ground, the wheels rose along with them, because the spirit of the living creatures was in the wheels.

Chrysolite is a crystalline substance that refracts light, and so would make a good medium to make something look

The living creature

13

sparkling. Each wheel seems to have had the appearance of a gyroscope, making it possible to move in all four directions without turning. Therefore the cherubim must be able to move to every possible corner of God's creation easily and swiftly. The eyes on the rims give the angelic transportation the ability to see and avoid all obstacles which might ruin their missions as they carry out the Lord's commands. The same energy or spirit that motivated the living creatures also propelled the wheels (verses 19-21). The motion of both is governed by the Lord. The cherubim did not go off on missions and in directions incompatible with God's will.

The wheeled structure is not defined in Ezekiel's vision. Some have thought it to be a battle chariot, opposing Nebuchadnezzar's military might. Others have defined it as a sort of chariot throne, much like Daniel saw in his vision (Daniel 7:9).

22Spread out above the heads of the living creatures was what looked like an expanse, sparkling like ice, and awesome. 23Under the expanse their wings were stretched out one toward the other, and each had two wings covering its body. 24When the creatures moved, I heard the sound of their wings, like the roar of rushing waters, like the voice of the Almighty, like the tumult of an army. When they stood still, they lowered their wings.

On the next level, above these most startling and majestic creatures was the Lord himself, separated from the cherubim by a sparkling, icy, awesome expanse. The audiovisual effects add to the awe which comes to us when we think about the Lord.

25Then there came a voice from above the expanse over their heads as they stood with lowered wings. 26Above the expanse over their heads was what looked like a throne of sapphire, and high above on the throne was a figure like that of a man. 27I saw that

from what appeared to be his waist up he looked like glowing metal, as if full of fire, and that from there down he looked like fire; and brilliant light surrounded him. [28]Like the appearance of a rainbow in the clouds on a rainy day, so was radiance around him.

This was the appearance of the likeness of the glory of the LORD. When I saw it, I fell facedown, and I heard the voice of one speaking.

The piercing purity of the Lord's holiness and the cleansing fire of his judgment are again obvious in this view of the Lord (27). And yet, the radiance around him was made up of the soft glow of his grace as it had been enunciated to Noah after the flood by the rainbow (28) — the Lord's blessings would unfailingly be dispersed throughout all generations. National disaster had come from the north. The Lord's holiness, his purity, his lightning-flashing anger was behind it. And yet, it did not overwhelm the glow of his gracious promises. His threats and even his implementation of discipline never remove or even diminish the predominance of his gracious forgiveness.

This vision was not intended to restrict God to a set tangible form. Ezekiel made sure we are aware of this by heaping up phrases: "like that of", "looked like", "what appeared to be", "appearance of the likeness of". This kind of language gives us the right to exercise the freedom to conclude that "these visual effects are symbolic of the different characteristics we know God possesses," as we have just done in the foregoing. The section closes with an expected reaction: Ezekiel fell down in awe. Then a voice was heard next. The verbal comment is needed to explain why God had appeared to him at such a time and in such a way.

General Comments on Chapter 1

All the repetition in the vision recorded for us in this chapter seems to indicate Ezekiel was having a difficult time

15

fully understanding all the details of what he had seen and heard. He compared what God had shown him with things we have seen, giving us at least a small grasp of what he saw by the power of the Lord. Sometimes Ezekiel seems to go back, take a second look and try a second time to describe what he saw so we might have a better chance to see it through his eyes.

This was not just a fireworks display put on by the Lord for Ezekiel to enjoy. It was something the Lord did to equip Ezekiel for his ministry: to strengthen him to preach judgment and to make him confident enough to point to God's promises. The reappearance of elements of this vision at later crucial points in his prophetic ministry indicates how practical the vision was for Ezekiel and for his ministry.

The difficult circumstances under which Ezekiel lived and worked demanded such a source of strength and confidence. After all, it seemed the God of Judah had just been defeated by Nebuchadnezzar's god, Marduk. Jerusalem and its temple would soon be destroyed. At that point Babylon would claim Marduk was in control of the universe, and the discouraged captives from Judah might be tempted to believe such a claim. They would easily doubt God's promise to protect his people. Ezekiel's vision was to arouse a potentially dispirited prophet to carry out his work among a potentially dispirited people.

In the vision the Lord was saying, "I can appear in the heartland of the conqueror's power. I can give you a display showing I am in control. I have power over animate and inanimate creation. I have the power to keep my promises and to carry out my threats."

Details in the vision familiar to those who knew what was in the temple at Jerusalem demonstrated this was the same God whom they had worshiped in Jerusalem and in the temple. The Old Testament does not give us an interpretation of each detail of the unusual vision God showed Ezekiel, a fact which led John Calvin to say: "I don't understand this vision." Even though we cannot understand God completely, even though the hints and traces he does give us of himself won't be made complete until later — "when he appears . . . we shall see him as he is" (1 John 3:2). Yet the vision does picture clearly God's might and mercy as extending over all the world. No matter where his people are or under what difficult conditions they are living, he is always able to deliver them and to let them enjoy the beauty of his grace.

Ezekiel's glorious vision in the opening chapter of his prophecy is one of many Old Testament references to the glory of the LORD. At times God would appear in majestic and spectacular ways. He appeared in a burning bush to Moses (Exodus 3); at the dedication of the temple of Solomon God appeared in a cloud which filled the temple — "the glory of the LORD filled his temple" (1 Kings 8:10,11). Such appearances assured God's people of his gracious presence. On other occasions the glory of the LORD was an awesome threat of judgment against God's enemies. Numbers 16:42 relates that "when the assembly gathered in opposition to Moses and Aaron . . . the glory of the LORD appeared" and sent a plague among the people. For Ezekiel the glory of the LORD was a comfort as the prophet struggled to bring God's word to exiles living in a strange land far from their home.

Ezekiel's Call

2 He said to me, "Son of man, stand up on your feet and I will speak to you." **2** As he spoke, the Spirit came into me and raised me to my feet, and I heard him speaking to me.

Since Ezekiel had fallen facedown at the splendor of the vision of God, the Lord told him, "Stand up on your feet."

The Lord had something important to tell Ezekiel for which he was to be ready.

Approximately ninety times in the book of Ezekiel the Lord addresses the prophet as "son of man." Perhaps this form of address was meant to teach Ezekiel something important. Although the Lord was granting him special visions, although the Lord was giving him the privilege of transmitting God's truth to his people, and although the Lord had picked him to fill the role of prophet-in-exile, Ezekiel was still a son of man. He was just a human being, a sinful son of Adam. It was not as priest or as pious man or as Israelite that Ezekiel was called to be the Lord's spokesman, but as a frail mortal who brought nothing but weakness to the task.

People in leadership positions, including leadership positions among God's people, are in circumstances perfect for fostering pride. Pride not only is a direct violation of God's command to love, but it gets in the way when people attempt to carry out service for God. It builds barriers and makes God-pleasing interpersonal relationship extremely difficult.

Since Ezekiel was a sinful son of man, he couldn't on his own stand in the presence of God, nor could he properly receive orders from the Lord. But the Lord made up for Ezekiel's spiritual insufficiencies. The Spirit stood him on his feet and made him ready to listen to the Lord. God is always the one who is responsible for making sinful humans into people who can stand in his presence. He makes them into people who have the courage to receive orders from him and to carry out those orders.

It might be our tendency to stay lying face down with Ezekiel, overcome with awe, when we are led to experience the mercy and majesty of the Lord. But the Lord doesn't let his people just lie around and bask in his glory. He has work for us to do. He lets us view the rainbow of his grace, orders us to stand up and listen to him, and then empowers us to do so.

³He said: "Son of man, I am sending you to the Israelites, to a rebellious nation that has rebelled against me; they and their fathers have been in revolt against me to this very day. ⁴The people to whom I am sending you are obstinate and stubborn. Say to them, 'This is what the Sovereign LORD says.' ⁵And whether they listen or fail to listen — for they are a rebellious house — they will know that a prophet has been among them. ⁶And you, son of man, do not be afraid of them or their words. Do not be afraid, though briers and thorns are all around you and you live among scorpions. Do not be afraid of what they say or terrified by them, though they are a rebellious house. ⁷You must speak my words to them, whether they listen or fail to listen, for they are rebellious. ⁸But you, son of man, listen to what I say to you. Do not rebel like that rebellious house; open your mouth and eat what I give you."

Ezekiel was to take his message to people descended from Israel. Because of God's choice of their nation to produce the Savior these people had a special national relationship with God. Most of them, nevertheless, had rebelled against the Lord. They had insisted on following other gods. They had insisted on disobeying God's will. This is why they were in exile. But even their years of exile had not led most of them to repent of their rebellious ways. In spite of their lack of inclination to repent and in spite of what appeared to be a lost cause, God still sent his prophet to these people.

Here we have an excellent view of the patient, long-suffering Lord. He suffered the rejection of his people for a long time, but it didn't hinder him from trying to bring them to repentance. Reminders of the Lord's patient endurance help keep us from becoming frustrated when we don't seem to be successful in reaching others with the Lord's call to repentance.

Ezekiel was to inform these descendants of Abraham, Isaac and Jacob that his message was not his own. It was the message of the God of the covenant with Abraham, Isaac and Jacob — the same God who had made the covenant with Moses and the nation. The Lord hadn't changed. Nor had the covenant changed. Through his prophet the Lord was trying to get the people to see that they had changed. That was the problem.

Ezekiel was to disregard the people's willingness or unwillingness to receive his message. He was not to stop transmitting the Lord's message even if they refused to listen to it. Thus, even the rejecters would have to admit that a prophet, a transmitter of the Lord's message, had been at work among them, especially after Jerusalem fell as the prophet had said it would. Transmitters of the Lord's message always must make it clear that what they are saying is what the Sovereign Lord says. We need to be ready to point to God's written Word so people are aware we are not just giving them our opinions. Witnesses for the Lord also can never plot their course of action on the basis of the reaction of their hearers. We are to witness because God has commanded it, not because we are getting a good reception.

Ezekiel was not to be intimidated by their rejection, their challenge of his authority, or their ridicule of his message, although they would truly fill the role of thorns in his side and scorpions in his house. If he would refuse to listen to the Lord, if he would refuse to carry out the work because it seemed to be a lost cause, if he thought some of the symbolic actions were too difficult or wretched — then Ezekiel would be doing exactly what the rebellious people had been doing.

⁹Then I looked, and I saw a hand stretched out to me. In it was a scroll, ¹⁰which he unrolled before me. On both sides of it were written words of lament and mourning and woe.

3 And he said to me, "Son of man, eat what is before you, eat this scroll; then go and speak to the house of Israel." ²So I opened my mouth, and he gave me the scroll to eat.

³Then he said to me, "Son of man, eat this scroll I am giving you and fill your stomach with it." So I ate it, and it tasted as sweet as honey in my mouth.

God designed food to be assimilated by the body. In much the same way God's words were to be assimilated into the prophet's very existence, into his very bone and fiber. Thus the command to eat the scroll. Once the prophet made the message his own — and only then — could he go and speak the message to Israel. The content of the scroll was a message of lament and mourning and woe. The message was not pleasing. And yet when Ezekiel ate it, it tasted sweet. In spite of the painful content of the message, in spite of the difficult circumstances described on the scroll, nothing could prevent Ezekiel from experiencing joy at being a messenger for the Lord.

Applying God's law to other people is never a pleasant task. We know the message may very well not please those to whom it is directed, and if it is accepted it will produce lament and mourning. Consequently we are inclined to avoid announcing this part of the Lord's message. We can counterbalance our reluctance with the knowledge that it is a God-given privilege to transmit his message, including the unpleasant parts.

⁴He then said to me: "Son of man, go now to the house of Israel and speak my words to them. ⁵You are not being sent to a people of obscure speech and difficult language, but to the house of Israel — ⁶not to many peoples of obscure speech and difficult language,

whose words you cannot understand. Surely if I had sent you to them, they would have listened to you. [7]But the house of Israel is not willing to listen to you because they are not willing to listen to me, for the whole house of Israel is hardened and obstinate. [8]But I will make you as unyielding and hardened as they are. [9]I will make your forehead like the hardest stone, harder than flint. Do not be afraid of them or terrified by them, though they are a rebellious house."

[10]And he said to me, "Son of man, listen carefully and take to heart all the words I speak to you. [11]Go now to your countrymen in exile and speak to them. Say to them, 'This is what the Sovereign LORD says,' whether they listen or fail to listen."

These verses are a repetition of 2:3-7 with two additions. First, the Lord reminded the prophet his job was actually easy in one area. Ezekiel didn't have to learn a new language. The incidental statement is made, "If the Lord had sent Ezekiel to foreigners they would have listened to him." Second, since those who should have listened (Israel) didn't, the Lord promised his prophet the ability to withstand the rebuffs and rejection which would come his way.

By this time the prophet certainly had no illusions about instant success. He was painfully aware that he was dealing with people who already had been so rebellious they were suffering the consequences of it. Ezekiel realized why the Lord would make him unyielding and hard like flint. He needed to be as unyielding with the truth as the people were in their rebellion. He needed to be able to resist their attacks on him as vigorously as they had resisted the Lord's message to them. Once more Ezekiel was reminded to speak *all* the words of the Lord, even the ones not pleasing to him or to Israel. Ezekiel would be outnumbered and he would be outshouted, but he would not be overcome.

It is not always easy to speak God's truth to those who are closest to us, to those who have the same language, life style and customs. It can be easier being foreign missionaries among strangers than witnesses to Jesus among our friends. This is true because we let our emotions and feelings overwhelm our mission. In these instances we need the Lord's gifts — an unyielding, hardened spirit and a forehead harder than flint.

¹²Then the Spirit lifted me up, and I heard behind me a loud rumbling sound — May the glory of the Lord be praised in his dwelling place! — ¹³the sound of the wings of the living creatures brushing against each other and the sound of the wheels beside them, a loud rumbling sound. ¹⁴The Spirit then lifted me up and took me away, and I went in bitterness and in the anger of my spirit, with the strong hand of the Lord upon me. ¹⁵I came to the exiles who lived at Tel Abib near the Kebar River. And there, where they were living, I sat among them for seven days — overwhelmed.

The rushing sound of the wheels and of the wings of the living creatures immediately reminded Ezekiel of the appearance of the likeness of the glory of the Lord which he had seen earlier. The Lord used this flashback to tell Ezekiel, "The same Lord whose glory you observed in that vision is the one who is commissioning you to be a prophet among the exiles." The vision was the basis for the call.

Ezekiel's initial reaction to his commission was one of anger and bitterness. Why was the chosen nation so stubborn in opposing God? And why did Ezekiel get stuck with the task of preaching to these people who would not listen? Why did he have to announce such a dreadful message of lamentation, mourning and woe to his own people?

God did not allow Ezekiel to get carried away with these thoughts. After all, the Lord was still in control. Nevertheless, for seven days Ezekiel was so overwhelmed with his anger and bitterness over the difficult task before him, that he was paralyzed, unable to move ahead with the task.

Whenever a task is so big it seems insurmountable, our first reaction is, "I can't handle it." Such an attitude can paralyze us. We feel ill-equipped and unable to handle the task. We tend to forget that the Lord who gave the directive is also able to supply us with the ability and willingness to carry out the directive.

Warning to Israel

¹⁶At the end of seven days the word of the LORD came to me: ¹⁷"Son of man, I have made you a watchman for the house of Israel; so hear the word I speak and give them warning from me. ¹⁸When I say to a wicked man, 'You will surely die,' and you do not warn him or speak out to dissuade him from his evil ways in order to save his life, that wicked man will die for his sin, and I will hold you accountable for his blood. ¹⁹But if you do warn the wicked man and he does not turn from his wickedness or from his evil ways, he will die for his sin; but you will have saved yourself.

²⁰"Again, when a righteous man turns from his righteousness and does evil, and I put a stumbling block before him, he will die. Since you did not warn him, he will die for his sin. The righteous things he did will not be remembered, and I will hold you accountable for his blood. ²¹But if you do warn the righteous man not to sin and he does not sin, he will surely live because he took warning, and you will have saved yourself."

Because Ezekiel was just sitting there, on dead center as it were, God came to him and said, "I gave you a vision of myself. I also gave you your orders so you might benefit the souls of these rebellious people. Because I have given you this responsibility, I hold you accountable for carrying it out."

Death, the punishment for sin God announced in Eden, would be carried out whether the prophet carried out his task or not. But the prophet would be judged by the Lord on the basis of whether he had faithfully carried out the task given him. Those who have received the Lord's message need to be reminded that they have a responsibility toward the souls of others. God has given his people a trust. When they faithfully transmit God's message of sin and grace, of warning and comfort, they save themselves from the Lord's anger against unfaithful servants.

God often allows stumbling blocks to come into people's lives. He brings us face to face with circumstances which ask us to decide whether to follow him or not — circumstances which demand from us a choice between him and this world with its materialism and immorality. With his help we step over these stumbling blocks to a stronger faith and life. If we try to surmount them on our own we will stumble and fall, and the righteous products of our faith will be forgotten.

²²The hand of the LORD was upon me there, and he said to me, "Go up and go out to the plain, and there I will speak to you." ²³So I got up and went out to the plain. And the glory of the LORD was standing there, like the glory I had seen by the Kebar River, and I fell facedown.

The elements found in this section are the same as in 1:28 — 2:2.

²⁴Then the Spirit came into me and raised me to my feet. He spoke to me and said: "Go, shut yourself inside your house. ²⁵And you, son of man, they will tie with ropes; you will be bound so that you cannot go out among the people. ²⁶I will make your tongue stick to the roof of your mouth so that you will be silent and unable to rebuke them, though they are a rebellious house. ²⁷But when I speak to you, I will open your mouth and you shall say to

them, 'This is what the Sovereign LORD says.' Whoever will listen let him listen, and whoever will refuse let him refuse; for they are a rebellious house.

At first glance these words seem to contradict God's previous words to Ezekiel. The prophet had just been told to be a watchman and to warn others (3:16-21). Now he was told to go into seclusion! The symbolism of being tied up with ropes indicated he would be rendered incapable of going out among the people. The Lord would make him unable to speak to the people, even though they certainly needed to hear what he had to say.

The solution to this apparent contradiction is verse 27, "when I speak to you." The prophet was to remain in seclusion and in silence. He was not to interact with the people, if the only thing he had to offer was his own opinion. Ezekiel was to speak only when the Lord spoke to him, when the Lord opened his mouth and when he could truthfully say to the people, "This is what *the Lord* says." Whenever God's people give their own opinions in place of the Lord's truth, it would be better to remain silent than to lead others astray. There is a time and place for our personal opinions, but not when we are called upon to speak God's truth. When speaking for the Lord we need to be very careful, so we are able to assert with confidence that what we are speaking is "what the Sovereign Lord says."

Introduction to Action-Parables

Some people, I am sure, would read the following sections (chapters 4-24) and say, "What is described here is unreal; nobody would have or could have done those things. There has to be an alternate explanation." Others would say, "What benefit would such actions produce? God would not have told his prophet to do such foolish things. Since we

26

don't have a record of Ezekiel actually having done them, he probably didn't."

We need not be so quick to reject these action-parables (one commentator has called them "charades"). Think of it this way. The exiles must have sensed that the Lord worked in a special way in the life of Ezekiel (3:15). Because they were aware of this, some of them made Ezekiel's house a regular stop on their visits in the community (8:1; 20:1). So Ezekiel had a ready-made stage or public forum right at home. When the Lord had told him to do some of the strange actions which we'll soon hear about, Ezekiel would go out in front of his house where everybody could see him, and do what God had told him to do. Those who were present in the neighborhood, passing by, or had come to talk to Ezekiel would say, "What does this strange thing Ezekiel is doing mean?" This would give Ezekiel a chance to give them the explanation. He could also relate the command of the Lord behind the action as well as the application to the lives of the people.

Because the exiles were a tightly knit group, whether they lived in a ghetto or not, you can imagine how quickly the action-parables were passed along throughout the group. Someone who had seen Ezekiel might say, "You wouldn't believe what Ezekiel is doing now!" And so the message would be passed. The next group would go to see him, and would say the same thing.

For the action-parables in which duration was an active ingredient, the procedure most likely was this: Part of each day, when there would be the possibility of an audience, Ezekiel would play his role. After all, the actions would be worthless and pointless unless there was someone to observe them. Then, perhaps at sundown, Ezekiel would go back into his house and resume his normal conduct.

Taking the actions in chapter 4 as our example, we might assume the following. Ezekiel went out in front of his house first thing in the morning, when there was some traffic past his house. He lay down in the required direction near the model of the besieged city which he had built, with his arm ready for action, but tied up. He presented this object lesson to teach his fellow exiles what the Lord was planning for Jerusalem. When he thought most of the traffic for the day had ceased, he released himself and performed the other symbolic actions which he couldn't do while lying down and tied up. Then he went inside for the evening. These symbolic action-parables were done four years before the actual siege of Jerusalem took place. It is obvious God was trying to prepare the exiles for the crushing news they would be hearing from Jerusalem.

The Siege of Jerusalem Symbolized

4 "Now, son of man, take a clay tablet, put it in front of you and draw the city of Jerusalem on it. ²Then lay siege to it: Erect siege works against it, build a ramp up to it, set up camps against it and put battering rams around it. ³Then take an iron pan, place it as an iron wall between you and the city and turn your face toward it. It will be under siege, and you shall besiege it. This will be a sign to the house of Israel.**

The clay tablet was the book of the ancient Near East. On tablets of soft clay which were then baked to make them durable the Assyrians and Babylonians wrote their private contracts, records and historical inscriptions. Archaeologists have uncovered whole libraries of these clay tablets. The result of Ezekiel's artistic endeavors was a clay tablet with the city of Jerusalem drawn on it, and models of siege works, probably movable towers from which archers could shoot over the walls, a ramp, enemy camps for soldiers, and battering rams all around the clay model of the city. This model of a besieged city was left for all to see as a semi-permanent visual reminder of the threats of the Lord. It also served as a centerpiece and reference point for the other symbolic actions of the prophet.

In this particular action-parable, Ezekiel was to play the role of God. He was to turn his face in opposition to the city, so they would realize that it was not only the Babylonian army which was besieging Jerusalem, but God himself. The iron pan placed as an iron wall between Ezekiel (God) and the city probably represented the "sins that had separated them from their God" (Isaiah 59:2) and the resultant unchangeable will of God to carry out the punishment this city deserved.

The action-parable, then, was more than just an announcement that Jerusalem would soon come under seige. It was also a statement that this tragedy was not just produced by men's political actions and warfare. No, it was God's judgment. God was going to besiege the city because she had rebelled against him. This parable should have led the exiles to ask, "Why will God direct his anger against Jerusalem in this way?" Such a question would give Ezekiel a chance to remind them of their rebellion against the Lord.

Whenever our faith is being besieged by the unbelief all around us or whenever our resolve to live a godly life is besieged by the prevalent godlessness of our world, it is a reflex reaction to say, "God, why are you letting this happen to me?" Our all-wise Lord allows these sieges to come into our lives for our best interest. At such times it would be well to ask God for understanding. Then we will see what benefit he had in mind for us when he allowed these sieges to enter our lives.

Acknowledgement of God's directing presence in our lives is often the only thing that can get us through a difficult situation. The other alternative is to think all things are arbitrary, produced either by some blind forces or by the whims of the sinful human beings around us. Such a mindset can lead to the meaninglessness, despair and hopelessness we see all around us.

[4]"Then lie on your left side and put the sin of the house of Israel upon yourself. You are to bear their sin for the number of days you lie on your side. [5]I have assigned you the same number of days as the years of their sin. So for 390 days you will bear the sin of the house of Israel.

[6]"After you have finished this, lie down again, this time on your right side, and bear the sin of the house of Judah. I have assigned you 40 days, a day for each year. [7]Turn your face toward the siege of Jerusalem and with bared arm prophesy against her. [8]I will tie you up with ropes so that you cannot turn from one side to the other until you have finished the days of your siege.

In this action-parable Ezekiel played the role of Israel and Judah. Lying on his left side with his head near the model of Jerusalem he had drawn on the clay tablet would make him face north toward the ten tribes which were known as the kingdom of Israel. He was to lie there as if he were a sick man who couldn't move. He was burdened with the sickness of the sins of Israel. This was not a bearing of sin as a substitute or a bearing of sins as an atonement as Jesus did for us, but just a symbolic reminder that Israel would have to bear the burden of God's anger over her sins. In fact, this action-prophecy was already being fulfilled. The 390 years is probably just a reference to the long period of God's anger against Israel. Samaria, proud capital of the northern kingdom of Israel, had already been destroyed and its people taken captive in 722 B.C., approximately 125 years before Ezekiel's time.

Lying on his right side and looking toward the clay model of Jerusalem, Ezekiel would be facing south toward the kingdom of Judah. He was to be a picture of Judah's bearing the burden of God's anger against her sin but for a much shorter period, 40 years. This period of God's judgment had just started recently with the early deportations to Babylon.

All attempts to find exact chronological dates and historical events to fit the 390 and 40 year periods have proven futile. Taking the two periods of 390 and 40 years to be representative of a long period and a short period seems to be the best approach. The combined period of 430 years does have roots in the history of the nations. The exile in Egypt had been for a total of 430 years (Exodus 12:40). Ezekiel's use of 430 might have said to the exiles: "Just as in the past we became subject to another nation, so God has and will let it happen again."

The Lord had the prophet tied up. This symbolic gesture conveyed the idea that the people would not be able to move out from under God's anger until he had finished besieging them.

The bared arm and the command to prophesy against Jerusalem mixed the picture a bit. Here the prophet was playing the role of prophet while at the same time portraying the nation against whom he was prophesying. The bared arm indicated the Lord whom the prophet represented was ready for action against the besieged city. In fact he was already in action.

Although the exiles heard that God's hand of judgment would be raised against Israel and Judah until his result was produced, the comparatively short period of 40 in contrast to 390 was a source of hope. The number 40 indicated that the people of Judah could look forward to an end of God's siege against them in a comparatively short time. God's grace, his loving forgiveness, is always there. Often our problem is that we are so wrapped up in our own lives, surrounded by and pervaded by the consequences of sin, all we can see is his bared arm and the siege. His gracious promises seem to be hidden behind his frowning face.

⁹"Take wheat and barley, beans and lentils, millet and spelt; put them in a container and make them into bread for yourself. You are to eat it during the 390 days you lie on your side. ¹⁰Weigh out twenty shekels of food to eat each day and eat it at set times. ¹¹Also measure out a sixth of a hin of water and drink it at set times. ¹²Eat the food as you would a barley cake; bake it in the sight of the people, using human excrement for fuel." ¹³The LORD said, "In this way the people of Israel will eat defiled food among the nations where I will drive them."

¹⁴Then I said, "Not so, Sovereign LORD! I have never defiled myself. From my youth until now I have never eaten anything found dead or torn by wild animals. No unclean meat has ever entered my mouth."

¹⁵"Very well," he said, "I will let you bake your bread over cow manure instead of human excrement."

¹⁶He then said to me: "Son of man, I will cut off the supply of food in Jerusalem. The people will eat rationed food in anxiety and drink rationed water in despair, ¹⁷for food and water will be scarce. They will be appalled at the sight of each other and will waste away because of their sin.

With the "charades" of the clay tablet with the diagram of the siege of Jerusalem and by lying on his side for specified periods of time Ezekiel had acted out God's judgment on Judah and Jerusalem. Now God instructed the prophet to perform still another such symbolical action.

Ezekiel was to mix a number of different ingredients to bake bread. This mixture seems to imply that the person had to scrape all this together to get enough to fill a small ration each day. Apparently the amount was one-half the normal amount needed for an adult, about eight ounces of bread (twenty shekels) and two-thirds of a quart of water (a sixth of a hin). This action-parable indicated there would be a lack of food and water when Jerusalem would be under siege. It also indicated that even that meager food allowance would be unclean.

Because of the scruples of the prophet's conscience, the Lord allowed him to use a common fuel, dried cow manure, instead of human waste as fuel, since his point had already been made. The prophet's objections against eating anything "found dead or torn by wild animals" or "unclean" were based on Levitical law (Leviticus 7:24; 19:6,7).

The interpretation of this action-parable is given in verses 16 and 17. Because of the sins of the people, the Lord would make food and water scarce during Jerusalem's last days and also during the exile. But what might be considered worse — God would put the Jews in circumstances which would make them no different from people of any other nation. Circumstances would force them to abandon their levitical cleanness so that all the evidence of their distinctive position as a separate, different, set-apart-for-the-Lord people would be lost. The siege of Jerusalem and the resultant exile would have such a drastic effect.

As usual, the Lord's warning against sin was meant to bring about results. He pointed to the disgusting consequences of sin in order to warn his people ahead of time, so they might repent and turn to him. This is also the reason God brings the law to us. He wants to warn us that living contrary to his will not only is displeasing to him, but also is drastically disruptive to our lives.

5 **"Now, son of man, take a sharp sword and use it as a barber's razor to shave your head and your beard. Then take a set of scales and divide up the hair. ²When the days of your siege come to an end, burn a third of the hair with fire inside the city. Take a third and strike it with the sword all around the city. And scatter a third to the wind. For I will pursue them with drawn sword. ³But take a few strands of hair and tuck them away in the folds of your garment.**

⁴Again, take a few of these and throw them into the fire and burn them up. A fire will spread from there to the whole house of Israel.

This chapter brings us the fourth in the series of Ezekiel's action prophecies about the fall of Jerusalem.

As easily as Ezekiel could whisk away his hair with a razor, so easily would the Lord sweep away the people — as numerous as hair — with the sword of Nebuchadnezzar. Some would perish in the city during the siege. These Ezekiel pictured by burning one-third of the hair on the clay tablet on which he had drawn the besieged city of Jerusalem. Some would perish by the sword as they fled from the city. These Ezekiel pictured by chopping the hair scattered around the picture of Jerusalem. Some would be scattered into exile. These he pictured with the hair thrown to the wind. Destruction would even follow this group into exile.

For the historic fulfillment of these prophecies, see 2 Kings 25:1-21; 2 Chronicles 36:15-21; Jeremiah 39. Some at first would seem to escape, tucked into the Lord's garment. Even a few of these would be burned by the Lord's anger, which would be directed not just against the inhabitants of Jerusalem, but also against the whole nation, in Judah and in exile.

⁵"This is what the Sovereign LORD says: This is Jerusalem, which I have set in the center of the nations, with countries all around her. ⁶Yet in her wickedness she has rebelled against my laws and decrees more than the nations and countries around her. She has rejected my laws and has not followed my decrees.

⁷"Therefore this is what the Sovereign LORD says: You have been more unruly than the nations around you and have not followed my decrees or kept my laws. You have not even conformed to the standards of the nations around you.

God had placed Jerusalem in the center of the nations. From this point God's truth of salvation was to radiate to the nations. Years before, God had told Abraham (Genesis 12:3) the people descended from him would be specially blessed in order to be a special blessing to the rest of the world. Yet Israel had rebelled against the Lord. The chosen people had been worse than the surrounding heathen nations; at least they had produced an outward social righteousness up to the potential which their knowledge of God's righteousness permitted. Jerusalem and the people of Israel were living far below the level God might have expected of people so richly blessed. God's choice, God's law, God's prophets — all were awesome benefits. Yet the people had abandoned him and rebelled (2 Kings 21:9).

Centuries later another prophet, greater than Ezekiel, spoke a similar message to the Jewish people. "From everyone who has been given much, much will be demanded; and from the one who has been entrusted with much, much more will be asked" (Luke 12:48). God's New Testament people are the spiritual center of the nations. We have been blessed abundantly with priceless spiritual blessings, not so we might become spiritually obese, but so we might share them. Such great blessings place on us equally great responsibilities. God judges very critically when we don't shoulder the responsibilities which his great blessings place on us.

8"Therefore this is what the Sovereign LORD says: I myself am against you, Jerusalem, and I will inflict punishment on you in the sight of the nations. 9Because of all your detestable idols, I will do to you what I have never done before and will never do again. 10Therefore in your midst fathers will eat their children, and children will eat their fathers. I will inflict punishment on you and will scatter all your survivors to the winds. 11Therefore as surely as I live, declares the Sovereign LORD, because you have defiled my sanctuary with all your vile images and detestable practices, I myself will withdraw my favor; I will not look on you with pity or spare you. 12A third of your people will die of the plague or perish

by famine inside you; a third will fall by the sword outside your walls; and a third I will scatter to the winds and pursue with drawn sword.

Instead of being a channel of blessing to the nations, Jerusalem would be an object lesson of warning to them. One reason for Jerusalem's complacent attitude was that the Lord in his mercy had never let her be destroyed. This was about to change. In the middle of the siege, things would get so bad that the people in Jerusalem would actually practice cannibalism. The reason for God's fierce anger against his people was their false worship. In God's view the worst sin was and is false worship. This occurred throughout the history of his Old Testament people. They were constantly accommodating their worship to the various nature religions of the area. Chief among these pagan religions were the worship of Baal and the fertility cults. God's chosen people even gave themselves to the worship of the sun, moon and stars.

We live in a society which considers itself to have advanced far beyond the ancient, primitive nature religions. We need to be reminded that to God the worst sin is worshiping a different god. Different gods are more prominent today than ever, the most popular of whom is the god called "old Number One," alias Self-Interest, or Self-Gratification.

[13]"Then my anger will cease and my wrath against them will subside, and I will be avenged. And when I have spent my wrath upon them, they will know that I the LORD have spoken in my zeal.
[14]"I will make you a ruin and a reproach among the nations around you, in the sight of all who pass by. [15]You will be a reproach and a taunt, a warning and an object of horror to the nations around you when I inflict punishment on you in anger and in wrath and with stinging rebuke. I the LORD have spoken. [16]When I shoot at you with my deadly and destructive arrows of

famine, I will shoot to destroy you. I will bring more and more famine upon you and cut off your supply of food. **¹⁷I will send famine and wild beasts against you, and they will leave you childless. Plague and bloodshed will sweep through you, and I will bring the sword against you. I the LORD have spoken."**

If the exiles were looking for any ray of hope in Ezekiel's message, the only thing they would find was this: there would be an end to the Lord's anger. It would cease when he got his point across: "I am the Covenant Savior God who never changes. I keep my promises and carry out my threats. I am not a harmless wooden or stone idol which can be mocked with no consequence. Instead of nations learning from Jerusalem that I am the Savior God as they should, they will learn from Jerusalem I do not tolerate sin."

For these false worshipers in the city of Jerusalem and in the land of Judah, Jerusalem was no longer the central location for worshiping the true God of the covenant. They were running after other gods. For them Jerusalem had become a rabbit's foot, a good luck charm, insuring that the Lord would not let them be destroyed. They were sure he would keep his holy city free from destruction. And so God declared through Ezekiel: "Forget it. Just wait. See what will happen to your rabbit's foot."

As he does frequently, the Lord used what most people call natural disasters to help carry out his punishment and discipline. From the historic fulfillment, we learn what the Lord had spoken was reliable. It was just as good as done.

In a world convinced it can shape its god to fit any mold which makes it most comfortable, we need to remember that God is not jello. His anger over sin and unbelief is real. His punishment is real. Ask the people in the Jerusalem of 587 B.C. His anger is stirred especially when our indifference toward him turns our relationship from a spiritual family tie into an impersonal religion, maintained superficially as an insurance policy against the possibility of eternal discomfort. When we see the natural disasters occurring all around us, we ought to think of another destruction promised by the Lord, the agony of a collapsing world (Matthew 24,25).

Discussion of Cause and Effect

Prophecy Against the Mountains of Israel

6 The word of the LORD came to me: [2]"Son of man, set your face against the mountains of Israel; prophesy against them [3]and say: 'O mountains of Israel, hear the word of the Sovereign LORD. This is what the Sovereign LORD says to the mountains and hills, to the ravines and valleys: I am about to bring a sword against you, and I will destroy your high places. [4]Your altars will be demolished and your incense altars will be smashed; and I will slay your people in front of your idols. [5]I will lay the dead bodies of the Israelites in front of their idols, and I will scatter your bones around your altars. [6]Wherever you live, the towns will be laid waste and the high places demolished, so that your altars will be laid waste and devastated, your idols smashed and ruined, your incense altars broken down, and what you have made wiped out. [7]Your people will fall slain among you, and you will know that I am the LORD.**

Some of the exiles had begun to face toward Jerusalem when they prayed. Perhaps they thought this would make their prayers more acceptable. The Lord directed Ezekiel to face Jerusalem and the mountains of Israel, not, however, to pray concerning them, but to prophesy against them. The mountains and high places were the locations for the false worship which had taken over among the people. Many of these sites had been old Canaanite worship places consisting of an altar, a pillar and an image.

Before King David established Jerusalem as the capital and before God's ark was placed in the temple, worship of the true God at other locations had been allowed (1 Samuel 9:14; 1 Kings 3:4). After King Solomon built the temple in Jerusalem, worship at other locations was discouraged, because it led to a blurring of the distinction between the worship of the true God and the worship of regional gods. It also led to local corruptions of the true worship. After the northern ten tribes split from the southern kingdom, worship centers in the border cities of Dan and Bethel became competition for the worship at Jerusalem. This was repugnant to God, for it led people away from worshiping him.

In Ezekiel 6 God promised to do to the people what they had done to him. As they had abandoned him by worshiping other gods, so he would abandon them. He would let them be conquered or killed, and the land destroyed by Nebuchadnezzar, king of Babylon. As they had dishonored him, so he would dishonor them by allowing their dead bodies to lie around unburied before the altars of their false gods. It was as if God were saying, "You want to sacrifice to these gods? Your lives will be taken and your bodies laid out as sacrifices to them. That will be a fitting climax to your worship of these false gods!"

Through all this destruction God was announcing: "You will know that I am the Lord." This phrase occurs fifty-four times in the simple form and eighteen more times in an expanded form in this book. Since all of this loving treatment of the people of Israel over the years had not taught them to trust and follow him, he would now withdraw his blessings. Through God's judgment Israel would learn that God was and is the unchangeable, independent Lord of the covenant. God can make this point by dispensing either his grace or his judgment.

8" 'But I will spare some, for some of you will escape the sword when you are scattered among the lands and nations. 9Then in the

nations where they have been carried captive, those who escape will remember me — how I have been grieved by their adulterous hearts, which have turned away from me, and by their eyes, which have lusted after their idols. They will loathe themselves for the evil they have done and for all their detestable practices. 10And they will know that I am the Lord; I did not threaten in vain to bring this calamity on them.

The destruction of the nation of Israel would not mean total annihilation. The Lord had to keep his promises to Abraham through these descendants of his. For some of those who survived, the destruction of their nation and land would be a successful object lesson. They would be led to acknowledge it was their sin of idolatry which caused God's anger. They would admit the justice of God's punishment. They would acknowledge that the Lord doesn't make threats and then not keep them. They would hate themselves for having abandoned the Lord after all of his blessings to them.

In other words, these people would admit the Lord was and is the unchangeable, independent Lord of the covenant. This was the goal the Lord had in mind when he allowed the destruction. Some would be brought to repentance.

11" 'This is what the Sovereign Lord says: Strike your hands together and stamp your feet and cry out "Alas!" because of all the wicked and detestable practices of the house of Israel, for they will fall by the sword, famine and plague. 12He that is far away will die of the plague, and he that is near will fall by the sword, and he that survives and is spared will die of famine. So will I spend my wrath upon them. 13And they will know I am the Lord, when their people lie slain among their idols around their altars, on every high hill and on all the mountaintops, under every spreading tree and every leafy oak — places where they offered fragrant incense to all their idols. 14And I will stretch

out my hand against them and make the land a desolate waste
from the desert to Diblah — wherever they live. Then they will
know that I am the LORD.' "

God told Ezekiel to clap his hands and stamp his feet to
call further attention to his message. This action served to
emphasize the importance of what he had to say. When
someone jumps up and down and yells, we tend to listen just
because he is making a spectacle of himself. So, here, Ezekiel.

The destruction would include people far and near. It
wouldn't be confined just to the shrines on the high places,
but would include the groves and parks, too, some of which
had become places of false worship. It would include the
entire land, from the desert to Diblah. We are more accustomed to the terms "from Dan (north) to Beersheba
(south)." Here we have "from the desert (south) to Diblah."
The location of Diblah has not been pinpointed, so some
think it should read Riblah, a known city in the far north.
(The Hebrew *d* and *r* look almost alike and might account
for a copyist's error in transcribing the text.) In any case, the
meaning is obvious. The entire land from south to north
would be a desolate waste.

The End Has Come

7 The word of the LORD came to me: ²"Son of man, this is what
the Sovereign LORD says to the land of Israel: The end! The
end has come upon the four corners of the land. ³The end is now
upon you and I will unleash my anger against you. I will judge you
according to your conduct and repay you for all your detestable
practices. ⁴I will not look on you with pity or spare you; I will
surely repay you for your conduct and the detestable practices
among you. Then you will know that I am the LORD.

The destruction threatened and described was so vivid to
the Lord and his prophet that even though it lay in the future

Ezekiel saw it as an accomplished fact. Ezekiel was to present his message in such a vivid way also. He was not to speak in vague terms, or merely talk of the possibility of punishment. He was to speak as if standing amidst the ruins after the destruction was complete! Not just his message alone, but even his method of presentation to the exiles was to attract their attention.

5"This is what the Sovereign LORD says: Disaster! An unheard-of disaster is coming. 6The end has come! The end has come! It has roused itself against you. It has come! 7Doom has come upon you — you who dwell in the land. The time has come, the day is near; there is panic, not joy, upon the mountains. 8I am about to pour out my wrath on you and spend my anger against you; I will judge you according to your conduct and repay you for all your detestable practices. 9I will not look on you with pity or spare you; I will repay you in accordance with your conduct and the detestable practices among you. Then you will know that it is I the LORD who strikes the blow.

All of the repetition about destruction in these sections was purposeful. It was necessary because all the people both those still in Judah, and the exiles in far-off Babylon — had convinced themselves that Jerusalem was untouchable. Only constant repetition of the threatened judgment would get this thought through: "Jerusalem is not exempt from punishment."

10"The day is here! It has come! Doom has burst forth, the rod has budded, arrogance has blossomed! 11Violence has grown into a rod to punish wickedness; none of the people will be left, none of that crowd — no wealth, nothing of value. 12The time has come, the day has arrived. Let not the buyer rejoice nor the seller grieve, for wrath is upon the whole crowd. 13The seller will not recover the land he has sold as long as both of them live, for the vision concerning the whole crowd will not be reversed.

Because of their sins, not one of them will preserve his life.
¹⁴Though they blow the trumpet and get everything ready, no one
will go into battle, for my wrath is upon the whole crowd.

This section, containing the same thoughts as the previous two, is an example of Ezekiel's literary skill. The
arrogance and violence of the sinful nation would be punished by the arrogant violence of the Babylonians. Crowds
of people and their wealth, which usually provided security,
would be gone. The Lord said, "Forget about daily affairs
and your business. Don't rejoice over a bargain; don't grieve
over a loss; and don't think that your property will be
returned to you in the Jubilee Year (Leviticus 25:10). Everything and everybody will be either wiped out or taken
away." The Lord's judgment would even rob them of their
courage. They wouldn't even have the courage to defend
themselves.

¹⁵"Outside is the sword, inside are plague and famine; those
in the country will die by the sword, and those in the city will
be devoured by famine and plague. ¹⁶All who survive and escape will be in the mountains, moaning like doves of the valleys, each because of his sins. ¹⁷Every hand will go limp, every
knee will become as weak as water. ¹⁸They will put on sack-
cloth and be clothed with terror. Their faces will be covered
with shame and their heads will be shaved. ¹⁹They will throw
their silver into the streets and their gold will be an unclean
thing. Their silver and gold will not be able to save them in the
day of the LORD's wrath. They will not satisfy their hunger or
fill their stomachs with it, for it has made them stumble into sin.
²⁰They were proud of their beautiful jewelry and used it to make
their detestable idols and vile images. Therefore I will turn these
into an unclean thing for them. ²¹I will hand it all over as
plunder to foreigners and as loot to the wicked of the earth, and
they will defile it. ²²I will turn my face away from them, and

**they will desecrate my treasured place; robbers will enter it and
desecrate it.**

Here Ezekiel describes the terror and grief which would
accompany the fall of Jerusalem. People would learn the
hard way that their wealth, which had often led them into
the sin of self-security and rejection of the Lord did not
exempt them from judgment. Their money could not buy
food. There was none to be bought. Nor could it buy off the
enemy. The very wealth with which the Lord had blessed
them and which they had used to make their false gods,
would be looted by the Babylonians and used in the worship
of their false gods!

And then would come the ultimate disgrace. The Lord
would withdraw from his temple, and leave that, too, for
foreigners to desecrate.

**²³"Prepare chains, because the land is full of bloodshed and the
city is full of violence. ²⁴I will bring the most wicked of the nations
to take possession of their houses; I will put an end to the pride of
the mighty, and their sanctuaries will be desecrated. ²⁵When
terror comes, they will seek peace, but there will be none. ²⁶Calamity upon calamity will come, and rumor upon rumor. They
will try to get a vision from the prophet; the teaching of the law by
the priest will be lost, as will the counsel of the elders. ²⁷The king
will mourn, the prince will be clothed with despair, and the hands
of the people of the land will tremble. I will deal with them
according to their conduct, and by their own standards I will
judge them. Then they will know that I am the LORD."**

"Prepare chains!" the Lord said, "I need them to bind the
captives." He also used whatever else he had to, including
the most wicked of nations, Babylon, in order to carry out
his judgment. When there was obviously no hope, then the
people would finally turn to the prophet, priest or elder. But

the Lord wouldn't use them to dispense his message of peace anymore. What a devastating picture of despair the Lord painted for the exiles!

Why does the Lord let us read about his promised destruction and punishment? St. Paul furnishes an answer, "These things occurred as examples to keep us from setting our hearts on evil things as they did. . . . These things happened to them as examples and were written down as warnings for us, on whom the fulfillment of the ages has come" (1 Corinthians 10:6,11).

The Glory of the Lord Departs
Idolatry in the Temple

The Lord had communicated his message through the symbolic actions of the prophet in chapters 4 and 5, and through the lips of the prophet in chapters 6 and 7. Now he would make his truth known by means of visions in chapters 8-11.

8 **In the sixth year, in the sixth month on the fifth day, while I was sitting in my house and the elders of Judah were sitting before me, the hand of the Sovereign LORD came upon me there. ²I looked, and I saw a figure like that of a man. From what appeared to be his waist down he was like fire, and from there up his appearance was as bright as glowing metal. ³He stretched out what looked like a hand and took me by the hair of my head. The Spirit lifted me up between earth and heaven and in visions of God he took me to Jerusalem, to the entrance to the north gate of the inner court, where the idol that provokes to jealousy stood. ⁴And there before me was the glory of the God of Israel, as in the vision I had seen in the plain.**

Chapter 8 begins a new set of prophecies — about a year after the first appearance of the glory of the Lord (1:2), and about five years before Jerusalem fell to the Babylonians. It shouldn't surprise us that after a year of observing the action-parables we studied in chapters 4 and 5, the elders of Judah had begun to gather, maybe even regularly, at the home of Ezekiel. It is surprising, however, that while they recognized Ezekiel as a man who spoke for God, they refused to believe the message he spoke!

As in 1:3 and 3:22, we have here a formal statement of his status, indicating the Lord's impetus — "the hand of the Lord came upon me." We have the same description of the "figure like that of a man" as we had in 1:26,27, except this time what is above and below the waist are reversed. The repeated phrases make us aware that this, too, was a vision of the Lord. The Savior God appeared to Ezekiel in all of his heavenly majesty, to give the prophet further evidence that Judah was ripe for judgment.

In a vision God showed Ezekiel the present and future of far-off Jerusalem. He was allowed to see symbolic occurrences there. The things Ezekiel observed in this vision should not have been allowed to happen in the temple complex, even if the people's hearts were far from the Lord. The Jews still maintained the outward purity of the temple, and still performed the outward acts of the covenant religion. Yet various forms of idolatry had invaded and infected their hearts and lives.

"The idol that provokes to jealousy" could refer to the altar to the starry host (2 Chronicles 33:4-7) or to the Asherah pole (2 Kings 21:7) which King Manasseh had placed in the temple. The term may be symbolically representative of the worship of any false god which had taken over in the hearts of the people. God always demands undivided allegiance from his people. He is jealous in that sense. And God enforces his demand to receive the allegiance that is rightly his. Even though these gods didn't really exist, Israel was running after them. In their idolatry the people were attacking the majesty of the true God and calling down on themselves his righteous retaliation.

The glory of the Lord, the visual representation of the Lord's majesty, belonged in the temple, his symbolic home. The cloud symbolizing the Lord's presence, dwelt in the Most Holy Place, above the ark. It was incongruous to the Lord and should have been to his people that an idol, a false god, was right there together with the glory of the Lord! It is interesting to note Ezekiel wrote "the glory of the God of Israel" and not "the glory of the LORD." This was a reminder the temple belonged to the God who had adopted Israel as his special people. The God of Israel was saying he would not tolerate worship of any other god in his temple.

Since the hearts of God's people are temples of the Holy Spirit, it is just as incongruous for any other god to be represented there along with the Lord. With Martin Luther we recognize that anything which we fear, love or trust more than God is in reality our god. Therefore we need to ask the Lord constantly to cleanse our hearts of these idols, so we do not provoke him to jealousy as Judah did. Although in the New Testament age the Lord hasn't called any political, geographical nation to be his adopted people, he still does not tolerate the worship of some other god by any human being. In a world which allows for an endless variety of gods and for a complete lack of precise definition of God, we need to be concerned that all our religious and worship actions confess this truth: any god besides Father, Son — the God-man Jesus Christ — and Holy Ghost is a false god.

5Then he said to me, "Son of man, look toward the north." So I looked, and in the entrance north of the gate of the altar I saw this idol of jealousy.

⁶And he said to me, "Son of man, do you see what they are doing — the utterly detestable things the house of Israel is doing here, things that will drive me far from my sanctuary? But you will see things that are even more detestable."

Although no worshipers were observed in this part of the vision, the presence of the idol in the Lord's temple implied the idol at least in part had replaced the true God in the hearts of the people. For this reason God promised to leave his sanctuary, the place he had chosen for his earthly dwelling. Their idolatry would drive him away. It would also rob them of all the blessings of his special presence among them.

⁷Then he brought me to the entrance to the court. I looked, and I saw a hole in the wall. ⁸He said to me, "Son of man, now dig into the wall." So I dug into the wall and saw a doorway there.

⁹And he said to me, "Go in and see the wicked and detestable things they are doing here." ¹⁰So I went in and looked, and I saw portrayed all over the walls all kinds of crawling things and detestable animals and all the idols of the house of Israel. ¹¹In front of them stood seventy elders of the house of Israel, and Jaazaniah son of Shaphan was standing among them. Each had a censer in his hand, and a fragrant cloud of incense was rising.

¹²He said to me, "Son of man, have you seen what the elders of the house of Israel were doing in the darkness, each at the shrine of his own idol? They say, 'The LORD does not see us; the LORD has forsaken the land.' " ¹³Again, he said, "You will see them doing things that are even more detestable."

Going further into the temple, the Spirit showed Ezekiel some worse abominations. Digging through the wall and finding a hidden doorway indicates that these religious activities were being carried out in hidden, secret places. Most likely the elders represented here didn't want anybody else to know what they were doing. Maybe they even thought they could hide from God. Their worship of crawling things and unclean animals was an accommodation to Egyptian worship. In Egypt, people worshiped cats, crocodiles, hawks and beetles. The fact that Israel's elders participated in this ungodliness demonstrated that these practices were widespread even among the religious leaders of the nation.

We don't know who Jaazaniah was who apparently was leading the false worship. Ironically his name means "the Lord hears." The Lord's question to Ezekiel in verse 12 implied that God had in fact heard, even though this practice was being carried out in secret.

When they were warned about their idolatry, the elders denied the Lord knew what they were doing. For proof they cited the difficulties they were having with the other nations around them. Their attitude was, "Obviously God has forsaken us, therefore, he doesn't care if we worship other gods." They had turned things around so much, they couldn't see that it was *their* abandonment of him which had caused their problems!

Human beings have an innate desire to relate to the supreme being. God has planted that desire within mankind. When the truth about God is repressed or abandoned, the vacuum created in our souls cries out to be filled. Satan saw to it that the people of Judah had many choices from which to pick to fill the spiritual void in their souls after they had abandoned the covenant of love the Lord had made with them.

We have just as many options available to us. The number of idols clamoring to take first place in our hearts is almost countless. Money, pleasure, self-fulfillment and a thousand other gods cry out for our devotion. The Lord, however, continues to ask for first place in our hearts. And he does so without apology.

¹⁴Then he brought me to the entrance to the north gate of the house of the LORD, and I saw women sitting there, mourning for Tammuz. ¹⁵He said to me, "Do you see this, son of man? You will see things that are even more detestable than this."

The women had accommodated themselves to worshiping Tammuz, the Mesopotamian fertility god, the supposed producer of new life. The cult worshiped Tammuz by celebrating his marriage to the goddess Inana and by mourning his early death. This pagan worship symbolized the rising to life of the vegetation each spring and the death of all of it each autumn. Here was just another of the many ungodly choices which some of the people of Judah had made. This was another path to destruction, followed by those who had forsaken the worship of the true Creator.

¹⁶He then brought me into the inner court of the house of the LORD, and there at the entrance to the temple, between the portico and the altar, were about twenty-five men. With their backs toward the temple of the LORD and their faces toward the east, they were bowing down to the sun in the east.
¹⁷He said to me, "Have you seen this, son of man? Is it a trivial matter for the house of Judah to do the detestable things they are doing here? Must they also fill the land with violence and continually provoke me to anger? Look at them putting the branch to their nose! ¹⁸Therefore I will deal with them in anger; I will not look on them with pity or spare them. Although they shout in my ears, I will not listen to them."

Now Ezekiel's vision took him into the inner court of the temple in Jerusalem. There twenty-five men, most likely representing the priests, performed symbolic actions which had to be the crowning insult to the Lord. Turning their backs on God's temple they worshiped the sun!

The people, the elders, the women and even the priests were abandoning the Lord. They were calling down God's punishment upon themselves for their idolatry. This is why the Lord could say they were responsible for the violence in the land. They had turned their backs on him; he was now turning his back on them. God would refuse to spare them or to listen to their cries, because he knew what was in their hearts. "Look at them putting the branch to their nose!" Apparently this was a gesture of contempt for the Lord. He showed these things to Ezekiel in exile to prove he was justified in destroying the wicked city.

Why is the world in which we live in such a mess? The simple, yet biblical answer is: It is this way because people have denied the Lord his place as Lord of their lives and have gone off on their own selfish ways. When that happens, God's judgment strikes. Often his punishment is to let people suffer the consequences of their sinful, foolish insistence on doing things their way instead of God's way.

Idolaters killed

9 **Then I heard him call out in a loud voice, "Bring the guards of the city here, each with a weapon in his hand." ²And I saw six men coming from the direction of the upper gate, which faces north, each with a deadly weapon in his hand. With them was a man clothed in linen who had a writing kit at his side. They came in and stood beside the bronze altar.**

The Lord made use of the guards in Jerusalem to carry out his commands in this vision. They were the logical choice to do this, since they had weapons with them. Consistently, the destruction was pictured as coming from the north, the direction from which invading armies usually entered Israel. One man clothed not like the guards, but like a priest, was assigned a different function. He was prepared for that function, since he had a writing kit. These servants of God all came and stood in the temple awaiting their orders.

³Now the glory of the God of Israel went up from above the cherubim, where it had been, and moved to the threshold of the temple. Then the LORD called to the man clothed in linen who had the writing kit at his side ⁴and said to him, "Go throughout the city of Jerusalem and put a mark on the foreheads of those who grieve and lament over all the detestable things that are done in it."

⁵As I listened, he said to the others, "Follow him through the city and kill, without showing pity or compassion. ⁶Slaughter old men, young men and maidens, women and children, but do not touch anyone who has the mark. Begin at my sanctuary." So they began with the elders who were in front of the temple.

The glory of the God of Israel came to the threshold of the temple to give the orders. The man clothed in linen and with the writing kit at his side was to mark those believers who grieved over the idolatry being practiced in Jerusalem. This is an obvious indication that the Lord was perfectly aware which people were his.

God then ordered the guards to kill everybody else. They were to begin the slaughter at the sanctuary. The elders who should have taken the lead in keeping the people faithful to the Lord would be punished first, for they had failed to carry out their responsibility. Jesus emphasized this truth when he said, "From everyone who has been given much, much will be demanded; and from the one who has been entrusted with much, much more will be asked" (Luke 12:48).

⁷Then he said to them, "Defile the temple and fill the courts with the slain. Go!" So they went out and began killing through-

out the city. ⁸While they were killing and I was left alone, I fell facedown, crying out, "Ah, Sovereign LORD! Are you going to destroy the entire remnant of Israel in this outpouring of your wrath on Jerusalem?"

⁹He answered me, "The sin of the house of Israel and Judah is exceedingly great; the land is full of bloodshed and the city is full of injustice. They say, 'The LORD has forsaken the land; the LORD does not see.' ¹⁰So I will not look on them with pity or spare them, but I will bring down on their own heads what they have done."

¹¹Then the man in linen with the writing kit at his side brought back word, saying, "I have done as you commanded."

In ancient Israel, contact with a dead body made a person ceremonially unclean for seven days. God's orders to make the temple unclean certainly meant: "Go ahead and defile it. This building isn't for me anymore. You might as well make it ceremonially unclean, since it is spiritually unclean. Why? Because the people who are using it have abandoned me and are worshiping other gods!"

Ezekiel panicked. He thought all of Israel would be destroyed. God explained he was doing only what the sin of the people deserved. The linen-clothed writer reported he had done as commanded. He had marked the believers as belonging to the Lord. So, even if they were killed in the siege of Jerusalem or on their way into exile, or if they were lost in exile, God would know them as his own. They would not be lost forever, as most of their countrymen would be.

Even though Ezekiel was a thousand miles away in far-off Babylon, his heart must have sunk when in the vision he heard the man clothed in linen announce to God: "I have done as you commanded." And Ezekiel knew that the terrible slaughter of Jerusalem's citizens was now an accomplished fact.

The Glory of the Lord Departs from the Temple

10 I looked, and I saw the likeness of a throne of sapphire above the expanse that was over the heads of the cherubim. ²The LORD said to the man clothed in linen, "Go in among the wheels beneath the cherubim. Fill your hands with burning coals from among the cherubim and scatter them over the city." And as I watched, he went in.

³Now the cherubim were standing on the south side of the temple when the man went in, and a cloud filled the inner court. ⁴Then the glory of the LORD rose from above the cherubim and moved to the threshold of the temple. The cloud filled the temple, and the court was full of the radiance of the glory of the LORD. ⁵The sound of the wings of the cherubim could be heard as far away as the outer court, like the voice of God Almighty when he speaks.

⁶When the LORD commanded the man in linen, "Take fire from among the wheels, from among the cherubim," the man went in and stood beside a wheel. ⁷Then one of the cherubim reached out his hand to the fire that was among them. He took up some of it and put it into the hands of the man in linen, who took it and went out. ⁸(Under the wings of the cherubim could be seen what looked like the hands of a man.)

⁹I looked, and I saw beside the cherubim four wheels, one beside each of the cherubim; the wheels sparkled like chrysolite. ¹⁰As for their appearance, the four of them looked alike; each was like a wheel intersecting a wheel. ¹¹As they moved, they would go in any one of the four directions the cherubim faced; the wheels did not turn about as the cherubim went. The cherubim went in whatever direction the head faced, without turning as they went. ¹²Their entire bodies, including their backs, their hands and their wings, were completely full of eyes, as were their four wheels. ¹³I heard the wheels being called "the whirling wheels." ¹⁴Each of the cherubim had four faces: One face was that of a cherub, the second the face of a man, the third the face of a lion, and the fourth the face of an eagle.

¹⁵Then the cherubim rose upward. These were the living creatures I had seen by the Kebar River. ¹⁶When the cherubim moved, the wheels beside them moved; and when the cherubim spread their wings to rise from the ground, the wheels did not leave their side. ¹⁷When the cherubim stood still, they also stood still; and when the cherubim rose, they rose with them, because the spirit of the living creatures was in them.

¹⁸Then the glory of the Lᴏʀᴅ departed from over the threshold of the temple and stopped above the cherubim. ¹⁹While I watched, the cherubim spread their wings and rose from the ground, and as they went, the wheels went with them. They stopped at the entrance to the east gate of the Lᴏʀᴅ's house, and the glory of the God of Israel was above them.

²⁰These were the living creatures I had seen beneath the God of Israel by the Kebar River, and I realized that they were cherubim. ²¹Each had four faces and four wings, and under their wings was what looked like the hands of a man. ²²Their faces had the same appearance as those I had seen by the Kebar River. Each one went straight ahead.

The glory of the Lord first appeared to Ezekiel in chapter 1. It equipped him for the life of ministry to which God had called him. Now Ezekiel sees it again, but in a much more unpleasant context. For one thing, the glory of the Lord, that visible evidence of God's loving presence, was going to leave the temple and the city that had rejected him. And, secondly, the vision God showed Ezekiel let him see that the burning coals taken from among the cherubim would be scattered over the city, to destroy it as God said it deserved.

Again, in this vision the orders to destroy Jerusalem came from the Lord. There is one change. It is not clear why one of the four faces is the face of a cherub instead of an ox (1:10). Much has been written to try to explain the change, but we really don't know why the Lord made the change.

The climax of chapter 10 is found in verses 18 and 19. The glory of the Lord has left the temple. Already in verse 4 it had moved to the courtyard, as though it was reluctant to leave. And now it has left completely. The temple was no longer the Lord's, so why should the visual reminder of his presence stay? The outward should reflect the inward. He wasn't in the hearts of the people. Why should he stay in the temple?

Within each of us there wages a war between God and our sinful nature. Unless our failure to use the Word of the Lord is properly checked and our insistence on having our own selfish, sinful ways is halted, such actions can only drive the Lord to remove his presence from the temples of our hearts. Observing God's departure from the temple in Jerusalem ought to make us aware of the possibility of such an occurrence. We need to ask his help to avoid spiritual disaster.

Judgment on Israel's Leaders

11 **Then the Spirit lifted me up and brought me to the gate of the house of the Lord that faces east. There at the entrance to the gate were twenty-five men, and I saw among them Jaazaniah son of Azzur and Pelatiah son of Benaiah, leaders of the people. ²The Lord said to me, "Son of man, these are the men who are plotting evil and giving wicked advice in this city. ³They say, 'Will it not soon be time to build houses? This city is a cooking pot, and we are the meat.' ⁴Therefore prophesy against them; prophesy, son of man."**

Ezekiel's vision continued. He saw twenty-five men. The phrase "giving wicked advice in the city" hints that they may have been political leaders. We don't know anything more about these men than what is given here, except to say this was a different Jaazaniah from the one in 8:11; that Jaazaniah was "son of Shaphan."

Whoever these men were they were contradicting God's prophets who were saying, "God will soon destroy this city." These leaders were saying, "We don't believe the city is in danger. Soon it will be the building season again, just as usual. We are sure we are safe. This city is an iron shield protecting us. We are just as safe and protected as meat in a pot is protected from the fire by the pot."

⁵Then the Spirit of the LORD came upon me, and he told me to say: "This is what the LORD says: That is what you are saying, O house of Israel, but I know what is going through your mind. ⁶You have killed many people in this city and filled its streets with the dead.

The Lord didn't have to rely on their words to determine what they were thinking. He knew that in their hearts they had abandoned him. He knew their advice would lead the people to rebel against Babylon, and that in turn would lead the Babylonian king to unleash his fury on Jerusalem. In this way the leaders were responsible for the many dead who would fill the streets. Again the Lord speaks in the past tense, as if it were already done. Jerusalem's doom was certain.

⁷"Therefore this is what the Sovereign LORD says: The bodies you have thrown there are the meat and this city is the pot, but I will drive you out of it. ⁸You fear the sword, and the sword is what I will bring against you, declares the Sovereign LORD. ⁹I will drive you out of the city and hand you over to foreigners and inflict punishment on you. ¹⁰You will fall by the sword, and I will execute judgment on you at the borders of Israel. Then you will know that I am the LORD. ¹¹This city will not be a pot for you, nor will you be the meat in it; I will execute judgment on you at the borders of Israel. ¹²And you will know that I am the LORD, for you have not followed my decrees or kept my laws but have conformed to the standards of the nations around you."

The Lord here referred to the picture of the meat and the pot, the iron shield, first used by the leaders (11:3). Instead of serving as a shield, the city would furnish no protection. "This city will not be a pot for you, . . . I will execute judgment on you at the borders of Israel."

The details of the prophecy were carried out precisely as written here. Even the detail that the leaders were not cooked in the pot was carried out when they were led to Riblah, north of Israel's border, and there judged (compare verse 10 with Jeremiah 52:24-27).

The lesson to be learned from all this once again was "You will know that I am the LORD." God had not lost his love for them. He had not changed his mind about them or broken his covenant with them. Rather, they had lost their love for him. They had changed their minds about him and broken their covenant with him.

13Now as I was prophesying, Pelatiah son of Benaiah died. Then I fell facedown and cried out in a loud voice, "Ah, Sovereign LORD! Will you completely destroy the remnant of Israel?"

14The word of the LORD came to me: 15"Son of man, your brothers — your brothers who are your blood relatives and the whole house of Israel — are those of whom the people of Jerusalem have said, 'They are far away from the LORD; this land was given to us as our possession.'

As proof of what God predicted in the vision, Pelatiah, one of Jerusalem's wicked leaders, died. When Ezekiel saw this in his vision he was distressed, although he was the one God sent to proclaim judgment and destruction. Even while he was thundering God's anger, Ezekiel's heart still beat with love for those against whom he was prophesying.

When we bring God's law to people and threaten them with his punishment, we can't do this unemotionally or in a detached way. We do it as an expression of our love for

58

them. When we tell people God must punish them because of their sins, we at the same time will pray to the Lord to lead them to repent, so they might be saved.

As before (8:8), Ezekiel's reaction to Pelatiah's death was, "LORD, will you destroy everybody?" Then the Lord had to remind Ezekiel: "Not all of God's people are in Jerusalem." The exiles in Babylon were his brothers and blood relatives, too. The inhabitants of Jerusalem hadn't felt that way. They had said, "*They* (the exiles) are far away from the Lord; this land was given to *us* as our possession." They had said this contemptuously, perhaps to the departing exiles. Apparently those who remained in Jerusalem felt that the exiles must have been abandoned by God or he would not have let *them* be taken away from his land in the deportation, as though residence in Palestine was proof of nearness to the Lord! This simply was not the case. Those in Babylon were still the people of Israel, no matter where they lived.

In fact, through Ezekiel's vision the Lord was getting through to some of those in exile and leading them to repentance.

Promised Return of Israel

16"Therefore say: 'This is what the Sovereign LORD says: Although I sent them far away among the nations and scattered them among the countries, yet for a little while I have been a sanctuary for them in the countries where they have gone.'

17"Therefore say: 'This is what the Sovereign LORD says: I will gather you from the nations and bring you back from the countries where you have been scattered, and I will give you back the land of Israel again.'

18"They will return to it and remove all its vile images and detestable idols. 19I will give them an undivided heart and put a new spirit in them; I will remove from them their heart of stone and give them a heart of flesh. 20Then they will follow my decrees and be careful to keep my laws. They will be my people, and I will

59

be their God. ²¹But as for those whose hearts are devoted to their vile images and detestable idols, I will bring down on their own heads what they have done, declares the Sovereign LORD."

In ancient times when a nation was led into exile, that usually marked the end of the nation. They never came back. Through Ezekiel God served notice that this wouldn't be the case with the people of Judah. Not all those in exile would be destroyed. In fact, God would be their refuge while they were in Babylon. Those individuals whom the Lord would bring back would abhor worship of false gods. These people were to be the basis of the New Testament church when the Messiah would come.

There would be a small remnant at Christ's time, too. They would be the Old Testament believers whose hearts of stone, which by nature were hardened to the Lord's message, would be changed by the Holy Spirit into hearts of flesh. With hearts of flesh they would believe the gospel and respond to it with love.

Even after the lesson which the exile should have taught, and even when Messiah would be there, some would still be "devoted to their vile images and detestable idols." On their heads the Lord promised to bring down what they had done.

²²Then the cherubim, with the wheels beside them, spread their wings, and the glory of the God of Israel was above them. ²³The glory of the LORD went up from within the city and stopped above the mountain east of it. ²⁴The Spirit lifted me up and brought me to the exiles in Babylonia in the vision given by the Spirit of God.

Then the vision I had seen went up from me, ²⁵and I told the exiles everything the LORD had shown me.

Here is the end of the present vision Ezekiel saw — and what a tragic end! The glory of the Lord, that visual representative of Jehovah in cloud and flame, left the city of

Jerusalem and stopped at the mountain east of the city, the mountain we know as the Mount of Olives. The Lord abandoned his city. Though reluctantly, indicating it was ripe for destruction.

The vision of Jerusalem was over. Back in Babylon, Ezekiel now told the elders what he had seen.

It is so easy to equate the presence of the Lord with something outward, like a church building, a church organization, a congregation, or a synod. The Lord's removal of his presence from the earthly temple and the city of Jerusalem reminds us that his presence is a spiritual presence in the hearts and lives of people. If the Lord's presence isn't in our hearts, if we have edged him out of our lives, he won't be in our church buildings, our congregations or our church organizations either. Only if God continues to live in our hearts through his Word, will he continue to be present in the outward manifestations of our internal relationship.

Predictions of Captivity

Exile Symbolized

12 The Word of the LORD came to me: ²"Son of man, you are living among a rebellious people. They have eyes to see but do not see and ears to hear but do not hear, for they are a rebellious people.**

Sinful human nature can be stubborn. Even though the exiles had felt God's hand of judgment, even though they had been forcibly torn from their homeland and forced to live in a strange land a thousand miles away from home, many of the exiles still held on to the idea that Jerusalem was a charmed city and wouldn't be touched by any destruction. This meant that Ezekiel had his work cut out for him. God therefore outlined another one of the action-prophecies Ezekiel was to deliver to the exiles.

³"Therefore, son of man, pack your belongings for exile and in the daytime, as they watch, set out and go from where you are to another place. Perhaps they will understand, though they are a rebellious house. ⁴During the daytime, while they watch, bring out your belongings packed for exile. Then in the evening, while they are watching, go out like those who go into exile. ⁵While they watch, dig through the wall and take your belongings out through it. ⁶Put them on your shoulder as they are watching and carry them out at dusk. Cover your face so that you cannot see the land, for I have made you a sign to the house of Israel."

⁷So I did as I was commanded. During the day I brought out my things packed for exile. Then in the evening I dug through the wall with my hands. I took my belongings out at dusk, carrying them on my shoulders while they watched.

Why was it necessary to repeat the symbolic message that Jerusalem would be destroyed and its inhabitants taken into exile? This was a message the Jewish exiles had refused to hear. But that was no excuse for Ezekiel to stop preaching.

When we read this repetition, we say, "Why? Why repeat?" But, when we look at our own lives, we recognize the need for it. Whenever people don't accept our message, we stop trying very quickly. We react that way over and over again. So, we need to be encouraged over and over again not to give up. That's what God was doing for Ezekiel with the repeated encouragements. He was getting Ezekiel to continue to bring the Lord's message in spite of the seeming lack of progress in accomplishing anything — "perhaps they will understand."

Not only do we need to continue sharing the message, but we also need to hear it over and over. Our own hardness of heart needs to be broken down constantly and replaced with a heart of flesh.

Six years earlier the people to whom Ezekiel was presenting this charade had done exactly what the prophet was now acting out — assembling the pitiful little pack which exiles carry with them into captivity. Thus, they immediately caught the meaning of his actions. Ezekiel's digging through the wall reminds us that the houses in Babylon were made of mud brick. This action symbolized the desperation of the people trying to escape the siege of Jerusalem. They would attempt to sneak out in any way possible.

The prophet's covering his face might have meant that the people couldn't bear to look at the beloved land they were now leaving, or that they were so ashamed and filled with sorrow that they couldn't bear to look at anybody else. A bit later we'll look at still another possible meaning to this symbolic action.

⁸"In the morning the word of the LORD came to me: ⁹"Son of man, did not that rebellious house of Israel ask you, 'What are you doing?'

¹⁰"Say to them, 'This is what the Sovereign LORD says: This oracle concerns the prince in Jerusalem and the whole house of Israel who are there.' ¹¹Say to them, 'I am a sign to you.'

"As I have done, so it will be done to them. They will go into exile as captives.

¹²"The prince among them will put his things on his shoulder at dusk and leave, and a hole will be dug in the wall for him to go through. He will cover his face so that he cannot see the land. ¹³I will spread my net for him, and he will be caught in my snare; I will bring him to Babylonia, the land of the Chaldeans, but he will not see it, and there he will die. ¹⁴I will scatter to the winds all those around him — his staff and all his troops — and I will pursue them with drawn sword.

¹⁵"They will know that I am the LORD when I disperse them among the nations and scatter them through the countries. ¹⁶But I will spare a few of them from the sword, famine and plague, so that in the nations where they go they may acknowledge all their detestable practices. Then they will know that I am the LORD."

Ezekiel's charade had the desired effect. The people asked, "What does this all mean?" Zedekiah, the prince of Israel, would go into exile with the rest of the inhabitants of Jerusalem. Ezekiel never called Zedekiah "king" because the real king was Jehoiachin, who was already in exile. Ezekiel and the rest of those already in Babylonia always considered Zedekiah a temporary leader placed on the throne by the Babylonians, thus the term "prince." The people would try to sneak Zedekiah out through the wall. It wouldn't work. He would be captured. His eyes would be put out and he would be taken to Babylon where he would die, never having seen Babylonia (Jeremiah 39:4-7; 52:4-11; 2 Kings 25:1-7). The symbol of covering one's face in verse 6 might have been a hint at this blindness.

Why was all this happening? Look at the number of times God uses the pronoun "I" in verses 14 and 15. Those who were spared would serve a confessional purpose. When asked by other people among whom they would be scattered, "Why did your God let this happen to you?" they could properly answer, "Because we broke our covenant with the LORD." To the next group of exiles coming to Babylon, those already there, on the basis of Ezekiel's message, could say, "Even if Jerusalem is in ruins, God still lives. He is among us here." They would know that what God said — "I am the LORD" — was true. The true God was in control. He was using the momentous fall of Jerusalem and exile for his purposes.

To confess God before men is always the function of God's people. We can confidently speak to the person whose circumstances in life have led him to conclude life is meaningless and consists only of one mess after another. We can share this assurance, "In spite of circumstances, the Lord lives and he is among us." In spite of the consequences of sin all around us, we have Christ's word and promise, "I am with you always" (Matthew 28:20). Often that promise gives us the strength and courage to carry on.

¹⁷The word of the Lᴏʀᴅ came to me: ¹⁸"Son of man, tremble as you eat your food, and shudder in fear as you drink your water. ¹⁹Say to the people of the land: 'This is what the Sovereign Lᴏʀᴅ says about those living in Jerusalem and in the land of Israel: They will eat their food in anxiety and drink their water in despair, for their land will be stripped of everything in it because of the violence of all who live there. ²⁰The inhabited towns will be laid waste and the land will be desolate. Then you will know that I am the Lᴏʀᴅ.' "

This is pretty much a repetition of 4:9-17. Food and the necessities of life would be lacking in the siege of Jerusalem. Ezekiel was to tremble as he ate his scant rations, to symbolize that life among the besieged would be filled with fear and despair. This was another frightening result of the sinfulness and violence of the people of Jerusalem and Israel in rebelling against God and his commandments. The nightmare of the siege would be their fault. They should blame themselves for it.

²¹The word of the Lᴏʀᴅ came to me: ²²"Son of man, what is this proverb you have in the land of Israel: 'The days go by and every vision comes to nothing'? ²³Say to them, 'This is what the Sovereign Lᴏʀᴅ says: I am going to put an end to this proverb, and they will no longer quote it in Israel.' Say to them, 'The days are near when every vision will be fulfilled. ²⁴For there will be no more false visions or flattering divinations among the people of Israel. ²⁵But I the Lᴏʀᴅ will speak what I will, and it shall be fulfilled without delay. For in your days, you rebellious house, I will fulfill whatever I say, declares the Sovereign Lᴏʀᴅ.' "

Most people in the land of Israel said, "There have been many prophets of doom. They all said God would punish us.

But it never happens. We just don't believe these prophets or their messages anymore." The Lord would put an end to that kind of talk. When he turned the Babylonian army loose on Jerusalem, exactly what Ezekiel predicted happened.

When that happened, all those false prophets who kept saying the opposite of the Lord's prophets would have to close up shop. Many false prophets had begun to say what the people wanted to hear. They prophesied, "Nothing will happen. Everything will be fine." These false visions and flattering divinations would come to a screeching halt along with everything else when Jerusalem fell.

Ezekiel's message was getting very precise when he could say that all this would happen "in your days."

26The word of the Lord came to me: 27"Son of man, the house of Israel is saying, 'The vision he sees is for many years from now, and he prophesies about the distant future.'

28"Therefore say to them, 'This is what the Sovereign Lord says: None of my words will be delayed any longer; whatever I say will be fulfilled, declares the Sovereign Lord.' "

Some of Ezekiel's countrymen were not quite as skeptical about the prophetic warnings. They said, "We won't say these predictions of doom aren't true. We will just say they will be fulfilled in the future. The doom they predict is still a long way off and has nothing to do with us now." To them Ezekiel was to say, "Wrong! The time of God's judgment is very near."

Unbelievers will make use of whatever rationalizations they can for their refusal to believe God's word. As in Ezekiel's day, people in our day say it is obvious God's promises about coming to judge and destroy are not valid. We don't have to worry that they will be fulfilled. And why

66

not? "Because it has been so long since he made them. If they were going to be kept, they would have been kept long ago. Jesus, come again? Are you kidding me? He talked about that 2,000 years ago." St. Peter vividly describes just this attitude: ". . . in the last days scoffers will come, scoffing and following their own evil desires. They will say, 'Where is this "coming" he promised? Ever since our fathers died, everything goes on as it has since the beginning of creation. . . .' " Such scoffing will no more prevent Christ's return to judge the world than the scoffers of Ezekiel's time prevented the destruction of Jerusalem. When God is ready he will carry out his promises.

From another viewpoint the unbelieving person might say, "It is obvious God's promises to return to judge and destroy the world are not valid for us. He has much more history which needs to be carried out before his purposes for the universe have been accomplished." In contrast to this kind of talk, we take every thought captive to make it obedient to Christ (2 Corinthians 10:5). Our Savior has promised to return. And in following his word we keep watch, because we do not know the day or the hour when he will come again (Matthew 25:13).

False Prophets Condemned

13 The word of the LORD came to me: **²"Son of man, prophesy against the prophets of Israel who are now prophesying. Say to those who prophesy out of their own imagination: 'Hear the word of the LORD! ³This is what the Sovereign LORD says: Woe to the foolish prophets who follow their own spirit and have seen nothing! ⁴Your prophets, O Israel, are like jackals among ruins. ⁵You have not gone up to the breaks in the wall to repair it for the house of Israel so that it will stand firm in the battle on the day of the LORD. ⁶Their visions are false and their divinations a lie. They say, "The LORD declares," when the LORD has not sent**

them; yet they expect their words to be fulfilled. ⁷Have you not seen false visions and uttered lying divinations when you say, "The LORD declares," though I have not spoken?

With this chapter another new message came to Ezekiel, which he was to relay to the Jews in exile. This message was aimed at false prophets and prophetesses who were at work among God's people.

These prophets were making up their own message. They claimed it came from God, but in reality it didn't. They hadn't seen visions from God as Ezekiel had (1:1). They were fools in the spiritual sense (Psalm 14:1), denying spiritual truth.

God compares them to jackals. These animals inhabited desolate places, without benefit to anyone but threatening danger to all. When Jerusalem would lie in ruin, these false prophets would be just like jackals, "wandering about" and howling over the fall of that great city, something which they had denied would ever happen. These prophets would have been much more helpful had they done what they should have. But they had made no attempt to fortify Israel against the coming destruction by calling the people to repentance and faith.

Their false visions had denied that God's destruction would befall Jerusalem and they had predicted a speedy return of the exiles to Judah. Such lies only served to reinforce the false security of the people and allowed them to remain in their unbelief and impenitence. What was even worse — these false prophets even began to believe their message themselves. They allowed sinful unbelief, and tolerated idolatry without comment. Such an approach, in and of itself, should have identified them as false prophets. One of the marks God had given his people by which to identify false prophets was "they will allow idolatry and what they say won't happen" (Deuteronomy 13:1-5; 18:21,22). If they claimed visions and practiced divinations and the Lord wasn't the source, then there could be only one other source — the devil.

We Christians need to be concerned about properly distinguishing between law and gospel and applying the proper teaching of Scripture at the proper time. If we apply the gospel when the law is needed or the law when the gospel is needed, we will be reinforcing false security and impenitence. We will be doing just what those false teachers in Babylon were doing.

Why do we who have been Christians thirty, forty, fifty years or more still study the Word regularly? It is so easy to teach our own opinion, and actually think our message is what the Lord says. We need to study the Word regularly to conform our message to the message from the Lord.

When people today claim to see visions or foretell the future, we need to apply the same test from the Lord. Is their god the God of the Bible? Is their savior the Christ proclaimed in Scripture? Do their predictions always come to pass like those of God's true prophets? If the answer to these questions is no, we can be sure the source of their revelations is not the Lord.

8" 'Therefore this is what the Sovereign LORD says: Because of your false words and lying visions, I am against you, declares the Sovereign LORD. 9My hand will be against the prophets who see false visions and utter lying divinations. They will not belong to the council of my people or be listed in the records of the house of Israel, nor will they enter the land of Israel. Then you will know that I am the Sovereign LORD.

A three-part punishment was in store for these false prophets. 1) They would lose their authority and respect among the people because their prophecies would prove to be false. Consequently, they would fall from their leadership positions. 2) They would not be listed among God's people after the exile. 3) They would not return with the exiles after the Babylonian captivity would come to an end.

¹⁰" 'Because they lead my people astray, saying, "Peace," when there is no peace, and because, when a flimsy wall is built, they cover it with whitewash, ¹¹therefore tell those who cover it with whitewash that it is going to fall. Rain will come in torrents, and I will send hailstones hurtling down, and violent winds will burst forth. ¹²When the wall collapses, will people not ask you, "Where is the whitewash you covered it with?"**

The false prophets spoke reassuring words: "There will be no problem for Jerusalem and the exiles will soon be OK." The Lord compares this message to a whitewashed, flimsy wall. It is attractive to the eye and gives the illusion of safety. But it offers no protection and is easily knocked down by the first wind that comes along.

The wall of lies of the false teachers not only offered no protection from the coming destruction, but actually hid from the people the seriousness of their spiritual condition. This wall of lies would be knocked down when the Babylonian armies would batter down the walls of Jerusalem.

¹³" 'Therefore this is what the Sovereign LORD says: In my wrath I will unleash a violent wind, and in my anger hailstones and torrents of rain will fall with destructive fury. ¹⁴I will tear down the wall you have covered with whitewash and will level it to the ground so that its foundation will be laid bare. When it falls, you will be destroyed in it; and you will know that I am the LORD. ¹⁵So I will spend my wrath against the wall and against those who covered it with whitewash. I will say to you, "The wall is gone and so are those who whitewashed it, ¹⁶those prophets of Israel who

prophesied to Jerusalem and saw visions of peace for her when there was no peace, declares the Sovereign LORD." '

God promised to destroy Jerusalem. The false prophets would lose their credibility, their positions and their occupations along with their capital city.

Why is dishonesty even more damaging in the spiritual realm than in any other realm? Because souls are involved. If we as preachers, teachers and witnesses for Jesus tell people only what they want to hear, when it is not the truth of God, we might become popular and maybe even quite successful. But if our whitewash job leads people to a false sense of spiritual satisfaction or safety, we are personally responsible when those people fall into sin, give in to the devil or lose their faith altogether. God sees through the whitewash. He will deal with deceivers for what they have done to the souls of others. We need to carefully teach all things which Jesus has commanded.

17"Now, son of man, set your face against the daughters of your people who prophesy out of their own imagination. Prophesy against them 18and say, 'This is what the Sovereign LORD says: Woe to the women who sew magic charms on all their wrists and make veils of various lengths for their heads in order to ensnare people. Will you ensnare the lives of my people but preserve your own? 19You have profaned me among my people for a few handfuls of barley and scraps of bread. By lying to my people, who listen to lies, you have killed those who should not have died and have spared those who should not live.

There were women in the Jewish community in Babylon who despite God's clear warnings against dabbling in the occult (Leviticus 19:26; Deuteronomy 18:10) did just that. We are not told exactly what these women intended to accomplish. Perhaps their charms and veils were meant to

71

cast spells on people to hinder their lives. The expression "preserve your own" seems to indicate they carried out their practices for a fee and thus preserved their own lives.

By causing people to practice occult forms of magic along with the worship of the Lord, they caused the destruction of those who should not have died. At the same time they spared their own lives, which should have been destroyed because of their corrupt superstitious practices.

20" 'Therefore this is what the Sovereign LORD says: I am against your magic charms with which you ensnare people like birds and I will tear them from your arms; I will set free the people that you ensnare like birds. 21I will tear off your veils and save my people from your hands, and they will no longer fall prey to your power. Then you will know that I am the LORD. 22Because you disheartened the righteous with your lies, when I had brought them no grief, and because you encouraged the wicked not to turn from their evil ways and so save their lives, 23therefore you will no longer see false visions or practice divination. I will save my people from your hands. And then you will know that I am the LORD.' "

As is always the case, this false practice had produced the opposite of what the Lord desired. God's people should have been encouraged by the Lord's message; instead they were being disheartened by the practice and message of these false prophetesses. Those who should have been urged to repent were by these false superstitious practices cemented in their sins. The Lord promised to get rid of the outward signs of their supposed magic powers and free the people from the power of their superstitious practices.

Dabbling in the occult did not die out in ancient Babylon. It flourishes in our modern world. Perhaps the popularity of the occult is a result of people's desire to maintain some belief in the supernatural in a scientific age. Although many take a "What can it harm?" attitude toward such activities, we Christians cannot. At the very least, participation in occult practices opens us to the devil's influence by downgrading his activity into the category of a plaything. At worst, such participation can so divert our attention from the Lord that it leads us to seek truth from sources other than God's revealed truth and to accept other than scriptural answers to spiritual questions. When it comes to spiritual matters "seeking truth from other sources" is just another way of describing unbelief.

Idolaters Condemned

14 **Some of the elders of Israel came to me and sat down in front of me. ²Then the word of the LORD came to me: ³"Son of man, these men have set up idols in their hearts and put wicked stumbling blocks before their faces. Should I let them inquire of me at all? ⁴Therefore speak to them and tell them, 'This is what the Sovereign LORD says: When any Israelite sets up idols in his heart and puts a wicked stumbling block before his face and then goes to a prophet, I the LORD will answer him myself in keeping with his great idolatry. ⁵I will do this to recapture the hearts of the people of Israel, who have all deserted me for their idols.'**

⁶"Therefore say to the house of Israel, 'This is what the Sovereign LORD says: Repent! Turn from your idols and renounce all your detestable practices!

Once again we're told that the elders of Israel came to visit Ezekiel. It is clear from this that the Babylonians allowed the captive Jews a large measure of freedom, including freedom of movement, assembly and worship.

Some of the Jewish leaders approached Ezekiel on the pretense of desiring information from him. Most likely they asked about what was happening in Jerusalem and about what would happen to them in Babylon. What displeased the Lord was the insincerity of this inquiry. They were idolaters but were asking the Lord through Ezekiel, just in case.

God's question in verse 3 implied that such people wouldn't get an answer through the prophet. Anyone who worshiped a false god forfeited his right to inquire of the Lord. Their idols are called "wicked stumbling blocks" because they were causing the people's spiritual downfall, and would also cause the downfall of the nation and of Jerusalem. Although these elders deserved no answer from the Lord, he condescended to answer. But his answer would be in keeping with their idolatry, in other words, with their punishment. God could see right through their pious outward request into their hypocritical hearts. Behind the Lord's rough answer lay a merciful purpose — to recapture the hearts of his people. Thus, the order from God to issue a John the Baptist-like proclamation: "Repent!"

So often we go to the Lord with a request, but our heart is filled with self-sufficiency. The god Self doesn't let us trust in the Lord to fulfill our need. So often we go to the Lord with an inquiry, but our heart is filled with our own preconceived answers. The god of Human Wisdom doesn't let us trust in the Lord to give us the right answer. At such times the Lord has to answer us with his discipline to recapture his rightful position in our hearts.

7" 'When any Israelite or any alien living in Israel separates himself from me and sets up idols in his heart and puts a wicked stumbling block before his face and then goes to a prophet to inquire of me, I the LORD will answer him myself. 8I will set my face against that man and make him an example and a byword. I will cut him off from my people. Then you will know that I am the LORD.

The same warning given to the elders in verses 4 and 5 is here transmitted to the ordinary citizens. Although these citizens would have liked the Lord's prophet to tell the good news, they heard the very opposite.

⁹" 'And if the prophet is enticed to utter a prophecy, I the LORD have enticed that prophet, and I will stretch out my hand against him and destroy him from among my people Israel. ¹⁰They will bear their guilt — the prophet will be as guilty as the one who consults him. ¹¹Then the people of Israel will no longer stray from me, nor will they defile themselves anymore with all their sins. They will be my people, and I will be their God, declares the Sovereign LORD.'

When idolatrous people approached a false prophet, God would often use that prophet. He would "entice" him. That is, God would let the prophet say what the people wanted to hear. Although the secondary cause of the false prophet's activity is the false prophet's unbelief, the primary cause is the Lord who often allows people to go their own way and suffer the consequences. Here God would be punishing the deceiver and rejecter by letting him be deceived by his own delusions. As a judgment on prophet and people he would also let the false teacher prophesy falsely, and thus let him cement his listeners in their unbelief.

One of the most severe forms of discipline the Lord uses is to permit us to continue in our selfish ways — even "enticing" us to carry them out! This discipline is most effective because the drastic, disastrous results of our own selfishness often tell us better than anything else: "God's way is the best."

Inescapable Judgment

¹²The word of the LORD came to me: ¹³"Son of man, if a country sins against me by being unfaithful and I stretch out my hand against it to cut off its food supply and send famine upon it and kill its men and their animals, ¹⁴even if these three men — Noah, Daniel and Job — were in it, they could save only themselves by their righteousness, declares the Sovereign LORD.

¹⁵"Or if I send wild beasts through that country and they leave it childless and it becomes desolate so that no one can pass through it because of the beasts, ¹⁶as surely as I live, declares the Sovereign LORD, even if these three men were in it, they could not save their own sons or daughters. They alone would be saved, but the land would be desolate.

¹⁷"Or if I bring a sword against that country and say, 'Let the sword pass throughout the land,' and I kill its men and their animals, ¹⁸as surely as I live, declares the Sovereign LORD, even if these three men were in it, they could not save their own sons or daughters. They alone would be saved.

¹⁹"Or if I send a plague into that land and pour out my wrath upon it through bloodshed, killing its men and their animals, ²⁰as surely as I live, declares the Sovereign LORD, even if Noah, Daniel and Job were in it, they could save neither son nor daughter. They would save only themselves by their righteousness.

The people regarded Jerusalem as a good luck charm to keep them safe. They also regarded the presence of righteous people, believers among them, as an insurance policy against God's anger. "God will surely not punish us because he would also have to punish those faithful ones," they reasoned. "Not so," said the Lord. The destruction of Jerusalem was inevitable. God's judgment by famine, wild beasts, sword and plague had been so firmly decreed that even the presence of outstanding believers like Noah, Daniel and Job couldn't have prevented it.

²¹"For this is what the Sovereign LORD says: How much worse will it be when I send against Jerusalem my four dreadful judgments — sword and famine and wild beasts and plague — to kill its men and their animals! ²²Yet there will be some survivors — sons and daughters who will be brought out of it. They will come to you, and when you see their conduct and their actions, you will be consoled regarding the disaster I have brought upon Jerusalem

— every disaster I have brought upon it. [23]You will be consoled when you see their conduct and their actions for you will know that I have done nothing in it without cause, declares the Sovereign LORD."

If the presence of those three believers wouldn't have been able to stop the inevitable destruction of Jerusalem, how much worse it would be in reality, since there were no such righteous ones present to buffer God's anger! War brought famine, which brought death, which brought scavengers, which brought disease. God used all four when he poured out his wrath on the city and people who had rebelled against him. The survivors brought to Babylon would by their idolatrous actions prove to those already in exile that the Lord had dealt justly with Jerusalem. This would assure the exiles that God never acts unfairly.

Relationships with the Lord are personal. Our parents' faith does not cover our unbelief. Our spouse's sanctification does not cover our wickedness. Our family's dedication to the Lord does not cover our indifference.

It is sobering, indeed, to see God's disciplining hand at work. It helps us realize that without these punishments the straying might never be led back to the Lord.

Jerusalem, a Useless Vine

15 The word of the LORD came to me: [2]"Son of man, how is the wood of a vine better than that of a branch on any of the trees of the forest? [3]Is wood ever taken from it to make anything useful? Do they make pegs from it to hang things on? [4]And after it is thrown on the fire as fuel and the fire burns both ends and chars the middle, is it then useful for anything? [5]If it was not useful for anything when it was whole, how much less can it be made into something useful when the fire has burned it and it is charred?

⁶"Therefore this is what the Sovereign LORD says: As I have given the wood of the vine among the trees of the forest as fuel for the fire, so will I treat the people living in Jerusalem. ⁷I will set my face against them. Although they have come out of the fire, the fire will yet consume them. And when I set my face against them, you will know that I am the LORD. ⁸I will make the land desolate because they have been unfaithful, declares the Sovereign LORD."

A vine is good only because of the fruit it produces. Its wood is worthless. You can't make anything out of it. And if the wood of the vine is charred, it is even worse than worthless. Jerusalem had produced no fruits of repentance. Therefore, she was like a fruitless vine. Good only for being burned up. She had come through previous burnings of God's anger, including the Assyrian captivity of 722 B.C. and Babylonian siege of Jerusalem in 597 B.C. resulting in the exile of which Ezekiel was a part. Now, however, she would be consumed by the fire of God's wrath.

God always expects fruits from those whom he has attached to himself through the Savior. If there is no fruit, there is no connection with the Lord. People who claim to be God's but don't live to thank the Lord and to transmit his grace to others are like a useless vine. They are good only for the fire of the Lord's anger.

An Allegory of Unfaithful Jerusalem

16 The word of the LORD came to me: ²"Son of man, confront Jerusalem with her detestable practices ³and say, 'This is what the Sovereign LORD says to Jerusalem: Your ancestry and birth were in the land of the Canaanites; your father was an Amorite and your mother a Hittite. ⁴On the day you were born your cord was not cut, nor were you washed with water to make you clean, nor were you rubbed with salt or wrapped in cloths. ⁵No one looked on you with pity or had compassion enough to do any of these things for you. Rather, you were thrown out into the open field, for on the day you were born you were despised.

Ezekiel 16 is without a doubt one of the most graphic and one of the most moving chapters of the entire Bible. It is a frank discussion of the shameful guilt of the nation which God had chosen as his very own. Ezekiel compares Israel to an abandoned baby who is rescued but who rewards the love of her divine rescuer by turning to a life of prostitution. The prophet's frank language will offend only those who fail to realize what a dirty thing sin is in God's sight.

We have already seen how God was rightly angry with the "detestable practices" of the Israelites. Even though their roots went back to godly Abram of Ur, the Lord said here, "It certainly looks as if your ancestry and birth are from the heathen Canaanites, Amorites and Hittites." Spiritually the people seemed to be descended from these previous inhabitants of their land, for they had become just like them in customs, morals, religion and attitudes.

Throughout the chapter the people of Jerusalem and the entire nation of Israel are compared to a single person. The Lord starts with a description of the nation as a newborn baby. When this baby girl was born, nobody took care of her. Nobody washed her, nobody rubbed her with salt to cleanse her, nobody clothed her. Rather, she was abandoned as many female babies were among heathen people of the day.

If we think of the birth of the nation occurring in Egypt, the picture fits. Jacob and his sons were foreigners in a strange land. As we learn from the book of Exodus, the Egyptians came to hate and despise Israel, and finally attempted to attack and destroy her.

6" 'Then I passed by and saw you kicking about in your blood, and as you lay there in your blood I said to you, "Live!" 7I made you grow like a plant of the field. You grew up and developed and became the most beautiful of jewels. Your breasts were formed and your hair grew, you who were naked and bare.

By his gracious empowering word God had made this weak, kicking "baby" of a nation live. He cared for her and saw to her growth. In spite of overwhelming opposition in Egypt the nation grew.

Because of God's blessings she became beautiful, even though she still didn't have any earthly possessions to call her own.

8" 'Later I passed by, and when I looked at you and saw that you were old enough for love, I spread the corner of my garment over you and covered your nakedness. I gave you my solemn oath and entered into a covenant with you, declares the Sovereign LORD, and you became mine.

When this child had gained some maturity, the Lord spread the corner of his garment over her. This symbolized an indication of his intention to marry her. He pledged his loyalty to her. At Mt. Sinai the Lord actually entered into a covenant, a solemn contract with his beloved.

9" 'I bathed you with water and washed the blood from you and put ointments on you. 10I clothed you with an embroidered dress and put leather sandals on you. I dressed you in fine linen and covered you with costly garments. 11I adorned you with jewelry: I put bracelets on your arms and a necklace around your neck, 12and I put a ring on your nose, earrings on your ears and a beautiful crown on your head. 13So you were adorned with gold and silver; your clothes were of fine linen and costly fabric and embroidered cloth. Your food was fine flour, honey and olive oil. You became very beautiful and rose to be a queen. 14And your fame spread among the nations on account of your beauty, because the splendor I had given you made your beauty perfect, declares the Sovereign LORD.

After she had been given the land of Canaan for her home, God showered her with all sorts of physical blessings. During the reign of David and Solomon, the nation became a queen. Other nations became aware of what a rich, powerful and blessed land this little corner of the world had become.

¹⁵" 'But you trusted in your beauty and used your fame to become a prostitute. You lavished your favors on anyone who passed by and your beauty became his. ¹⁶You took some of your garments to make gaudy high places, where you carried on your prostitution. Such things should not happen, nor should they ever occur. ¹⁷You also took the fine jewelry I gave you, the jewelry made of my gold and silver, and you made for yourself male idols and engaged in prostitution with them. ¹⁸And you took your embroidered clothes to put on them, and you offered my oil and incense before them. ¹⁹Also the food I provided for you — the fine flour, olive oil and honey I gave you to eat — you offered as fragrant incense before them. That is what happened, declares the Sovereign LORD.

Because things were going so well, she began to trust herself instead of the Lord. She began to adopt heathen worship practice, thus prostituting herself with other gods while committing adultery toward her husband the Lord. The very blessings which she had received from her husband the Lord, she used to worship these false gods!

²⁰" 'And you took your sons and daughters whom you bore to me and sacrificed them as food to the idols. Was your prostitution not enough? ²¹You slaughtered my children and sacrificed them to the idols. ²²In all your detestable practices and your prostitution you did not remember the days of your youth, when you were naked and bare, kicking about in your blood.

She even went so far as to adopt the heathen practice of sacrificing children (Judges 11:29-39; 2 Kings 16:3; 21:6). How could she fall into all these evil practices? She had begun to take the blessings of the Lord for granted. She didn't even remember anymore that he had taken her when she was naked and kicking in her own blood, and made her into a richly blessed nation.

23" 'Woe! Woe to you, declares the Sovereign LORD. In addition to all your other wickedness, 24you built a mound for yourself and made a lofty shrine in every public square. 25At the end of every street you built your lofty shrines and degraded your beauty, offering your body with increasing promiscuity to anyone who passed by. 26You engaged in prostitution with the Egyptians, your lustful neighbors, and provoked me to anger with your increasing promiscuity. 27So I stretched out my hand against you and reduced your territory; I gave you over to the greed of your enemies, the daughters of the Philistines, who were shocked by your lewd conduct. 28You engaged in prostitution with the Assyrians too, because you were insatiable; and even after that, you still were not satisfied. 29Then you increased your promiscuity to include Babylonia, a land of merchants, but even with this you were not satisfied.

Her attitude toward the Lord kept disintegrating. It became so bad she began to accept and even invite religious philosophy and practice from anybody who came through the area on the international trade routes which passed through the land of Canaan. Worship sites built to a variety of gods dotted the landscape. Political alliances with Egypt (Isaiah 30:1-3; 31:1), with Assyria (2 Kings 16:7) and with Babylon (2 Kings 20:12-14) not only showed a lack of trust in the Lord, but involved her in worshiping the gods of these nations, something implied in an alliance between the gods of nations.

Just as some people are so sexually obsessed that no matter how much sexual activity they are engaged in they seem to want more, so the people of Israel seemed to be unable to satisfy their desire to fill their lives with the worship copied from the nations around them. Although the political-religious alliances were intended to keep the gods of the other nations on her side and thus keep her safe, the opposite happened. She began to lose her land little by little, after the heady expansion under David and Solomon.

God used some of the old enemies, whom Israel had failed to clear out of the land, to carry out this disciplining action against his people. The Philistines were longtime enemies of Israel. Earlier in the history of Israel they had become aware of the blessings which the God of the Covenant had given to this people. Now even the wicked Philistines were shocked to see that Israel would turn her back on all those blessings.

30" 'How weak-willed you are, declares the Sovereign LORD, when you do all these things, acting like a brazen prostitute! 31When you built your mounds at the head of every street and made your lofty shrines in every public square, you were unlike a prostitute, because you scorned payment.

32" 'You adulterous wife! You prefer strangers to your own husband! 33Every prostitute receives a fee, but you give gifts to all your lovers, bribing them to come to you from everywhere for your illicit favors. 34So in your prostitution you are the opposite of others; no one runs after you for your favors. You are the very opposite, for you give payment and none is given to you.

In her spiritual adultery Israel was even worse than an ordinary prostitute. She actually paid to have these foreigners come in with their idols so she could commit adultery with them against her husband the Lord. Israel and Judah often called in one of the foreign powers to help them against their enemies. In order to get help, she frequently had to pay tribute, or at least make a major contribution to the war chest of the power she invited in. Paying to be a prostitute! How low can you get!

35" 'Therefore, you prostitute, hear the word of the LORD! 36This is what the Sovereign LORD says: Because you poured out your wealth and exposed your nakedness in your promiscuity with your lovers, and because of all your detestable idols, and because you gave them your children's blood, 37therefore I am going to gather all your lovers, with whom you found pleasure, those you loved as well as those you hated. I will gather them against you from all around and will strip you in front of them, and they will see all your nakedness. 38I will sentence you to the punishment of women who commit adultery and who shed blood; I will bring upon you the blood vengeance of my wrath and jealous anger. 39Then I will hand you over to your lovers, and they will tear down your mounds and destroy your lofty shrines. They will strip you of your clothes and take your fine jewelry and leave you naked and bare. 40They will bring a mob against you, who will stone you and hack you to pieces with their swords. 41They will burn down your houses and inflict punishment on you in the sight of many women. I will put a stop to your prostitution, and you will no longer pay your lovers. 42Then my wrath against you will subside and my jealous anger will turn away from you; I will be calm and no longer angry.

The punishment promised by the Lord fit the crime. All those foreign powers who brought the false gods to Israel would gather against her to destroy her. In ancient Israel adultery was punishable by stoning, and murder — in this case of the children offered to idols — was also punishable by death. God would raise up nations to destroy everything constructed for the worship of the false gods along with all the indications of the Lord's blessings on the people. Israel would lose her "lofty [heathen] shrines" as well as the "clothes" and "fine jewelry" God had given her. In this way God would bring an end to the spiritual prostitution with false gods.

And when the prostitution would stop, so would the Lord's anger.

⁴³" 'Because you did not remember the days of your youth but enraged me with all these things, I will surely bring down on your head what you have done, declares the Sovereign LORD. Did you not add lewdness to all your other detestable practices?

⁴⁴" 'Everyone who quotes proverbs will quote this proverb about you: "Like mother, like daughter." ⁴⁵You are a true daughter of your mother, who despised her husband and her children; and you are a true sister of your sisters, who despised their husbands and their children. Your mother was a Hittite and your father an Amorite. ⁴⁶Your older sister was Samaria, who lived to the north of you with her daughters; and your younger sister, who lived to the south of you with her daughters, was Sodom. ⁴⁷You not only walked in their ways and copied their detestable practices, but in all your ways you soon became more depraved then they. ⁴⁸As surely as I live, declares the Sovereign LORD, your sister Sodom and her daughters never did what you and your daughters have done.

Israel's history seemed to prove more and more that the pagan Amorites and Hittites (verses 3 and 45) were her parents instead of Abram, the man of faith in the Lord. Now we are told that wicked Samaria and Sodom were her sisters. She copied them in their idolatry and ungodliness. In view of all the additional blessings Jerusalem and Judah had received, her unfaithfulness was far worse than that of Sodom and Samaria.

⁴⁹" 'Now this was the sin of your sister Sodom: She and her daughters were arrogant, overfed and unconcerned; they did not help the poor and needy. ⁵⁰They were haughty and did detestable things before me. Therefore I did away with them as you have seen. ⁵¹Samaria did not commit half the sins you did. You have done more detestable things than they, and have made your

85

sisters seem righteous by all these things you have done. ⁵²Bear your disgrace, for you have furnished some justification for your sisters. Because your sins were more vile than theirs, they appear more righteous than you. So then, be ashamed and bear your disgrace, for you have made your sisters appear righteous.

Sodom and the smaller city-states around her were rich but did not help those in need. They lived their lives in a manner totally displeasing to God. So God "rained down burning sulfur" and wiped them off the face of the earth (Genesis 19:24,25). Samaria was involved in idolatry. But next to Jerusalem and Judah, Samaria and Sodom seemed to be more righteous.

⁵³" 'However, I will restore the fortunes of Sodom and her daughters and of Samaria and her daughters, and your fortunes along with them, ⁵⁴so that you may bear your disgrace and be ashamed of all you have done in giving them comfort. ⁵⁵And your sisters, Sodom with her daughters and Samaria with her daughters, will return to what they were before; and you and your daughters will return to what you were before. ⁵⁶You would not even mention your sister Sodom in the day of your pride, ⁵⁷before your wickedness was uncovered. Even so, you are now scorned by the daughters of Edom and all her neighbors and the daughters of the Philistines — all those around you who despise you. ⁵⁸You will bear the consequences of your lewdness and your detestable practices, declares the LORD.

The Lord's mercy can lift even the lowest sinner from degradation and restore that sinner to communion with him. He promised to do that here. He would lead Jerusalem and Judah to recognize her sins were much worse than those of Sodom (representing people without God's written law) and Samaria (representing people who fall away from the Lord). He would lead them all to repent.

When things had been going well for her, Israel didn't even want to be reminded of what had happened to Sodom. But it would have been a good reminder for her of how the Lord deals with impenitent unbelievers. She had despised Sodom because of what happened to her. Now Jerusalem and Judah would be destroyed and despised by all the neighbors.

Let us apply this to ourselves, lest we in pride look down on others. We daily need God's grace.

59" 'This is what the Sovereign LORD says: I will deal with you as you deserve, because you have despised my oath by breaking the covenant. 60Yet I will remember the covenant I made with you in the days of your youth, and I will establish an everlasting covenant with you. 61Then you will remember your ways and be ashamed when you receive your sisters, both those who are older than you and those who are younger. I will give them to you as daughters, but not on the basis of my covenant with you. 62So I will establish my covenant with you, and you will know that I am the LORD. Then, when I make atonement for you for all you have done, you will remember and be ashamed and never again open your mouth because of your humiliation, declares the Sovereign LORD.' "

God's reaction to this adultery was twofold. First, he would punish, because she had broken the covenant and was unfaithful to her husband. But God is faithful in grace as well as in judgment. His second reaction was: "I will continue to be faithful to my side of the covenant. I'll even add an additional covenant that is everlasting (Jeremiah 31:31-34)."

When the people would see that God had not changed in spite of their adultery, that he still loved them, and that he was willing to forgive them, they would be ashamed of what they had done. Then some would return to the Lord. New sisters including Sodom and Samaria would be brought into the family of the Lord from all the nations of the world.

Ezekiel spoke of this previously when he said, "And your sisters, Sodom and her daughters and Samaria with her daughters, will return to what they were before; and you and your daughters will return to what they were before" (16:55). Centuries later St. Paul spoke of the new covenant which is a blessing to the whole world: "And this is my covenant with them when I take away their sins" (Romans 11:27).

The people of Jerusalem would know that God is faithful to his word, this time not in keeping his promises to punish the evildoers for their sins, but in keeping his promises to forgive and restore. Only the Lord of forgiveness could bring rebellious and adulterous people who had performed dreadful sins back to himself. If the people would keep all this in mind, they would not boast about themselves as "the people of God" on the basis of their own activity or their own ability. They would recognize they were his people only on account of his grace toward them.

This allegory which fit Jerusalem so well is really the life story of every sinner. Every human being is covered with the pollution of sin from birth and needs to be spiritually cleansed. Only the Lord can spiritually wash us, make us clean, rub us in salt and wrap us in cloth. Nobody except the Lord has the necessary pity or compassion to want to do any of this for us. Spiritually each of us by nature deserves to be thrown out and abandoned. But God has rescued us and made us his own through Jesus Christ.

The Lord is the only one who can come to the spiritually stillborn and say, "Live!" And when he says "Live" to people through his gospel which comes by the means of the Word and baptism, it actually happens. They live. They are reborn, made alive in Christ, to borrow phrases from the New Testament and Luther.

88

The Lord is the one who blesses us with the gifts of physical life, growth and health. Frequently he adds the gifts of wealth, conveniences and luxury. He commits himself to us as our husband. Other people become aware of all the blessings the Lord has placed into our lives as they observe us. But so often like ancient Israel, we begin to take his blessings for granted. We use them in pursuit of our own selfish interests and commit adultery with the gods of Self and World. We sometimes even go looking for and purchase or hire people and things which can only detract from our Husband and hinder our relationship with him.

So, the Lord frequently lets those very gods which have replaced him produce the discipline in our lives which he uses to bring us back to him. He allows selfishness to isolate us from his blessings. He permits the unbelieving world to treat us in accord with its rules so that we see the Lord's way as the only way to happiness. God considers people who have his Word and his blessings, and in spite of it, prostitute themselves to other gods, to be much more guilty than those who haven't received as much.

But God is always there with his promised grace and forgiveness. He wants us to be constantly aware he will still offer forgiveness no matter how prideful and self-sufficient we have become. The Lord doesn't change. His love doesn't change. His covenant made with us in baptism doesn't change. Only the gospel can lead us to crush our pride and boast in the Lord.

Two Eagles and a Vine

17 **The word of the LORD came to me: ²"Son of man, set forth an allegory and tell the house of Israel a parable. ³Say to them, 'This is what the Sovereign LORD says: A great eagle with powerful wings, long feathers and full plumage of varied colors**

**came to Lebanon. Taking hold of the top of a cedar, ⁴he broke off
its topmost shoot and carried it away to a land of merchants,
where he planted it in a city of traders.**

We usually think of parables as those interesting little
stories Jesus told, stories taken right out of everyday life and
illustrating some truth about how God saves people. But the
Old Testament prophets often taught in parables, too.
Isaiah taught the parable of the vineyard (5:1-7) and the
parable of the plowman (28:23-29). Jeremiah told the parable of the potter (18:1-11).

In this chapter the imagery changes from that of an unfaithful wife to the parable of two eagles and a vine.

The first eagle in Ezekiel's parable is Nebuchadnezzar and
Babylon. The cedar represents the kings of Judah. There
were two good reasons why God chose the cedar to represent the royal line of David. A cedar of Lebanon was a lofty,
regal tree. Many of them had been used in building the royal
palaces in Jerusalem. Jehoiachin, who was king of Judah
about a dozen years before Jerusalem fell to the Babylonians, was "broken off" by Nebuchadnezzar and carried away
to Babylon, the political and commercial capital of the
world.

**⁵" 'He took some of the seed of your land and put it in fertile
soil. He planted it like a willow by abundant water, ⁶and it
sprouted and became a low, spreading vine. Its branches turned
toward him, but its roots remained under it. So it became a vine
and produced branches and put out leafy boughs.**

Nebuchadnezzar took another "seed" of David and
planted it in the fertile soil of Jerusalem. That was Jehoiachin's uncle Zedekiah, who became the twentieth and last
king of Judah. Zedekiah was no more than a Babylonian
puppet king.

With Zedekiah as king Judah could have continued to exist and grow as a dependent state under Babylonian dominance, admittedly no longer a lofty cedar, but now a lowly vine. The nation could have produced branches and boughs under a native son.

7" 'But there was another great eagle with powerful wings and full plumage. The vine now sent out its roots toward him from the plot where it was planted and stretched out its branches to him for water. ⁸It had been planted in good soil by abundant water so that it would produce branches, bear fruit and become a splendid vine.'

Even though the vine, the puppet kingdom of Judah, was relatively well off and had everything it needed, it sent out tendrils to the other great eagle in the ancient Near East, Pharaoh Hophra of Egypt. For the historical details of this alliance, see 2 Kings 24:8-20; 2 Chronicles 36:9-13; Jeremiah 37; 52:1-11. Instead of helping Judah, her alliance with Egypt and rebellion against Babylon only hastened her downfall.

9"Say to them, 'This is what the Sovereign LORD says: Will it thrive? Will it not be uprooted and stripped of its fruit so that it withers? All its new growth will wither. It will not take a strong arm or many people to pull it up by the roots. ¹⁰Even if it is transplanted, will it thrive? Will it not wither completely when the east wind strikes it — wither away in the plot where it grew?' "

It doesn't take much imagination to guess what the Babylonian king would do when his puppet in Jerusalem began to flirt with the powerful kingdom on the Nile. The first eagle would move in and uproot the vine and strip it of its fruit. The words "It will not take a strong arm" show contempt for the weakness of the kingdom of Judah.

11Then the word of the LORD came to me: 12"Say to this rebellious house, 'Do you not know what these things mean?' Say to them: 'The king of Babylon went to Jerusalem and carried off her king and her nobles, bringing them back with him to Babylon. 13Then he took a member of the royal family and made a treaty with him, putting him under oath. He also carried away the leading men of the land, 14so that the kingdom would be brought low, unable to rise again, surviving only by keeping his treaty. 15But the king rebelled against him by sending his envoys to Egypt to get horses and a large army. Will he succeed? Will he who does such things escape? Will he break the treaty and yet escape?

God now had Ezekiel explain the details of the parable.

The characters involved, Kings Nebuchadnezzar and Jehoiachin, are referred to in verse 12. The member of the royal family who pledged loyalty to the Babylonians (verse 13) was Zedekiah (2 Chronicles 36:13). The king referred to in verse 15 is again Zedekiah. Egypt is the second eagle in the parable (verse 7). Other references and comments on attempts at an alliance with Egypt are in Isaiah 30:1-3; 36:6 and Ezekiel 29:6,7.

16" 'As surely as I live, declares the Sovereign LORD, he shall die in Babylon, in the land of the king who put him on the throne, whose oath he despised and whose treaty he broke. 17Pharaoh with his mighty army and great horde will be of no help to him in war, when ramps are built and siege works erected to destroy many lives. 18He despised the oath by breaking the covenant. Because he had given his hand in pledge and yet did all these things, he shall not escape.

Although Egypt did send an army north in 588, forcing the Babylonians to lift their siege of Jerusalem temporarily, this only caused Nebuchadnezzar to send in his whole army.

Then Egypt quickly retreated. The Lord was angry because Zedekiah had broken his treaty with Babylon.

The Lord doesn't differentiate between what is right in a private situation and what is right in a public situation. What is right is right and what is wrong is wrong, no matter what the context is. We ought to speak the truth to our family members, to our business competitors, and to foreign government representatives. We ought to keep our promises to our children, to our business partners and to our political constituency.

¹⁹" 'Therefore this is what the Sovereign LORD says: As surely as I live, I will bring down on his head my oath that he despised and my covenant that he broke. ²⁰I will spread my net for him, and he will be caught in my snare. I will bring him to Babylon and execute judgment upon him there because he was unfaithful to me. ²¹All his fleeing troops will fall by the sword, and the survivors will be scattered to the winds. Then you will know that I the LORD have spoken.

Why did God say this was his covenant and his oath? Wasn't it just an agreement between Zedekiah and Nebuchadnezzar, between Judah and Babylon? No, God himself had been called into the situation publicly. Earlier in chapter 17 we learned that "the king of Babylon went to Jerusalem and carried off her king and her nobles. . . . he took a member of the royal family and made a treaty with him, putting him under oath" (17:12,13). This oath would have been made in the name of the God of Judah, the Lord. He was to have been witness to the validity of the agreement. He was to have been the one responsible for punishing breaches of the agreement. The oath and covenant had been made in his name. Consequently, when Zedekiah broke it, he was despising God. He was telling others he didn't think God was interested enough in the situation to do anything about punishing his sin.

Whenever we call God into a situation, and then leave people with the impression he is irrelevant, disinterested, not important, or powerless, we misuse God's name and insult God. The Second Commandment states, "You shall not misuse the name of the Lord your God." Transgressions of the Second Commandment are often responsible for the non-Christian's lack of interest in learning about Jesus. His attitude is: "If you who claim to follow Jesus refer to him in such a common way that he seems to be no more important than you or me, too disinterested even to pay attention to the negative references to him, too weak to punish abuse of him, and too irrelevant to relate to everyday life, why should I even think about learning to know him?" If as many people used God's name to witness to Jesus Christ the Savior from sin as frequently as they use God's name thoughtlessly in their everyday conversation, God would be glorified and many more sinners saved.

22"'This is what the Sovereign Lord says: I myself will take a shoot from the very top of a cedar and plant it; I will break off a tender sprig from its topmost shoots and plant it on a high and lofty mountain. 23On the mountain heights of Israel I will plant it; it will produce branches and bear fruit and become a splendid cedar. Birds of every kind will nest in it; they will find shelter in the shade of its branches. 24All the trees of the field will know that I the Lord bring down the tall tree and make the low tree grow tall. I dry up the green tree and make the dry tree flourish.

"'I the Lord have spoken, and I will do it.'"

Nebuchadnezzar would not be the only one to top a cedar. The Lord would too. From the same family tree of David a tender sprig would be planted on the heights of Israel, grow into a splendid tree and provide shelter and shade. Already in Old Testament times, Hebrew commentators regarded this as a Messianic passage, pointing to the special Anointed One of the Lord. Although not precise in detail, the prophecy indicated someone from the family tree of David would exert a worldwide influence. All the trees (people) of the field (world) would know the Lord is a Fortress and Shelter, for he controls the history of individuals and of nations.

We might be familiar with other prophecies which refer to the Savior as a branch. Isaiah 11:1, for example, states, "A shoot will come from the stump of Jesse; from his roots a Branch will bear fruit." (See also Jeremiah 23:5,6; 33:14-16). These prophecies were fulfilled in Jesus Christ to whom God has given "the throne of his father David" and whose "kingdom will never end" (Luke 1:32,33).

When interpreting a parable one must beware of looking for precise references to exact spiritual details. Nevertheless, it is interesting to note Jesus himself used a reference to trees and birds in Matthew 13:31,32: "The kingdom of heaven is like a mustard seed. . . . when it grows, it becomes a tree . . . so that birds of the air come and perch in its branches."

Here in the middle of Ezekiel's strong pronouncements of judgment, God has surprised us with this little passage of gospel promise. Against a dark backdrop of judgment and condemnation God's glowing love shines all the brighter. The Lord reminds us that no matter how sinful we have become, his love and promises are there. No matter how much we have left him out of our lives, he is never far away. Just the opposite. His love and his promises remove the sin, and clear away everything which has replaced him in our lives and hearts. We are not so unlike the people of 2500 years ago. Like them we tend to follow our sinful desires. Human nature doesn't change. The good news is that God hasn't changed either! His love is everlasting.

The Soul Who Sins Will Die

18 **The word of the LORD came to me: ²"What do you people mean by quoting this proverb about the land of Israel:**

> **" 'The fathers eat sour grapes,**
> **and the children's teeth are set on edge'?**

There's a tendency in each of us to blame someone else for our troubles. Ezekiel's warning that Jerusalem would be punished because of the accumulated sins of the nation led the people to complain about being punished for the sins of others. They probably said it was all King Manasseh's fault. He had been notorious for his "detestable sins" (2 Kings 21:10-15).

The people accused God of being unfair. Behind their complaint was the idea they were not as guilty as their fathers had been and didn't deserve what was about to happen. By quoting the proverb they meant to say: "Our fathers sinned and the children have to suffer the consequences."

³"As surely as I live, declares the Sovereign LORD, you will no longer quote this proverb in Israel. ⁴For every living soul belongs to me, the father as well as the son — both alike belong to me. The soul who sins is the one who will die.

God answered their objection. He created everyone. Each individual has a direct relationship with him. God expects each person to respond to his love with a life of love. Everyone is responsible to the Lord for his way of life. The Lord punishes the sinner for his own sins. God does not punish anyone for someone else's sin. To illustrate this, Ezekiel described three men — father, son and grandson. First he described the father:

> **⁵"Suppose there is a righteous man**
> **who does what is just and right.**

⁶He does not eat at the mountain shrines
  or look to the idols of the house of Israel.
He does not defile his neighbor's wife
  or lie with a woman during her period.
⁷He does not oppress anyone,
  but returns what he took in pledge for a loan.
He does not commit robbery
  but gives his food to the hungry
  and provides clothing for the naked.
⁸He does not lend at usury
  or take excessive interest.
He withholds his hand from doing wrong
  and judges fairly between man and man.
⁹He follows my decrees
  and faithfully keeps my laws.
That man is righteous;
  he will surely live,
                    declares the Sovereign LORD.

Who is a perfectly righteous man who always does what is just and right? No one. This answer is taken for granted in the context. Ezekiel offers no doctrinal explanation right here about God's love and his forgiveness, about man's complete innate spiritual incompetence and dependence on the Lord to be righteous in God's sight. All of those concepts are assumed. From the preceding context of the book of Ezekiel, it is clear that righteous living is a product of loyalty to God; we usually call it faith in God. A man strives to do what is just and right as an expression of his close relationship with God and as a product of the Lord's presence in his heart. The term "righteous" is frequently applied to believers. For instance, Genesis 6:9 describes Noah as "a righteous man, blameless among the people of his time."

Evidence of the righteous man's proper relationship with the Lord was obvious when one observed his actions. The righteous man could not participate in worship festivals for false gods, nor even look trustingly toward false gods. He would not commit adultery, or violate the biblical laws regarding uncleanness. The laws about uncleanness (Leviticus 15:24) were intended to teach that nothing impure could even appear in the Lord's presence. Any bodily condition associated with or even suggestive of impurity was marked as unclean and caused exclusion from the sanctuary, symbolically excluding a person from the presence of the Lord. Cleansing after a period of ceremonial uncleanness was required to restore one's previous status.

It was a sin to keep what had been taken in pledge for a loan, if that article was necessary for the borrower's survival (Exodus 22:26,27). When a fellow Israelite was in financial need it was also wrong to charge him interest on the loan, since this disrupted the family spirit which the Lord wanted his people to cultivate (Deuteronomy 23:19,20).

With these outward actions toward the people around him and toward God's law, the man showed he was right with God (Matthew 25:31-46). Such a man will live. That is, his life will continue with God's blessings. The exiles in Babylon considered themselves spiritually dead, cut off from the temple in Jerusalem. But Ezekiel was telling them they could be alive, living under God's blessings. The "alive" unrepentant people living close to the temple were actually "dead." They were continuing their unbelieving ways, thus cutting themselves off from the Lord and his blessings.

[10]"Suppose he has a violent son, who sheds blood or does any of these other things [11](though the father does none of them):

> "He eats at the mountain shrines.
> He defiles his neighbor's wife.
> [12]He oppresses the poor and needy.
> He commits robbery.

>He does not return what he took in pledge.
>He looks to the idols.
>He does detestable things.
>[13]He lends at usury and takes excessive interest.

Will such a man live? He will not! Because he has done all these detestable things, he will surely be put to death and his blood will be on his own head.

Here Ezekiel presents the second generation. The son referred to here is directly responsible to God. His father's righteousness won't save him. Such a man has no one to blame but himself when he faces the consequences of his wicked ways. "His blood will be on his own head."

We should take this warning to heart. We may come from a long line of Christians. Certainly that's something to be thankful for, but it's no guarantee we'll be saved. Our salvation depends on our relationship with the Lord. May God keep us in his grace!

[14]But suppose this son has a son who sees all the sins his father commits, and though he sees them, he does not do such things:

>[15]"He does not eat at the mountain shrines
>   or look to the idols of the house of Israel.
>He does not defile his neighbor's wife.
>[16]He does not oppress anyone
>   or require a pledge for a loan.
>He does not commit robbery,
>   but gives his food to the hungry
>   and provides clothing for the naked.
>[17]He withholds his hand from sin
>   and takes no usury or excessive interest.
>He keeps my laws and decrees.

He will not die for his father's sin; he will surely live. [18]But his father will die for his own sin, because he practiced extortion, robbed his brother and did what was wrong among his people.

Here is the third generation. The grandson recognized the sins of his father and did not repeat them. Consequently, the father's sins are not charged against the son.

¹⁹"Yet you ask, 'Why does the son not share the guilt of his father?' Since the son has done what is just and right and has been careful to keep all my decrees, he will surely live. ²⁰The soul who sins is the one who will die. The son will not share the guilt of the father, nor will the father share the guilt of the son. The righteousness of the righteous man will be credited to him, and the wickedness of the wicked will be charged against him.

The question really was: "Isn't this what is happening to us? Aren't we being punished for the sins of the fathers?" God's answer was "NO." They had perpetuated the sins of the fathers. They were being held responsible for and punished for their own sins.

This truth is not a contradiction of Exodus 20:5 where the Lord speaks of "punishing the children for the sins of the fathers unto the third and fourth generations of those who hate me." That passage describes a situation in which several generations in a row hate God and ignore his will. Each succeeding generation multiplies the sins of the previous generation. God acts in accordance with their hatred. But each person is held responsible for and is punished for his own sins.

²¹"But if a wicked man turns away from all the sins he has committed and keeps all my decrees and does what is just and right, he will surely live; he will not die. ²²None of the offenses he has committed will be remembered against him. Because of the righteous things he has done, he will live. ²³Do I take any pleasure in the death of the wicked? declares the Sovereign Lord. Rather, am I not pleased when they turn from their ways and live?

God wants "everyone to come to repentance" (2 Peter 3:9). What is more, the Lord's forgiveness totally obliterates past offenses, so that he doesn't remember them anymore. In the words of the Prophet Micah, he "treads our sins underfoot" and "hurls all our iniquities into the depths of the sea" (Micah 7:19).

24"But if a righteous man turns from his righteousness and commits sin and does the same detestable things the wicked man does, will he live? None of the righteous things he has done will be remembered. Because of the unfaithfulness he is guilty of and because of the sins he has committed, he will die.

It is possible for a man to turn away from the Lord and change back to a life of sin and selfishness in which he has no proper relationship with God. Then "none of the righteous things he has done will be remembered."

25"Yet you say, 'The way of the Lord is not just.' Hear, O house of Israel: Is my way unjust? Is it not your ways that are unjust? 26If a righteous man turns from his righteousness and commits sin, he will die for it; because of the sin he has committed he will die. 27But if a wicked man turns away from the wickedness he has committed and does what is just and right, he will save his life. 28Because he considers all the offenses he has committed and turns away from them, he will surely live; he will not die. 29Yet the house of Israel says, 'The way of the Lord is not just.' Are my ways unjust, O house of Israel? Is it not your ways that are unjust?

It seems that no matter what God did, Ezekiel's fellow countrymen criticized him as unjust for punishing them, for forgiving sinners, and for condemning the righteous man who turned away from the Lord.

30"Therefore, O house of Israel, I will judge you, each one according to his ways, declares the Sovereign LORD. Repent! Turn away from all your offenses; then sin will not be your downfall. 31Rid yourselves of all the offenses you have commit-

ted, and get a new heart and a new spirit. Why will you die, O house of Israel? [32]For I take no pleasure in the death of anyone, declares the Sovereign LORD. Repent and live!

The solution? "Repent!" God doesn't want people to be cut off from his blessings. He wants them to live. Man can't get a new heart and spirit on his own. God is the only one who can supply this. Ezekiel had stated this before (11:19), and he will say it again (36:26). The call to repentance expresses the need to acknowledge and turn away from sin, and to turn to God as the source of forgiveness.

Christianity is not a movement, an organization, or an attitude. It is a relationship between God and an individual person based on Jesus Christ the Savior from sin. The individual responds to what the Lord has given him in Christ Jesus; he asks the Lord to help him live a life reflecting the righteousness which Jesus has given him. And so the righteous man "lives," that is, he exists and will continue to do so under the blessings of God.

To attempt to base our relationship with God on ourselves without Jesus is to tell God that we think Christ's work is neither necessary nor beneficial. Then our life is not an effort to express our loyalty to the Lord. Such a misguided life can take about any track it wants, but it is headed away from the Lord and his blessings. In the strong language of Scripture, that is death.

This chapter gives us a rich banquet of the gospel. Even when we think he is unfair for doing it, God still forgives. Our God, although just and willing to carry out his drastic threats and punishments, doesn't like doing it. He would much rather bless and give life.

A Lament for Israel's Princes

19 **"Take up a lament concerning the princes of Israel [2]and say:**

" 'What a lioness was your mother
　　among the lions!
She lay down among the young lions
　　and reared her cubs.
3She brought up one of her cubs,
　　and he became a strong lion.
He learned to tear the prey
　　and he devoured men.
4The nations heard about him,
　　and he was trapped in their pit.
They led him with hooks
　　to the land of Egypt.

The entire chapter is poetry. In Hebrew it is a poem with a special kind of rhythm (three beats plus two beats) often used for funeral dirges. Although Ezekiel recognized Jerusalem was getting what she deserved, he still felt personal sorrow because religious and moral conditions had become so bad. Even the royal family of David had become evil. In chapter 18, God had said he held individuals responsible for their sins. In chapter 19 Ezekiel provides examples of several individuals and their punishment.

The lioness mentioned here was Judah. Back in Genesis 49:9 Jacob had referred to his son Judah in this manner: "You are a lion's cub, O Judah; you return from the prey, my son. Like a lion he crouches and lies down, like a lioness — who dares to rouse him?" Ezekiel now applied this picture to the descendants of Judah. Like a mighty lion, the nation of Judah had become strong and respected among the other nations of the world.

In each generation one of Judah's cubs would grow up to be "a strong lion." This represented the leaders of the people. Sad to say, these leaders misused their power and took advantage of the people, instead of being the type of rulers

God required (Deuteronomy 17:14-20). As Ezekiel's poem continues, our attention is focused on one of these leaders in particular. Because of his evil God used the neighboring nations to punish him: "The nations heard about him and he was trapped in their pit. . . ." The reference is to Jehoahaz, who was taken to Egypt by Pharaoh Necho (2 Kings 23:31-34). The hooks were on the collars around the necks of those who were led away in chains.

Jehoahaz and his nephew Jehoiachin, referred to later in this chapter, were both wicked kings who ruled during the last and troubled years of the kingdom of Judah. But they were probably no worse than a half dozen other kings of Judah. Why then should Ezekiel have singled them out here for special attention? Perhaps because their deportation (Jehoahaz to Egypt, Jehoiachin to Babylon) was a very obvious and very public expression of God's displeasure.

> 5" 'When she saw her hope unfulfilled,
>   her expectation gone,
>   she took another of her cubs
>   and made him a strong lion.
> 6He prowled among the lions,
>   for he was now a strong lion.
>   He learned to tear the prey
>   and he devoured men.
> 7He broke down their strongholds
>   and devastated their towns.
>   The land and all who were in it
>   were terrified by his roaring.
> 8Then the nations came against him,
>   those from regions round about.
>   They spread their net for him,
>   and he was trapped in their pit.
> 9With hooks they pulled him into a cage
>   and brought him to the king of Babylon.

> They put him in prison,
>> so his roar was heard no longer
>> on the mountains of Israel!

The hopes of the nation were dashed when her king was exiled. But then another of her sons took over. The scenario was the same. He too abused his power and acted tyrannically, undermining the welfare of the country which supported him and the fiber of his own people. Again God used the surrounding nations to carry out the punishment: "The LORD sent Babylonian, Aramean, Moabite and Ammonite raiders against him. He sent them to destroy Judah, in accordance with the word of the LORD proclaimed by his servants the prophets" (2 Kings 24:2).

The prince-lion was treated like a captured animal and taken to Babylon. The captivity of Jehoiachin (2 Kings 24:8-15) has been discussed previously several times. It was in that same deportation that Ezekiel himself had been taken to Babylon (1:2).

> 10" 'Your mother was like a vine in your vineyard
>> planted by the water;
>> it was fruitful and full of branches
>> because of abundant water.
> 11Its branches were strong,
>> fit for a ruler's scepter.
> It towered high
>> above the thick foliage,
>> conspicuous for its height
>> and for its many branches.
> 12But it was uprooted in fury
>> and thrown to the ground.
> The east wind made it shrivel,
>> it was stripped of its fruit;
>> its strong branches withered
>> and fire consumed them.

105

> ¹³**Now it is planted in the desert,**
>   **in a dry and thirsty land.**
> ¹⁴**Fire spread from one of its main branches**
>   **and consumed its fruit.**
>   **No strong branch is left on it**
>   **fit for a ruler's scepter.'**
> **This is a lament and is to be used as a lament."**

The picture now changes from that of lion to the world of plants. God had blessed Judah, Jerusalem and the royal family of David "like a vine" which "was fruitful and abundant in water." Although Judah had been a small nation, because of God's blessings it had become a strong nation. At the time of David and Solomon especially, and periodically afterward, it was very conspicuous when compared with the power, wealth and security of other nations similar in size.

Because of the Lord's promised punishment, Jerusalem, Judah and the royal family were just as good as uprooted in Ezekiel's eyes. In spite of all the past blessings of the Lord, the nation was withered and would soon be consumed in the fire. Its leaders and best citizens had already been stripped from the tree in 597 and transplanted in a much less productive area of the world. Already Judah was as good as totally consumed.

Since he had broken his treaty with Nebuchadnezzar, King Zedekiah was the final cause of the destruction of Jerusalem and of the downfall of the royal house of David. Thus the fire had spread from one of the main branches to the rest of Judah. In the process, all the results of God's blessings were consumed. When God's judgment struck, the nation was just a shadow of its former self, certainly not fit for a ruler, or even able to produce one. After Zedekiah had been arrested and deported, Judah and the royal house of David were totally inconsequential in the history of nations.

When this final destruction of Judah and Jerusalem would occur, an event which to Ezekiel was just as good as done and which is here presented as a past event, the people could use this dirge. "This is a lament," declared Ezekiel, "and is to be used as a lament." The prophet had prepared it for them ahead of time. However, Ezekiel was primarily a prophet, and not a poet. He taught them this dirge to remind them to repent of their sins which were causing God's anger to fall on them.

Human greatness and power, and the greatness and power of nations are subject to change, decay and destruction. The abuse of greatness and the sinfulness of men speed this process of decay and destruction. We might consider our nation to be a strong lion. From the history of the world we ought to learn that nothing is permanent. When any nation abandons God, he allows even the strong lion to be trapped, caged, hooked and humiliated.

The only permanent kingdom is the kingdom of our Lord and of his Christ. When Judah was no longer a strong enough branch to be fit for a ruler's scepter, the Anointed One came to be her king. When nations crumble and fall, our citizenship in Christ's kingdom remains untouched. We are his now and forever.

Warnings Prior to the Fall of the City
Rebellious Israel

20 **In the seventh year, in the fifth month on the tenth day, some of the elders of Israel came to inquire of the LORD, and they sat down in front of me.**

July 591 B.C.. Two years after the first vision (1:2) and four years before the destruction of Jerusalem. The elders of Judah again came to see Ezekiel. Perhaps they came to see if

107

the prophet had any good news about how soon they could go home. After Ezekiel's past tongue-lashings, it might surprise us they even came back, let alone for the third time. It seems the message of the Lord had touched their hearts at least enough for them to be curious about what more Ezekiel might have to say.

We frequently come up with a variety of "good reasons" why we can't listen to, study, read or meditate upon the Word of the Lord. Sometimes we even find ourselves in the outward circumstances of listening, studying or reading the Bible, but we have this gnawing feeling that we would just as soon not be doing it at this particular time. Then we chastise ourselves for struggling internally. This internal struggle is an evidence that the Lord's message has touched our hearts and is working in us. If this were not the case, there would be no struggle. We wouldn't even consider going to listen to Ezekiel. We wouldn't even be in the circumstances where the Word is being used.

²Then the word of the Lord came to me: ³"Son of man, speak to the elders of Israel and say to them, 'This is what the Sovereign Lord says: Have you come to inquire of me? As surely as I live, I will not let you inquire of me, declares the Sovereign Lord.'

In their present spiritual status, these men had no right to ask God anything. Of course no human being in his natural spiritual state has a right to ask God anything. Only by God's grace can we approach God as children approach their father. But before he would in grace let the elders approach him, God wanted them to hear and take to heart his judgment:

⁴"Will you judge them? Will you judge them, son of man? Then confront them with the detestable practices of their fathers ⁵and say to them: 'This is what the Sovereign Lord says: On the day I

chose Israel, I swore with uplifted hand to the descendants of the house of Jacob and revealed myself to them in Egypt. With uplifted hand I said to them, "I am the LORD your God." ⁶On that day I swore to them that I would bring them out of Egypt into a land I had searched out for them, a land flowing with milk and honey, the most beautiful of all lands. ⁷And I said to them, "Each of you, get rid of the vile images you have set your eyes on, and do not defile yourselves with the idols of Egypt. I am the LORD your God."

The repeated question has the force of a command. It is similar to the question issued by parents, "Are you going to wash the dishes?" followed in a few more minutes by "*Are you going to wash the dishes*!" If Ezekiel was to judge them, he had to get at the heart of the problem, the detestable practices of the fathers. God's choice of Israel as his own is here dated at the time he promised that he as the covenant God of unfailing forgiveness would lead them out of Egypt (Exodus 6:3-8). Already back then, over seven centuries before Ezekiel's time, God had told the Israelites to get rid of the "vile images" and "idols of Egypt."

⁸" 'But they rebelled against me and would not listen to me; they did not get rid of the vile images they had set their eyes on, nor did they forsake the idols of Egypt. So I said I would pour out my wrath on them and spend my anger against them in Egypt. ⁹But for the sake of my name I did what would keep it from being profaned in the eyes of the nations they lived among and in whose sight I had revealed myself to the Israelites by bringing them out of Egypt. ¹⁰Therefore I led them out of Egypt and brought them into the desert. ¹¹I gave them my decrees and made known to them my laws, for the man who obeys them will live by them. ¹²Also I gave them my Sabbaths as a sign between us, so they would know that I the LORD made them holy.

God did not annihilate the people of Israel while they were still in Egypt, because then the foreign nations would have ridiculed him. They would have said he lacked the power to keep his promises to rescue his people and to give blessings to all through the people whom he had chosen for himself (Numbers 14:15,16; Deuteronomy 9:27,28; Genesis 12:3). Because of his love for his people, certainly not because of their faithfulness to him, God revealed his word to them. He brought them out of Egypt and established his covenant with them on the basis of the laws given to Moses on Sinai.

A special sign of the covenant was the Sabbath. Nobody else had a practice like this. The Sabbath made the Israelites different from the Egyptians, later the Canaanites, and still later the Babylonians. God wanted his chosen people to be different. That's why he gave them these laws of the covenant. The covenant set them aside from the sinful world for God. They were thus holy — that is, set aside for God.

God's people are always different. If nobody can tell by observing us that we are not like everybody else in the world, it's not that the entire world has become Christian. Rather, we have become conformed to the people around us. It means we have blocked the Lord out of our lives so the Holy Ghost has not been able to implement in us a desire to put God's laws and decrees into practice. When we put God first in our lives, we are going to be different from the selfish people around us.

God is always ultimately interested in keeping his name from being profaned. His grace is behind this interest. Only if people are led to know the truth about God will they be attracted to him. Only if people are led to realize the Lord is the gracious One who loves and protects his people, will they be interested in his forgiveness and the eternal life he offers. Whatever he allows to happen in our lives has as its ultimate purpose to hinder us from giving him a wrong reputation among those around us who should be getting the truth about him from us.

13" 'Yet the people of Israel rebelled against me in the desert. They did not follow my decrees but rejected my laws — although the man who obeys them will live by them — and they utterly desecrated my Sabbaths. So I said I would pour out my wrath on them and destroy them in the desert. 14But for the sake of my name I did what would keep it from being profaned in the eyes of the nations in whose sight I had brought them out. 15Also with uplifted hand I swore to them in the desert that I would not bring them into the land I had given them — a land flowing with milk and honey, most beautiful of all lands — 16because they rejected my laws and did not follow my decrees and desecrated my Sabbaths. For their hearts were devoted to their idols. 17Yet I looked on them with pity and did not destroy them or put an end to them in the desert. 18I said to their children in the desert, "Do not follow the statutes of your fathers or keep their laws or defile yourselves with their idols. 19I am the LORD your God; follow my decrees and be careful to keep my laws. 20Keep my Sabbaths holy, that they may be a sign between us. Then you will know that I am the LORD your God."

The same circumstances repeated themselves in the desert. Once again Israel rebelled and angered the Lord. In fact, in Ezekiel's opinion, the history of Israel was one long period of rebellion against God, marked by infrequent intervals when faith was evident. Although God did allow an entire generation to die in the wilderness (Numbers 14:26-35), he did not allow the nation to be annihilated.

21" 'But the children rebelled against me: They did not follow my decrees, they were not careful to keep my laws — although the man who obeys them will live by them — and they desecrated my Sabbaths. So I said I would pour out my wrath on them and spend my anger against them in the desert. 22But I withheld my hand, and for the sake of my name I did what would keep it from being profaned in the eyes of the nations in whose sight I had brought them out. ²³Also with uplifted hand I swore to them in the desert that I would disperse them among the nations and scatter them through the countries, ²⁴because they had not obeyed my laws but had rejected my decrees and desecrated my Sabbaths, and their eyes⌊lusted⌋ after their fathers' idols. ²⁵I also gave them over to statutes that were not good and laws they could not live by; ²⁶I let them become defiled through their gifts — the sacrifice of every firstborn — that I might fill them with horror so they would know I am the LORD.'

Each generation of Israelites perpetuated the sins of the previous one. When God first gave the law at Mt. Sinai he had warned the people, "I will scatter you among the nations" (Leviticus 26:33) if they rebelled against him. Moses repeated this threat just before he died (Deuteronomy 28:64). Now Ezekiel reminded the people of these warnings.

As a judgment on their wickedness, the Lord gave them over to their own sinful thinking. Instead of dedicating their firstborn to him, as God had commanded (Exodus 22:29; 13:11-13), they sacrificed them to the pagan idols!

²⁷"Therefore, son of man, speak to the people of Israel and say to them, 'This is what the Sovereign LORD says: In this also your fathers blasphemed me by forsaking me: ²⁸When I brought them into the land I had sworn to give them and they saw any high hill or any leafy tree, there they offered their sacrifices, made offerings that provoked me to anger, presented their fragrant incense and poured out their drink offerings. ²⁹Then I said to them: What is this high place you go to?' " (It is called Bamah to this day.)

Things didn't change when God led them into the promised land either. They even used all the earthly blessings God bestowed on them to worship other gods. The word "Bamah" means "high place." It was on the hill tops, the high places, that the Israelites had practiced their wicked idolatry.

Judgment and Restoration

[30]"Therefore say to the house of Israel: 'This is what the Sovereign LORD says: Will you defile yourselves the way your fathers did and lust after their vile images? [31]When you offer your gifts — the sacrifice of your sons in the fire — you continue to defile yourselves with all your idols to this day. Am I to let you inquire of me, O house of Israel? As surely as I live, declares the Sovereign LORD, I will not let you inquire of me.

Even in the Babylonian exile the people of Judah were still practicing false worship. Is it any surprise, then, that the Lord wouldn't let their leaders inquire of him?

[32]" 'You say, "We want to be like the nations, like the peoples of the world, who serve wood and stone." But what you have in mind will never happen. [33]As surely as I live, declares the Sovereign LORD, I will rule over you with a mighty hand and an outstretched arm and with outpoured wrath. [34]I will bring you from the nations and gather you from the countries where you have been scattered — with a mighty hand and an outstretched arm and with outpoured wrath. [35]I will bring you into the desert of the nations and there, face to face, I will execute judgment upon you. [36]As I judged your fathers in the desert of the land of Egypt, so I will judge you, declares the Sovereign LORD. [37]I will take note of you as you pass under my rod, and I will bring you into the bond of the covenant. [38]I will purge you of those who revolt and rebel against me. Although I will bring them out of the land where they are living, yet they will not enter the land of Israel. Then you will know that I am the LORD.

What justification could the Jews find for their shameful conduct? Their response to the Lord was: "We don't like to be different from everybody else. Maybe we would get along better with the people around us if we would adopt some of their worship practices." But God was not about to let Israel lose its national identity by assimilating false, foreign worship practices. For then the Lord could not keep his promises to bring the Savior into the world through the descendants of Abraham.

This time the punishment of rebellious Israel would be carried out in Babylonia, here called "the desert of the nations." Just as God had previously judged the Israelites "in the desert of the land of Egypt," that is, the wilderness of Sinai, so he would now judge them in Babylon, the "desert" of the nations.

In this very picturesque paragraph Ezekiel added another comparison. In Babylon God would carefully inspect each of his people, as a shepherd does when he allows only his own sheep to go past his staff into the safety of the sheep pen. He would cull out the sheep that didn't belong to him and had rebelled against him. Those who repented he would allow to pass under his staff and would bring back under the security of his covenant. Just as earlier in history God had brought his people out of Egypt where they had been living, now he would bring them out of Canaan where they had been living. This time he would not bring them to the promised land of milk and honey, but to Babylon, the desert of nations. God's purpose was — and always is — to bring people to repentance. He purges from his people the rebels who can only be destructive to the covenant relationship.

Why does God want us to be spiritually separate from those who believe differently from us? He knows close spiritual contact with something which is not truth can easily affect us. He wants us to be his completely, to trust his Word totally. This relationship and attitude can only be damaged by falsehood. He gives us his commands to be spiritually separate because he knows what is safest for us. The Lord loves us and wants us to remain his.

[39] " 'As for you, O house of Israel, this is what the Sovereign LORD says: Go and serve your idols, every one of you! But afterward you will surely listen to me and no longer profane my holy name with your gifts and idols. [40]For on my holy mountain, the high mountain of Israel, declares the Sovereign LORD, there in the land the entire house of Israel will serve me, and there I will accept them. There I will require your offerings and your choice gifts, along with all your holy sacrifices. [41]I will accept you as fragrant incense when I bring you out from the nations and gather you from the countries where you have been scattered, and I will show myself holy among you in the sight of the nations. [42]Then you will know that I am the LORD, when I bring you into the land of Israel, the land I had sworn with uplifted hand to give to your fathers. [43]There you will remember your conduct and all the actions by which you have defiled yourselves, and you will loathe yourselves for all the evil you have done. [44]You will know that I am the LORD, when I deal with you for my name's sake and not according to your evil ways and your corrupt practices, O house of Israel, declares the Sovereign LORD.' "

"Go serve your idols, if that's what you want!" declared God in holy irony, "But after my discipline has purged from my people all the rebels, *then* you will no longer profane my name with idols." Through the discipline of the exile, those who were indifferent to the Lord would be culled out. Only those who continued to believe God's promises would be interested in going back to the promised land after the exile. Upon their return home, "the entire house of Israel" present in the homeland would serve the Lord. By bringing them home, the Lord would show that he always keeps his promises. The people, newly returned, would be characterized by repentance (verse 43). And they would acknowledge the Lord had dealt with them according to his unchanging covenant with them, and not on the basis of their evil ways.

Moreover, God declared, restoration to the homeland would cause people to know that "I am the LORD." Most of the time in the book of Ezekiel this phrase had meant: "You will know I am the LORD who will keep my promise to punish your sins." Here it would mean: "You will know I am the LORD who can keep my promise of the Messiah. In order to do so, I had to keep the nation intact. I have done this by restoring you to the status of an ethnic entity in the promised location."

From this nation would be born the Savior of mankind, Jesus Christ.

Prophecy Against the South

45The word of the LORD came to me: 46"Son of man, set your face toward the south; preach against the south and prophesy against the forest of the southland. 47Say to the southern forest: 'Hear the word of the LORD. This is what the Sovereign LORD says: I am about to set fire to you, and it will consume all your trees, both green and dry. The blazing flame will not be quenched, and every face from south to north will be scorched by it. 48Everyone will see that I the LORD have kindled it; it will not be quenched.' "

In case anyone got the idea that God's promises of restoration negated the promises of destruction, Ezekiel was to remind them of the fire of the Lord (19:14). That fire was about to consume everybody and everything in the south, in the area around Jerusalem.

49Then I said, "Ah, Sovereign LORD! They are saying of me, 'Isn't he just telling parables?' "

The inquirers said, "He is talking parables again and we can't understand a thing." Notice that almost the entire

conversation between Ezekiel and the inquirers had been a
history lesson. There were no parables until verse 45. If the
leaders who had come to inquire of Ezekiel didn't want to
accept Ezekiel's message from the Lord, then no matter in
what form the prophet presented it, they wouldn't understand his "parables."

The law and the gospel are opposites. They can't be made
to fit well together. The same God who promises and sends
the blazing flame and consuming fire promises to restore us
to our membership in his family and finally to take us to the
promised land of heaven. The only way God can function
toward us on the basis of both law and gospel and still be
consistent is through the Messiah. In Christ we see God's
law at work as he suffers God's wrath against sin. And in the
suffering Savior we behold the unique blessings of the gospel — God so loved the world that he gave his one and only
Son. . . .

Babylon, God's Sword of Judgment

21 **The word of the Lord came to me:** ²**"Son of man, set your
face against Jerusalem and preach against the sanctuary.
Prophesy against the land of Israel** ³**and say to her: 'This is what
the Lord says: I am against you. I will draw my sword from its
scabbard and cut off from you both the righteous and the wicked.**
⁴**Because I am going to cut off the righteous and wicked, my
sword will be unsheathed against everyone from south to north.**
⁵**Then all people will know that I the Lord have drawn my sword
from its scabbard; it will not return again.'**

If they didn't like parables, Ezekiel would talk plainly. No
more talk of trees and forests. Jerusalem, the temple and the
land of Israel would be the victims of God's judgment. The
Lord would swing his sword. Nebuchadnezzar would be the
sword of the Lord (verse 19). When national disasters come,

the righteous along with the wicked suffer the same consequences which overtake the entire community. It is often more difficult to acknowledge the Lord is still in control when disaster strikes than it is to acknowledge he is in control when times are good and we are enjoying the sunshine of God's goodness.

The Lord promised to keep his sword in action until the job was finished. Ezekiel may very well have been waving a sword while speaking the "song of the sword" recorded in this chapter.

⁶"Therefore groan, son of man! Groan before them with broken heart and bitter grief. ⁷And when they ask you, 'Why are you groaning?' you shall say, 'Because of the news that is coming. Every heart will melt and every hand go limp; every spirit will become faint and every knee become as weak as water.' It is coming! It will surely take place, declares the Sovereign LORD."

To go along with the rest of this action-prophecy Ezekiel was to groan and moan. When interested bystanders questioned him, he would remind them that the news of Jerusalem's coming destruction would paralyze everyone with fear. Although we are not faced with the army of Nebuchadnezzar, in a world dominated by the consequences of sin, we are faced with many developments which turn our knees to water. Then let's remember that the Lord is our strength and our fortress. He is the only one who can help us solve this problem of fear. Since the people of Jerusalem had left God out of the picture, they didn't have this solution.

⁸The word of the LORD came to me: ⁹"Son of man, prophesy and say, 'This is what the Lord says:

> **" 'A sword, a sword,**
> **sharpened and polished —**

¹⁰sharpened for the slaughter,
  polished to flash like lightning!
" 'Shall we rejoice in the scepter of my son ⌊Judah⌋? The sword despises every such stick.

    ¹¹" 'The sword is appointed to be polished,
      to be grasped with the hand;
   it is sharpened and polished,
      made ready for the hand of the slayer.
   ¹²Cry out and wail, son of man,
     for it is against my people;
     it is against all the princes of Israel.
   They are thrown to the sword
     along with my people.
   Therefore beat your breast.
¹³" 'Testing will surely come. And what if the scepter ⌊of Judah⌋, which the sword despises, does not continue? declares the Sovereign LORD.'

    ¹⁴"So then, son of man, prophesy
     and strike your hands together.
   Let the sword strike twice,
     even three times.
   It is a sword for slaughter —
     a sword for great slaughter,
     closing in on them from every side.
   ¹⁵So that hearts may melt
     and the fallen be many,
     I have stationed the sword for slaughter
     at all their gates.
   Oh! It is made to flash like lightning,
     it is grasped for slaughter.
   ¹⁶O sword, slash to the right,
     then to the left,
     wherever your blade is turned.
   ¹⁷I too will strike my hands together,
     and my wrath will subside.
   I the LORD have spoken."

To strike terror into the hard hearts of God's stubborn people, Ezekiel personified the sword which would soon wreak its havoc. Judah and Jerusalem had despised the advice of God's prophets and resisted God's loving discipline; now they were about to experience the bloody consequences.

By striking his hands together Ezekiel was not showing happy approval; he was calling attention to what was going on. God's anger, however, is not insatiable.

18The word of the LORD came to me: 19"Son of man, mark out two roads for the sword of the king of Babylon to take, both starting from the same country. Make a signpost where the road branches off to the city. 20Mark out one road for the sword to come against Rabbah of the Ammonites and another against Judah and fortified Jerusalem. 21For the king of Babylon will stop at the fork in the road, at the junction of the two roads, to seek an omen; He will cast lots with arrows, he will consult his idols, he will examine the liver. 22Into his right hand will come the lot for Jerusalem, where he is to set up battering rams, to give the command to slaughter, to sound the battle cry, to set battering rams against the gates, to build a ramp and to erect siege works. 23It will seem like a false omen to those who have sworn allegiance to him, but he will remind them of their guilt and take them captive.

Here is another of the symbolic actions Ezekiel was commanded to perform. Ezekiel was to draw a little map, perhaps of Aram (ancient Syria) where Nebuchadnezzar had established his military headquarters. On it there was to be a crossroads sign indicating two roads to the south. At this location Nebuchadnezzar would choose to go either to Rabbah (capital of the kingdom of Ammon, east of the Jordan) or to Jerusalem. These two capitals seem to have been the two principal cities in a revolt against Nebuchadnezzar in 589 B.C.

As was his custom, Nebuchadnezzar would consult the omens before making his choice. One name was put on each of several arrows. One arrow was picked after they had been placed into a quiver and shaken. The arrow with the name Jerusalem on it was picked: "Into his right hand will come the lot for Jerusalem." We are not told exactly how he would "consult his idols," except that livers of slain animals were examined. The color and the lines (such as in palm reading) were usually interpreted to indicate whether what was being contemplated met with the favor of the gods or not, whether it would be successful or not.

In their disbelief, the only thing the inhabitants of Jerusalem would think of would be their alliance with Nebuchadnezzar. They would conveniently forget that their King Zedekiah had violated the terms of that alliance.

Repentance often seems to be lacking in our lives because we do such a good job of remembering only what we want to. When we repress our awareness of our sins, we can see absolutely no need for penitence. Sometimes the Lord has to bring a sword into our lives to help us to remember.

24"Therefore this is what the Sovereign Lord says: 'Because you people have brought to mind your guilt by your open rebellion, revealing your sins in all that you do — because you have done this, you will be taken captive.

This has been the theme of the book of Ezekiel up to this point. God couldn't make it any clearer than this summary statement. He would punish the people for their sins.

25" 'O profane and wicked prince of Israel, whose day has come, whose time of punishment has reached it climax, 26this is what the Sovereign Lord says: Take off the turban, remove the crown. It will not be as it was: The lowly will be exalted and the exalted will be brought low. 27A ruin! A ruin! I will make it a ruin! It will not

be restored until he comes to whom it rightfully belongs; to him I will give it.'

Wicked King Zedekiah, whose time was up, should face the facts and remove all outward indications of royalty. The entire society would be turned upside down by Nebuchadnezzar. The royal house of David would be ruined. Nobody of that house would sit on the throne of David again, until the Messiah would come (Genesis 49:10; Isaiah 9:6,7; Luke 1:32). To him the crown "rightfully belongs." Indeed, he is the King of kings and his kingdom is everlasting.

²⁸"And you, son of man, prophesy and say, 'This is what the Sovereign LORD says about the Ammonites and their insults:

" 'A sword, a sword,
    drawn for the slaughter,
polished to consume
    and to flash like lightning!
²⁹Despite false visions concerning you
    and lying divinations about you,
you will be laid on the necks
    of the wicked who are to be slain,
whose day has come,
    whose time of punishment has reached its climax.
³⁰Return your sword to its scabbard.
    In the place where you were created,
in the land of your ancestry,
    I will judge you.
³¹I will pour out my wrath upon you
    and breathe out my fiery anger against you;
I will hand you over to brutal men,
    men skilled in destruction.
³²You will be fuel for the fire,
    your blood will be shed in your land,
you will be remembered no more;
    for I the LORD have spoken.' "

Although Nebuchadnezzar invaded Judah and Jerusalem first, the kingdom of Ammon would also fall under his sword. Ammon had once joined Nebuchadnezzar against Judah during Jehoiakim's reign (2 Kings 24:2), and thus followed an historic hostility toward Israel and Judah. This is what Ezekiel referred to in speaking of "the Ammonites and their insults."

Yet Ammon had also managed to incur the wrath of Babylon's king. Despite false prophecies, apparently given by prophets in Ammon, which said Nebuchadnezzar's sword wouldn't hurt Ammon, his sword would fall on the necks of the people of Ammon too. So certain was the destruction of the Ammonites that the Lord encouraged them to put the sword back in the scabbard and not even fight. Because of their gross idolatry and godlessness, God would use the sword of Nebuchadnezzar to carry out his disgust against them. These people were even more revolting to the Lord than the other heathen Canaanite nations because they were descendants of one of Lot's daughters (Genesis 19:38), and thus had their roots in the truth. For Ammon there was no promise of restoration.

Frequently we tend to complain when God disciplines us. We compare our lot with the situation of others and end up telling God he should punish his and our enemies instead of disciplining us. When we do that, we are assuming God's role. It is God's business, not ours, to punish his enemies. It is up to us to witness to them about the gospel of Jesus Christ so they don't remain enemies.

Jerusalem's Sins

22 The word of the LORD came to me: [2]"Son of man, will you judge her? Will you judge this city of bloodshed? Then confront her with all her detestable practices [3]and say: 'This is what the Sovereign LORD says: O city that brings on herself doom by shedding blood in her midst and defiles herself by making idols, **⁴you have become guilty because of the blood you have shed and have become defiled by the idols you have made. You have brought your days to a close, and the end of your years has come. Therefore I will make you an object of scorn to the nations and a laughingstock to all the countries. ⁵Those who are near and those who are far away will mock you, O infamous city, full of turmoil.**

If Ezekiel was going to do a good job of being the Lord's prosecuting attorney in this case, he would have to be aware of the sins of which the people of Jerusalem were guilty. There were several good reasons the city might be called a "city of bloodshed." It might be a reference to the blood of all the idol sacrifices which were carried out there. It might be a reference to the blood of the children offered as sacrifices (16:21) to the heathen god Moloch. It might be a reference to the judicial injustices which often resulted in the deaths of innocent people, of which Naboth and others were examples (1 Kings 21). Or, it might just be a loose use of the term to refer to the tremendous guilt of the city in all areas.

As in chapter 7, here the end is presented (4) as something about to happen immediately: "The end of your years has come."

⁶" 'See how each of the princes of Israel who are in you uses his power to shed blood. ⁷In you they have treated father and mother with contempt; in you they have oppressed the alien and mistreated the fatherless and the widow. ⁸You have despised my holy things and desecrated my Sabbaths. ⁹In you are slanderous men bent on shedding blood; in you are those who eat at the mountain shrines and commit lewd acts. ¹⁰In you are those who dishonor their fathers' bed; in you are those who violate women during their period, when they are ceremonially unclean. ¹¹In you one man commits a detestable offense with his neighbor's wife, another shamefully defiles his daughter-in-law, and another violates his sister, his own father's daughter. ¹²In you men accept bribes to shed blood; you take usury and excessive interest and make

124

unjust gain from your neighbors by extortion. And you have forgotten me, declares the Sovereign LORD.

Those in authority used their positions to take advantage of others. Their flagrant violations of the laws of Moses announced from Mount Sinai was an indication of how far they had drifted from the Lord. They disregarded laws about parents (Exodus 20:12), the alien, the fatherless and the widow (Exodus 22:21-24), holy things (Leviticus 10:10; 11:47), Sabbaths (Exodus 20:8), slander (Leviticus 19:16), idol festivals (Exodus 20:4,5), sexual impurity (Leviticus 18), bribery (Exodus 23:8) and usury (Exodus 22:25-27).

It is important to note that God considers not just idolatry and direct abandonment of the Lord as affronts to him. Loveless deeds which hurt others are an offense against him as well. The same God who said, "Love the LORD your God with all your heart and with all your soul and with all your strength" (Deuteronomy 6:5) has also said, "Love your neighbor as yourself" (Leviticus 19:18).

What do our actions toward others say to God? When we treat our aged parents with indifference, we are telling the Lord we don't appreciate all the blessings he has given us through them over the years. When we fail to look after the lonely, the needy, the fatherless and the widow, we are telling God we don't appreciate his blessings which have enabled us to stay out of those circumstances. When we slander and attack others, we are telling God we don't think his gift of life is something to be preserved and enjoyed. When we sexually use other people, we are telling him his gift of sexuality is only an appetite to be satisfied, not a special blessing to be reserved for a special permanent relationship with another human being. When we take bribes or excessive interest, we are telling him we don't trust his

125

judgment concerning how much of this world's goods we need to live in this world.

13" 'I will surely strike my hands together at the unjust gain you have made and at the blood you have shed in your midst. 14Will your courage endure or your hands be strong in the day I deal with you? I the LORD have spoken, and I will do it. 15I will disperse you among the nations and scatter you through the countries; and I will put an end to your uncleanness. 16When you have been defiled in the eyes of the nations, you will know that I am the LORD.' "

Ezekiel's striking his hands together (21:14) symbolized the anger of God, who now declared, "I will surely strike my hands together." Then, under the thundering wrath of God, would the people be so bold or brazen as they had been in dealing with their fellowmen?

Again God declared his threat of dispersing his people among the nations. Dispersion is presented here as the way God would put a stop to their uncleanness.

We need to remember that we constantly stand in the presence of God. The Almighty is always aware of precisely what we are doing. If we kept this in mind, we probably wouldn't act so harshly and unlovingly toward the people around us. Remembering that God is still a God who must punish sin will lead us (in the words of Luther's *Small Catechism*) to "fear his wrath and not do contrary to his commandments."

17Then the word of the LORD came to me: 18"Son of man, the house of Israel has become dross to me; all of them are the copper, tin, iron and lead left inside a furnace. They are but the dross of silver. 19Therefore this is what the Sovereign LORD says: 'Because you have all become dross, I will gather you into Jerusalem. 20As men gather silver, copper, iron, lead and tin into a furnace to melt

it with a fiery blast, so will I gather you in my wrath and put you inside the city and melt you. ²¹I will gather you and I will blow on you with my fiery wrath, and you will be melted inside her. ²²As silver is melted in a furnace, so you will be melted inside her, and you will know that I the LORD have poured out my wrath upon you.' "

Here God used another comparison to show how useless Judah had become to him, how unsuited to his high and holy purposes. God would use the city walls of Jerusalem as a smelting furnace. His people would be put into the furnace. He would be looking for silver, but would find only base metals. In a word, he would find nothing but dross. In the Lord's view there was no silver in Jerusalem. In its present condition it was of no value.

²³Again the word of the LORD came to me: ²⁴"Son of man, say to the land, 'You are a land that has had no rain or showers in the day of wrath.' ²⁵There is a conspiracy of her princes within her like a roaring lion tearing its prey; they devour people, take treasures and precious things and make many widows within her. ²⁶Her priests do violence to my law and profane my holy things; they do not distinguish between the holy and the common; they teach that there is no difference between the unclean and the clean; and they shut their eyes to the keeping of my Sabbaths, so that I am profaned among them. ²⁷Her officials within her are like wolves tearing their prey; they shed blood and kill people to make unjust gain. ²⁸Her prophets whitewash these deeds for them by false visions and lying divinations. They say, 'This is what the Sovereign LORD says' — when the LORD has not spoken. ²⁹The people of the land practice extortion and commit robbery; they oppress the poor and needy and mistreat the alien, denying them justice.

As further evidence of his displeasure, God would even withhold the blessing of rain to compound the problems caused by the siege. The political leaders had used their positions for crime and fraud. Instead of protecting the people they had taken advantage of them. Involving the nation in war, the leaders had caused the deaths of many men, and thus made many widows. The priests, who should have taught God's law, acted as if there was no law! The prophets, claiming to speak for God, whitewashed their evil deeds. And — perhaps worst of all — the people followed the ungodly examples of their leaders.

Do the leaders of a society drag it down by their ungodly actions? Are they the trend setters and the ones whose examples are followed? Or, do the leaders of a society merely reflect the level of existence of the people whom they lead? These questions always cause good arguments. But they are pointless questions. They always seem to be asked by those who want to shirk their own personal responsibility for the lack of godliness in society or in their own lives. A better question would be: "Is my ungodly life adding to the ungodliness of my society?" Or "Is my godly life detracting from the ungodliness of my society?"

30"I looked for a man among them who would build up the wall and stand before me in the gap on behalf of the land so I would not have to destroy it, but I found none. 31So I will pour out my wrath on them and consume them with my fiery anger, bringing down on their own heads all they have done, declares the Sovereign LORD."

The God of grace was always looking for someone to raise up as a leader of a reform movement, a person to lead the people to repentance so their doom might be averted. God wanted someone who would build up a wall of repentance and godly living among the people so the anger of the Lord and the battering ram of Nebuchadnezzar would be turned aside. But no one was to be found. Prophets like Jeremiah who tried had all been rebuffed, ridiculed and persecuted. So God had no choice but to step in with judgment.

A nation which openly defies the Lord and his will is going to be destroyed. Frequently historians look at a nation which has collapsed and point to factors inside the society which contributed to its destruction. Their finding is always that the society was flawed and destroyed itself. This might seem to be a correct evaluation. But we know the Lord rules over all creation and does not let open rebellion against him go unpunished. He is the one who lets a society devour itself when it insists on its rights and its liberties to the neglect of God's will. The fall of that nation, then, isn't really self-destruction. It is a punishment from the Lord.

Two Adulterous Sisters

23 **The word of the LORD came to me: ²"Son of man, there were two women, daughters of the same mother. ³They became prostitutes in Egypt, engaging in prostitution from their youth. In that land their breasts were fondled and their virgin bosoms caressed. ⁴The older was named Oholah, and her sister was Oholibah. They were mine and gave birth to sons and daughters. Oholah is Samaria, and Oholibah is Jerusalem.**

Chapter 23 is one of the most powerful sections of Ezekiel. It opens with comparing Samaria and Jerusalem, the capitals of Israel and Judah, to two sisters. They were "daughters of the same mother" because they had a common ancestor, namely Jacob, whose sons' descendants formed the twelve tribes. The undefined idolatry in Egypt has already been referred to (20:7). Samaria was probably called the older because her falling away from the Lord had occurred earlier. Oholah, which means "her own tent," is probably a reference to the false worship which Israel's wicked kings set up at Dan and Bethel after the division of the kingdom. Oholibah, which means "my tent is in her," undoubtedly refers to the presence of God's sanctuary at Jerusalem.

As in chapter 16, here again the Lord referred to the covenant relationship as a marriage between himself and his people. Here the language is explicitly sexual. Why? Probably to shock the sensibilities of those who were listening. Through the Prophet Ezekiel God was saying to his people: "What you are doing in your spiritual lives is just as revolting to me as if you would be involved in prostitution in your sexual lives. Spiritual adultery is the same to me as sexual prostitution."

So often we differentiate between physical-social sins and spiritual sins. Because physical-social sins have observable consequences, we give the impression they are "worse." We express anger over the wanton murders (physical) all around us because they directly affect the lives of others (social). We decry the lack of respect for property (physical), because it directly affects the lives of others (social). We bewail the lack of sexual restraint and the sexual perversions all around us (physical), because they, too, directly affect the lives of others (social).

But somehow failure to study the Word of God and to apply it to our life doesn't seem so bad. It doesn't have observable negative consequences on the outward lives of people around us. Failure to speak of God in a positive, constructive way "doesn't seem so bad" because it doesn't have any physical-social consequences.

The problem, of course, is that when we differentiate between spiritual and physical-social sins in this way, we fail to see our relationship with God as God had described it in the first three commandments. When God told the people of Judah that their spiritual sins made them prostitutes in his sight, his explicit language might bring the same point home to us.

Eventually, of course, a breakdown in our relationship with God will lead to wickedness in many other areas of life. The seeds of today's widespread moral decay were sown with a disrespect for the Bible and spiritual values. In the case of Israel and Judah spiritual apostasy was closely linked to gross immorality.

5Oholah engaged in prostitution while she was still mine; and she lusted after her lovers, the Assyrians — warriors 6clothed in blue, governors and commanders, all of them handsome young men, and mounted horsemen. 7She gave herself as a prostitute to all the elite of the Assyrians and defiled herself with all the idols of everyone she lusted after. 8She did not give up the prostitution she began in Egypt, when during her youth men slept with her, caressed her virgin bosom and poured out their lust upon her.

Samaria (Israel) kept the leftovers of the idolatry practiced in Egypt by having the calf-idols as the focus of worship in the northern kingdom (1 Kings 12:28-30). They were probably representations of Apis, the bull-god from Egypt. Contrary to God's command against military alliances with heathen neighbors, Hoshea tried an alliance with Egypt (2 Kings 17:4). In addition, Samaria was attracted to the power of the Assyrian empire. The alliances made with Assyria (2 Kings 15:19,20) violated the trust and unreserved dependence which the people had pledged to maintain with the Lord. The treaties also always required acknowledging the foreign gods and at the very least joining in outward participation in the worship of these foreign gods.

It is always easier to trust something you can see rather than God. It is much easier to be "secure" because of a sound financial program than to feel secure resting in God's promises. It is easier to feel safe because of the military might of one's nation or of one's allies than to feel safe because of the Lord's promises. And so often the two bases of trust become mutually exclusive, as was the case for Samaria.

9"Therefore I handed her over to her lovers, the Assyrians, for whom she lusted. ¹⁰They stripped her naked, took away her sons and daughters and killed her with the sword. She became a byword among women, and punishment was inflicted on her.

God's punishment had already fallen on Samaria before Ezekiel's time (722 B.C.). The nation to whom Israel had looked for help became her executioner!

¹¹"Her sister Oholibah saw this, yet in her lust and prostitution she was more depraved than her sister. ¹²She too lusted after the Assyrians — governors and commanders, warriors in full dress, mounted horsemen, all handsome young men. ¹³I saw that she too defiled herself; both of them went the same way.

Jerusalem (Judah) did not learn from the unhappy history of her sister to the north. She had seen what had happened to Samaria, and yet she was attracted to the world powers in the same way. Instead of turning to God, she also turned to Assyria (2 Kings 16:5-9) to help her solve her problems with Syria.

Sometimes people depreciate the Old Testament, say it is only a history book of the Jewish people, think it isn't worth much, and certainly don't regard it as God's message to us. It is a history book, that's true. We are given the history of the world and of God's people so we can learn from it. We can learn where those people failed. With the Lord's help, we can then try to avoid the same pitfalls. We can also learn that no matter what happens, the ages are His-Story. The nations are in God's hands.

¹⁴"But she carried her prostitution still further. She saw men portrayed on a wall, figures of Chaldeans portrayed in red, ¹⁵with belts around their waists and flowing turbans on their heads; all of them looked like Babylonian chariot officers, natives of Chaldea. ¹⁶As soon as she saw them, she lusted after them and sent messengers to them in Chaldea. ¹⁷Then the Babylonians came to her, to the bed of love, and in their lust they defiled her. After she had been defiled by them, she turned away from them in disgust. ¹⁸When she carried on her prostitution openly and exposed her nakedness, I turned away from her in disgust, just as I had turned away from her sister. ¹⁹Yet she became more and more promiscuous as she recalled the days of her youth, when she was a prostitute in Egypt. ²⁰There she lusted after her lovers, whose genitals were like those of donkeys and whose emission was like that of horses. ²¹So you longed for the lewdness of your youth, when in Egypt your bosom was caressed and your young breasts fondled.

Jerusalem-Judah was a progressive prostitute. Once she had turned from the Lord she moved from one partner to the next, whoever was convenient. When Babylon came on the scene and took over Assyria's dominant role in the ancient Near East (2 Kings 20:12,13), Judah played the same game with King Merodach-Baladan. Then Jerusalem, turning away "in disgust," renounced her relationship with Babylon (2 Kings 24:1) and tried to go back to an alliance with Egypt. As the language of Ezekiel shows, all of this thoroughly disgusted God.

An attitude of convenience is often at the root of a lack of godliness. If we approach any circumstance without a set of absolutes, we are going to evaluate the situation in terms of what is convenient. But the convenient way isn't necessarily the God-pleasing way. In fact, sometimes the convenient way is downright God-displeasing.

²²"Therefore, Oholibah, this is what the Sovereign LORD says: I will stir up your lovers against you, those you turned away from in

133

disgust, and I will bring them against you from every side — ²³the Babylonians and all the Chaldeans, the men of Pekod and Shoa and Koa, and all the Assyrians with them, handsome young men, all of them governors and commanders, chariot officers and men of high rank, all mounted on horses. ²⁴They will come against you with weapons, chariots and wagons and with a throng of people; they will take up positions against you on every side with large and small shields and with helmets. I will turn you over to them for punishment, and they will punish you according to their standards. ²⁵I will direct my jealous anger against you, and they will deal with you in fury. They will cut off your noses and your ears, and those of you who are left will fall by the sword. They will take away your sons and daughters, and those of you who are left will be consumed by fire. ²⁶They will also strip you of your clothes and take your fine jewelry. ²⁷So I will put a stop to the lewdness and prostitution you began in Egypt. You will not look on these things with longing or remember Egypt anymore.

The Lord would treat Oholibah in the same way he had treated Oholah. He would use the very nations she had chosen as her allies, including some of the lesser tribes from along the Tigris River, to punish Jerusalem. Although the nation of Babylon would be the sword cutting down God's people, it would be the Lord himself wielding that sword. The beauty of the Jewish nation, the best of its people, would be "cut off" and taken away, just as a prostitute was punished by having her nose or ears cut off. The captivity would put a stop to Judah's idolatrous and adulterous alliances with false gods.

²⁸"For this is what the Sovereign Lord says: I am about to hand you over to those you hate, to those you turned away from in disgust. ²⁹They will deal with you in hatred and take away everything you have worked for. They will leave you naked and bare, and the shame of your prostitution will be exposed. Your lewdness and promiscuity ³⁰have brought this upon you, because you

lusted after the nations and defiled yourself with their idols. ³¹You have gone the way of your sister; so I will put her cup into your hand.

Jerusalem had rebelled against her former political allies and now they would attack her. Those whom she had trusted, she now hated. The same consequences which Samaria, capital of the northern kingdom, had received, Jerusalem would face. God's furious judgment on Judah-Jerusalem is compared to a cup of judgment she must drink.

³²"This is what the Sovereign Lord says:
   "You will drink your sister's cup,
      a cup large and deep;
   it will bring scorn and derision,
      for it holds so much.
³³You will be filled with drunkenness and sorrow,
      the cup of ruin and desolation,
      the cup of your sister Samaria.
³⁴You will drink it and drain it dry;
      you will dash it to pieces
      and tear your breasts.
I have spoken, declares the Sovereign Lord.

The same scorn and derision which fell on Samaria from the heathen nations would now fall on Jerusalem. The ruin and desolation she would have to suffer would bring about a drunkenness of despair in which she would even mutilate herself.

³⁵"Therefore this is what the Sovereign Lord says: Since you have forgotten me and thrust me behind your back, you must bear the consequences of your lewdness and prostitution."

Was the desolation of Judah just the result of power politics, just the rise and fall of nations? No, the reason for Judah's fall was that she had forgotten the Lord.

³⁶The Lord said to me: "Son of man, will you judge Oholah and Oholibah? Then confront them with their detestable practices, ³⁷for they have committed adultery and blood is on their hands. They committed adultery with their idols; they even sacrificed their children, whom they bore to me, as food for them. ³⁸They have also done this to me: At that same time they defiled my sanctuary and desecrated my Sabbaths. ³⁹On the very day they sacrificed their children to their idols, they entered my sanctuary and desecrated it. That is what they did in my house.

The past punishment of Samaria and the future punishment of Jerusalem were now combined into a single summary of history and punishment. The same charges which were issued previously are repeated here. One addition is made. These worshipers of Moloch and child-sacrificers were so brazen they thought it was perfectly all right to go to worship the Lord right after they had finished their detestable actions!

Common respect for other human beings and what they believe demands toleration from all of us. However, religious indifference which sees no difference between the true God and the man-made gods of the world is offensive to the Lord. One often hears today that such toleration of false religion is necessary if we are to get along in a pluralistic world. But if our actions give credence and approval to falsehood and in the next breath we worship the Lord, it must disgust him just as much as it did when the inhabitants of Judah did it.

⁴⁰"They even sent messengers for men who came from far away, and when they arrived you bathed yourself for them, painted your eyes and put on your jewelry. ⁴¹You sat on an elegant couch, with a table spread before it on which you had placed the incense and oil that belonged to me.

Another disgusting aspect to the alliances with foreign powers and gods was that Israel and Judah actually took the initiative in establishing these alliances. Israel and Judah, not the foreign powers, were responsible for the spiritual prostitution occurring.

[42]"The noise of a carefree crowd was around her; Sabeans were brought from the desert along with men from the rabble, and they put bracelets on the arms of the woman and her sister and beautiful crowns on their heads. [43]Then I said about the one worn out by adultery, 'Now let them use her as a prostitute, for that is all she is.' [44]And they slept with her. As men sleep with a prostitute, so they slept with those lewd women, Oholah and Oholibah. [45]But righteous men will sentence them to the punishment of women who commit adultery and shed blood, because they are adulterous and blood is on their hands.

God finally got sick and tired of the idolatrous revelling and abandoned the sisters to their evil ways. Spiritual prostitution had now become a regular habit to Oholah and Oholibah. Their dealings now included the Sabeans from the desert kingdom of Sheba. It was not just something into which they had slipped on an occasion.

Now God promised to use "righteous men" as instruments of his judgment. These men would carry out God's just punishment.

[46]"This is what the Sovereign LORD says: Bring a mob against them and give them over to terror and plunder. [47]The mob will stone them and cut them down with their swords; they will kill their sons and daughters and burn down their houses.

The punishment God promised fit the crime. In the Old Testament stoning was the punishment for prostitution. And death by the sword was the punishment for murder.

⁴⁸"So I will put an end to lewdness in the land, that all women may take warning and not imitate you. ⁴⁹You will suffer the penalty for your lewdness and bear the consequences of your sins of idolatry. Then you will know that I am the Sovereign LORD."

God's punishment was intended to first put a stop to the shameful spiritual adultery, but also to warn others not to follow other gods.

The Cooking Pot

24 In the ninth year, in the tenth month on the tenth day, the word of the LORD came to me: ²"Son of man, record this date, this very date, because the king of Babylon has laid siege to Jerusalem this very day. ³Tell this rebellious house a parable and say to them: 'This is what the Sovereign LORD says:

" 'Put on the cooking pot; put it on
    and pour water into it.
⁴Put into it the pieces of meat,
    all the choice pieces — the leg and the shoulder.
Fill it with the best of these bones;
    ⁵take the pick of the flock.
Pile wood beneath it for the bones;
    bring it to a boil
    and cook the bones in it.

Approximately four and a half years after Ezekiel's first vision (1:2), the siege was laid against Jerusalem (in January of 588 B.C.). The siege lasted a year and a half. Ezekiel's four and a half years of calling the people of Judah to repentance hadn't done much. The people to whom he was prophesying were still a "rebellious" house.

Now, however, because the siege about which he had warned had actually begun, any hopes they had that Jerusalem might be spared were gone. In Ezekiel's parable of

138

judgment Jerusalem was the pot. The people were the meat and bones. The siege laid by Nebuchadnezzar and the war waged by him were the fire under the pot.

> ⁶" 'For this is what the Sovereign LORD says:
>
>> " 'Woe to the city of bloodshed,
>>> to the pot now encrusted,
>>> whose deposit will not go away!
>> Empty it piece by piece
>>> without casting lots for them.
>> ⁷" 'For the blood she shed is in her midst:
>>> She poured it on the bare rock;
>> she did not pour it on the ground,
>>> where the dust would cover it.
>> ⁸To stir up wrath and take revenge
>>> I put her blood on the bare rock,
>>> so that it would not be covered.

Jerusalem was no longer the "holy" city, but the city of bloodshed (22:1-5). She had become so brazen she made no attempt to cover her crimes or to bring her criminals to justice. Blood was shed and left out on the bare rock for all to see. God made use of this evidence to prove his anger and revenge were justified.

The pieces of meat would be taken out of the pot individually and sent into exile. No one would get special treatment by "lady luck" — casting lots. The people of the city were so polluted that the pot itself had to be described as "encrusted with a deposit that won't go away."

When our sinfulness has had public consequences, sometimes the Lord deals out his discipline in a public way. If a child's disobedience is flagrant, his parents may have to discipline the child in front of the other children. This public rebuke also says something to the other children. When the sentence pronounced on a convicted criminal is made public, this says something to the rest of society. God may find it necessary to inflict an entire society when that society has become brazen enough to carry out its sins for all to see.

⁹" 'Therefore this is what the Sovereign LORD says:

" 'Woe to the city of bloodshed!
 I, too, will pile the wood high.
¹⁰So heap on the wood
 and kindle the fire.
Cook the meat well,
 mixing in the spices;
 and let the bones be charred.
¹¹Then set the empty pot on the coals
 till it becomes hot and its copper glows
 so its impurities may be melted
 and its deposit burned away.
¹²It has frustrated all efforts;
 its heavy deposit has not been removed,
 not even by fire.

¹³" 'Now your impurity is lewdness. Because I tried to cleanse you but you would not be cleansed from your impurity, you will not be clean again until my wrath against you has subsided.

¹⁴" 'I the LORD have spoken. The time has come for me to act. I will not hold back; I will not have pity, nor will I relent. You will be judged according to your conduct and your actions, declares the Sovereign LORD.' "

Not only would the city and its inhabitants ("the meat and bones") be cooked by the siege of Nebuchadnezzar's army, but the pot itself (the city emptied of inhabitants) would be melted down. The only way to get rid of the pollution of Jerusalem was to melt it down and burn away its impurities. None of the Lord's previous attempts at chastisement had produced the desired repentance. A reference (verse 13) to chapter 23 reminded the hearers of the cause of all this — spiritual lewdness. Nothing could deter the Lord from his announced intentions as he declared, "I have spoken.... I will not hold back; I will not have pity, nor will I relent...." The writer to the Hebrews summed up the judgment of God in this way: "It is a dreadful thing to fall into the hands of the living God" (10:31).

Sometimes the residue of our sins cannot be easily removed. The consequences appear to be so long-term we can't see whether we will ever get out from under them. Once in a while the only thing the Lord can do is melt down the pot and lead us into exile, a sort of Babylon. There we might start a new life, producing fruits of repentance in a setting in which all residue of our former sins has been completely removed. New surroundings might not only be more comfortable for us, but they might also make it possible for us to be more productive in our service to the rest of God's people.

Ezekiel's Wife Dies

¹⁵The word of the LORD came to me: ¹⁶"Son of man, with one blow I am about to take away from you the delight of your eyes. Yet do not lament or weep or shed any tears. ¹⁷Groan quietly; do not mourn for the dead. Keep your turban fastened and your sandals on your feet; do not cover the lower part of your face or eat the customary food ⌊of mourners⌋."

Although Ezekiel was a prophet of unflinching endurance when announcing God's punishment, he was not a man without human feelings. He considered his wife the delight of his eyes. Her sudden death must have come as a shock. God commanded Ezekiel not to implement all the customary outward indications of mourning, but to repress all the natural feelings in regard to the loss of his wife! He was not to hire mourners to wail aloud. He was not to put ashes on his head and walk around barefoot. He was to leave his face uncovered as if things were normal. He was not to accept the food brought in by sympathetic friends and relatives.

18So I spoke to the people in the morning and in the evening my wife died. The next morning I did as I had been commanded.

Ezekiel, always the Lord's obedient servant, did as he was commanded.

19Then the people asked me, "Won't you tell us what these things have to do with us?"

Again, the Lord's purpose was to instruct his people. When they asked the meaning of Ezekiel's unusual behavior, he could tell them the message God had for them.

Our activities in connection with the death of loved ones often bring questions from those around us who are not Christians. We can use these opportunities to bring the Lord's thoughts to the inquirers, as Ezekiel did. We can indicate we groan quietly for ourselves because we miss our loved one. But we do not mourn as those who have no hope, since we know the dead believer is with the Lord. We don't give up our life's daily activities, because we know life really hasn't stopped for our loved one. It has just changed modes. It is now life with the Lord. We don't need to express special shame before the Lord on behalf of the loved one, because we know our dear one is acceptable to the Lord. We know his sins have been washed away in the blood of Christ, and he is wearing the holiness which Jesus won by living a perfect life as his Substitute.

20So I said to them, "The word of the LORD came to me: 21Say to the house of Israel, 'This is what the Sovereign LORD says: I am

about to desecrate my sanctuary — the stronghold in which you take pride, the delight of your eyes, the object of your affection. The sons and daughters you left behind will fall by the sword. ²²And you will do as I have done. You will not cover the lower part of your face or eat the customary food ⌊of mourners⌋. ²³You will keep your turbans on your heads and your sandals on your feet. You will not mourn or weep but will waste away because of your sins and groan among yourselves. ²⁴Ezekiel will be a sign to you; you will do just as he has done. When this happens, you will know that I am the Sovereign Lord.'

God had taken away Ezekiel's wife, the delight of Ezekiel's eyes. Now the Almighty was about to take away the temple, the beautiful delight of the eyes of the nation. Just as Ezekiel didn't mourn in the usual way for his wife, so the loss of Jerusalem and the temple would be too great a loss to express in human emotions.

Instead, the people would groan inside, when they realized that their sins had caused this tragedy. Ezekiel's lack of mourning for his wife would be a sign. It would be a reminder to them, when they would do the same thing over Jerusalem, that the Lord had predicted all of this through Ezekiel. By this God would again prove he was the Lord.

²⁵"And you, son of man, on the day I take away their stronghold, their joy and glory, the delight of their eyes their heart's desire, and their sons and daughters as well — ²⁶on that day a fugitive will come to tell you the news. ²⁷At that time your mouth will be opened; you will speak with him and will no longer be silent. So you will be a sign to them, and they will know that I am the Lord."

When Jerusalem fell, a messenger-fugitive would come to Babylon to tell the exiles the news. From that point on, the limitations which had been placed on Ezekiel (3:26-37) would be lifted. Up to this time, he had spoken to them only when directed to do so by the Lord. What he had said under direct orders from the Lord is recorded for us in chapters 4-24. At all other times during this four and a half year period he had withdrawn into his house and acted as if he were tied with ropes and as if his tongue were stuck to the roof of his mouth (3:24-26). But when the messenger arrived with the news indicating that all of Ezekiel's predictions from the Lord had come true, all restrictions would be lifted. This fulfillment of Ezekiel's predictions should have been a sign, a proof to them the Lord was the source of the message of Ezekiel.

Many people claim to find parallels between what the Lord says in the Bible and things happening in the world today, even when there aren't really any parallels. But when parallels are there, we can use them as Ezekiel did. We can point to scriptural predictions and say, "We should have expected it. Everything is turning out exactly as God said it would." Such linkage is a powerful reminder that the One behind all of Scripture is the Sovereign Lord himself.

PART II

PROPHECIES AGAINST HOSTILE NATIONS
EZEKIEL 25 — 32

Chapters 25 to 32 of Ezekiel form a bridge between the book's main sections. In the first major section (chapters 4-24), God's spokesman foretold the doom of Jerusalem. In the second major section (chapters 33-48), Ezekiel would promise restoration for the chastened people.

In this middle bridging section, the Lord, through Ezekiel, indicated he was the God of all the nations, not just of Israel and Judah. He would judge the surrounding nations for their sins with the same justice he used on Israel and Judah. The result of the Lord's judgment upon these other nations is indicated in Ezekiel 28:24-26. "No longer will the people of Israel have malicious neighbors.... When I gather the people of Israel from the nations where they have been scattered.... they will live in their own land.... in safety... when I inflict punishment on all their neighbors who maligned them."

A Prophecy Against Ammon

25 **The word of the LORD came to me: [2]"Son of man, set your face against the Ammonites and prophesy against them. [3]Say to them, 'Hear the word of the Sovereign LORD. This is what the Sovereign LORD says: Because you said "Aha!" over my sanctuary when it was desecrated and over the land of Israel when it was laid waste and over the people of Judah when they went into**

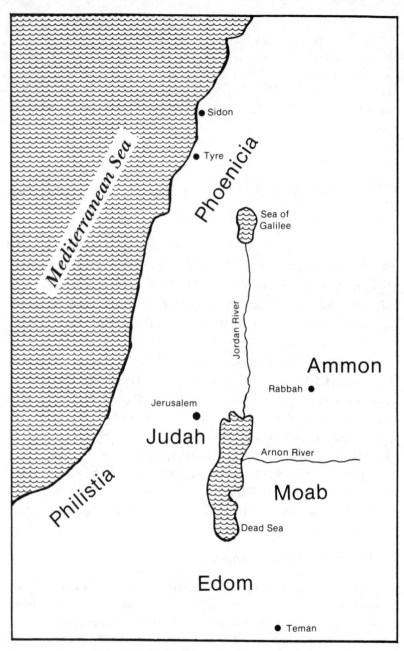

Judah and surrounding nations
(Ammon, Moab, Edom, Philistia, Phoenicia)

exile, 4therefore I am going to give you to the people of the East as a possession. They will set up their camps and pitch their tents among you; they will eat your fruit and drink your milk. 5I will turn Rabbah into a pasture for camels and Ammon into a resting place for sheep. Then you will know that I am the LORD. 6For this is what the Sovereign LORD says: Because you have clapped your hands and stamped your feet, rejoicing with all the malice of your heart against the land of Israel, 7therefore I will stretch out my hand against you and give you as plunder to the nations. I will cut you off from the nations and exterminate you from the countries. I will destroy you, and you will know that I am the LORD.' "

The Ammonites were descendants of Lot by his younger daughter (Genesis 19:37,38). They had inhabited land east and north of the Dead Sea. Ammon was often allied with other nations against Israel. The Ammonites offered no assistance to Israel while she was on her journey from Egypt to Canaan (Deuteronomy 23:3,4). Ammon joined Moab and Amalek in subjugating Israel for eighteen years (Judges 3:12,13). After an amazingly brazen action showing ridicule for King David, they hired the Syrians to try to defeat David (2 Samuel 10:1-19). By A.D. 200 they had lost their identity among the Arabian nomads. Their god was Moloch. Their capital was Rabbah, or Rabbath Ammon, today called Amman, the capital of modern Jordan.

The immediate cause of the Lord's anger against Ammon was their bitter anger against the people of Israel. The Ammonites had participated in (2 Kings 24:2) and rejoiced over the destruction of the temple, the land of Israel, and the nation.

A Prophecy against Moab

8"This is what the Sovereign LORD says: 'Because Moab and Seir said, "Look, the house of Judah has become like all the other

147

nations," [9]therefore I will expose the flank of Moab, beginning at its frontier towns — Beth Jeshimoth, Baal Meon and Kiriathaim — the glory of that land. [10]I will give Moab along with the Ammonites to the people of the East as a possession, so that the Ammonites will not be remembered among the nations; [11]and I will inflict punishment on Moab. Then they will know that I am the LORD.' "

The Moabites were descendants of Lot by his older daughter (Genesis 19:37,38). They inhabited land east of the Dead Sea and like the Ammonites had a long history of bitter enmity toward Israel. Moab refused to let Israel cross through its land on the journey back to Canaan from Egypt (Judges 11:17). The King of Moab hired Balaam to curse Israel (Numbers 22:4-6). King Eglon with help from Ammon and Amalek subjugated Israel for eighteen years (Judges 3:12,13).

Moab also participated with Babylon in overthrowing Jerusalem (2 Kings 24:2). Her attitude toward Jerusalem and Judah seems to have been: "Judah isn't any different from any other nation. She has fallen to the power of Babylon just like so many others. The temple and Judah's God, which always were assumed to be the source of special protection, have been shown to be nothing special at all. Nebuchadnezzar's destruction of them should have proven it once and for all." In God's sight, this amounted to despising Israel's sacred calling.

God promised to break Moab's defense by letting her fortified border and frontier towns be captured. This would expose the relatively unprotected interior. It is difficult to ascertain why Seir (Edom) and Ammon are included in this section, since Ammon has already been discussed, and Edom is about to be discussed (12-14). The punishments intended for Ammon and Moab are clearly differentiated.

Moab's punishment definitely seems to have been less severe.

A Prophecy Against Edom

12"This is what the Sovereign LORD says: 'Because Edom took revenge on the house of Judah and became very guilty by doing so, 13therefore this is what the Sovereign LORD says: I will stretch out my hand against Edom and kill its men and their animals. I will lay it waste, and from Teman to Dedan they will fall by the sword. 14 I will take vengeance on Edom by the hand of my people Israel, and they will deal with Edom in accordance with my anger and my wrath; they will know my vengeance, declares the Sovereign LORD.' "

The Edomites, descendants of Esau (Genesis 25:30), inhabited the land south of the Dead Sea. They, too, had refused to let Israel cross through their land (Numbers 20:18-21) en route to Canaan. Edom's King Hadad became one of Solomon's greatest enemies (1 Kings 11:14-23). Edom attacked Israel at the time of King Jehoshaphat, but was defeated (2 Chronicles 20:22). When Nebuchadnezzar besieged Jerusalem, the Edomites joined in, plundering the city and helping to slaughter the people (Obadiah 8-14). After Jerusalem fell Edom again prospered until the time of the Maccabees. In 126 B.C. one of the Maccabees, John Hyrcanus, subjugated Edom and incorporated it into the Jewish state. The area was called Idumea by Greek and Roman writers.

A unique element of this oracle of judgment was that Israel itself would carry out God's judgment against Edom. This actually occurred under the Maccabees. Teman seems to have been a city or district in the north of Edom. Dedan was either a district or a tribe along the southern border. Seir is a mountain range running through and beyond Edom.

A Prophecy Against Philistia

[15]"This is what the Sovereign LORD says: 'Because the Philistines acted in vengeance and took revenge with malice in their hearts, and with ancient hostility sought to destroy Judah, [16]therefore this is what the Sovereign LORD says: I am about to stretch out my hand against the Philistines, and I will cut off the Kerethites and destroy those remaining along the coast. [17]I will carry out great vengeance on them and punish them in my wrath. Then they will know that I am the LORD, when I take vengeance on them.' "

The Philistines inhabited the coastal strip in southwestern Palestine. The name Palestine is related to the name Philistine. Philistia was a federation of five city-states, each under an independently powerful ruler. This intercity rivalry made the coalition very powerful militarily. Their location on the major trade routes from Mesopotamia to Egypt made them strategically and economically important. Their long Mediterranean coastline made them a viable seafaring commercial power. And their fertile soil made them agriculturally independent.

The biblical books of Judges, Samuel, Kings and Chronicles document the historic and almost constant conflict between Israel and Philistia.

After the fall of Jerusalem, again because of their strategic location, the Philistines suffered conquest at the hands of both the Egyptians and Babylonians (Jeremiah 47). "Kerethites" seems to have been just another name for Philistines. It may be related to Crete, the ancestral home of the Philistines.

God was saying to these nations: "I have the right to punish my people for their sins. I have chosen to use Babylon as my instrument for carrying out that punishment. Yet you have had no right arbitrarily to punish my people either in the past or at present. Therefore, I will punish you for your action against my people, because it was really action against me."

The doom directed against each of these heathen nations at the end of each brief section is reminiscent of the doom and gloom directed at Jerusalem and Judah throughout the first major segment of Ezekiel's prophecy (chapters 4-24). But there is a difference. In the second major segment of the prophecy (chapters 33-48), there will be promises of restoration for the chastened people of God. There are no such promises here for these other nations. A remnant of God's people would still survive as a national entity, so it could carry out its role as the Messiah-producer. None of these other nations had such a function assigned by the Lord. After the Lord judged them, they simply disappeared from the pages of history.

God is the ruler of nations, the controller of history. Sometimes he must discipline us harshly. But this discipline doesn't hinder his promise that he will protect us from our enemies and destroy them if necessary. We need such reminders as we are daily locked in battle with God's and our enemies.

A Prophecy Against Tyre

Tyre and Sidon were the principal cities of the Phoenicians on the Mediterranean coast north of Israel. At Ezekiel's time Tyre was the more prominent of the two. Despite its insignificant size, Phoenicia was one of the most influential civilizations in the ancient world. Its people were shipbuilders, navigators, traders and colonists. Phoenician ships had sailed as far as Britain and around Africa.

David and Solomon had used Phoenicia as their source for timber and craftsmen for palace and temple building projects (1 Kings 5-9). Neither David nor Solomon attempted to annex Phoenicia into their expanded kingdoms. Wicked King Ahab (1 Kings 16:29-31) married Jezebel, a princess of Sidon, for political and economic reasons. The Bible gives the impression that although Tyre and Sidon had achieved technical skill and accumulated vast wealth, they were not concerned about the human cost of their huge profits.

The Prophecy

26 In the eleventh year, on the first day of the month, the word of the LORD came to me: ²"Son of man, because Tyre has said of Jerusalem, 'Aha! The gate to the nations is broken, and its doors have swung open to me; now that she lies in ruins I will prosper,' ³therefore this is what the Sovereign LORD says: I am against you, O Tyre, and I will bring many nations against you, like the sea casting up its waves. ⁴They will destroy the walls of Tyre and pull down her towers; I will scrape away her rubble and make her a bare rock. ⁵Out in the sea she will become a place to spread fishnets, for I have spoken, declares the Sovereign LORD. She will become plunder for the nations, ⁶and her settlements on the mainland will be ravaged by the sword. Then they will know that I am the LORD.**

This was the same year (586 B.C.) Jerusalem fell to Nebuchadnezzar. Tyre's reaction to Jerusalem's fall was: "Good! Now Jerusalem will no longer be around to divert the attention of the people away from me. Now in this region the nations will only have me to look to as a role model. My prosperity can only increase as a result. Besides, Jerusalem will no longer be able to tax or control any of the overland traffic from the east on its way to my markets."

The Lord promised to use the very nations which looked to Tyre as the merchant leader of the world to destroy her.

The picture of the sea casting up its waves over Tyre was appropriate, because Tyre was built on a rocky island a short distance from the coast of Phoenicia. This strategic location made her virtually impregnable against any land attack.

But God said everything would be scraped off the rock and the only thing left would be the rock itself, so solitary and lonely that henceforth it would be useful only as a place for fishermen to spread their nets to dry. Even the dependent Phoenician towns on the mainland would not escape.

⁷"For this is what the Sovereign LORD says: From the north I am going to bring against Tyre Nebuchadnezzar king of Babylon, king of kings, with horses and chariots, with horsemen and a great army. ⁸He will ravage your settlements on the mainland with the sword; he will set up siege works against you, build a ramp up to your walls and raise his shields against you. ⁹He will direct the blows of his battering rams against your walls and demolish your towers with his weapons. ¹⁰His horses will be so many that they will cover you with dust. Your walls will tremble at the noise of war horses, wagons and chariots when he enters your gates as men enter a city whose walls have been broken through. ¹¹The hoofs of his horses will trample all your streets; he will kill your people with the sword, and your strong pillars will fall to the ground. ¹²They will plunder your wealth and loot your merchandise; they will break down your walls and demolish your fine houses and throw your stones, timber and rubble into the sea. ¹³I will put an end to your noisy songs, and the music of your harps will be heard no more. ¹⁴I will make you a bare rock and you will become a place to spread fishnets. You will never be rebuilt, for I the LORD have spoken, declares the Sovereign LORD.

The instrument for bringing judgment on Phoenicia would be Nebuchadnezzar. He was called king of kings because Babylonia was an empire consisting of many countries whose kings were subservient to him.

When infantry advanced toward a fortified walled city, they raised their shields above them to form a turtle shell type of protection against projectiles fired down from the walls.

The size of the army was calculated in terms of the dust raised by the horses and the shaking of the walls because of the noise of the siege. The destruction of Tyre would mean the end of all its songs of revelry and music.

Nebuchadnezzar besieged Tyre for thirteen years after he had conquered Jerusalem. Years later it was destroyed by Alexander the Great, in 332 B.C., but was rebuilt. As a viable city it lasted until the time of the Crusades. After its destruction in the Middle Ages, it was not rebuilt. Today it is an insignificant city in Lebanon.

This history subsequent to the prophecy of Ezekiel leads us to several possible explanations of verse 14. We might say that Nebuchadnezzar was the first in a long string of conquerors who eventually brought destruction to Tyre at the time of the Crusades and now the island fortress has not been rebuilt. Or it is possible that God's threat of absolute destruction at the hand of Nebuchadnezzar was similar to his threat of destruction against Nineveh through the Prophet Jonah, a threat which God did not carry out because of Nineveh's repentance.

15"This is what the Sovereign Lord says to Tyre: Will not the coastlands tremble at the sound of your fall, when the wounded groan and the slaughter takes place in you? 16Then all the princes of the coast will step down from their thrones and lay aside their robes and take off their embroidered garments. Clothed with terror, they will sit on the ground, trembling every moment, appalled at you. 17Then they will take up a lament concerning you and say to you:

> " 'How you are destroyed, O city of renown,
> peopled by men of the sea!

You were a power on the seas,
    you and your citizens;
you put your terror
    on all who lived there.
[18]Now the coastlands tremble
    on the day of your fall;
the islands in the sea
    are terrified at your collapse.'

Because of her commercial contacts throughout the world, the fall of Tyre would have ramifications for all her trading partners, including her colonies in the Mediterranean world. The leaders of these other nations would give outward indication of their grief and would even take up a lament.

[19]"This is what the Sovereign LORD says: When I make you a desolate city, like cities no longer inhabited, and when I bring the ocean depths over you and its vast waters cover you, [20]then I will bring you down with those who go down to the pit, to the people of long ago. I will make you dwell in the earth below, as in ancient ruins, with those who go down to the pit, and you will not return or take your place in the land of the living. [21]I will bring you to a horrible end and you will be no more. You will be sought, but you will never again be found, declares the Sovereign LORD."

The destruction of the city of Tyre would put her and her inhabitants in the same category as all other nations in world history who down through the centuries had passed into death and oblivion.

A Lament for Tyre

27 The word of the LORD came to me: [2]"Son of man, take up a lament concerning Tyre. [3]Say to Tyre, situated at the gateway to the sea, merchant of peoples on many coasts, 'This is what the Sovereign LORD says:

" 'You say, O Tyre,
"I am perfect in beauty."
⁴Your domain was on the high seas;
your builders brought your beauty to perfection.
⁵They made all your timbers
of pine trees from Senir;
they took a cedar from Lebanon
to make a mast for you.
⁶Of oaks from Bashan
they made your oars;
of cypress wood from the coasts of Cyprus
they made your deck, inlaid with ivory.
⁷Fine embroidered linen from Egypt was your sail
and served as your banner;
your awnings were of blue and purple
from the coasts of Elishah.
⁸Men of Sidon and Arvad were your oarsmen;
your skilled men, O Tyre, were aboard as your seamen.
⁹Veteran craftsmen of Gebal were on board
as shipwrights to caulk your seams.
All the ships of the sea and their sailors
came alongside to trade for your wares.
¹⁰" 'Men of Persia, Lydia and Put
served as soldiers in your army.
They hung their shields and helmets on your walls,
bringing you splendor.
¹¹Men of Arvad and Helech
manned your walls on every side;
men of Gammad
were in your towers.
They hung their shields around your walls;
they brought your beauty to perfection.

Tyre's location gave her access to the sea toward both Egypt and Asia Minor. She was truly a gateway to the sea.

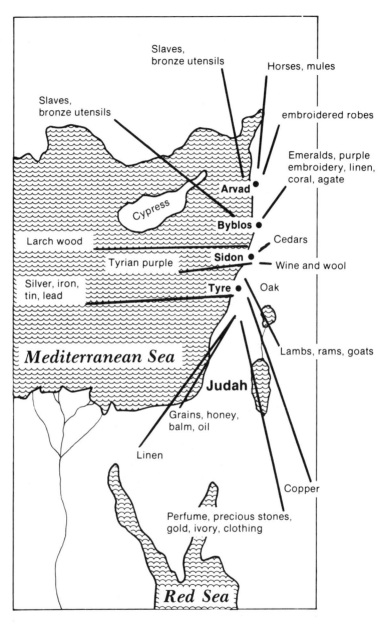

Slaves, bronze utensils

Horses, mules

Slaves, bronze utensils

embroidered robes

Emeralds, purple embroidery, linen, coral, agate

Cypress

Arvad

Byblos

Larch wood

Cedars

Tyrian purple

Sidon

Wine and wool

Silver, iron, tin, lead

Tyre

Oak

Lambs, rams, goats

Mediterranean Sea

Judah

Grains, honey, balm, oil

Linen

Copper

Perfume, precious stones, gold, ivory, clothing

Red Sea

Mediterranean world
(indicating trading of Phoenicia)

157

Tyre had great pride in herself. She had a perfect, beautiful location which was virtually unapproachable militarily. Her buildings reflected the pride of her people in her beauty.

Since her wealth and beauty came from her seagoing commerce, Ezekiel aptly described her as a stately merchant ship. The varying locations which served as sources for the parts of the ship and its gear remind us that her trade extended to all parts of the ancient world.

The list of commodities carried by Phoenician ships was impressive: Pine from Mount Hermon (Senir) on the border of Syria and Lebanon. Cedar from Lebanon. Oak from Bashan (east of the Sea of Galilee). Cypress from Cyprus. Linen from Egypt. Cloth from Elishah (Cyprus). Oarsmen from Sidon and Arvad (100 miles north of Tyre). Craftsmen from Gebal (50 miles north). Mercenaries from Persia, Lydia (western Turkey) and Put (west of Egypt). Soldiers from Arvad, Helech (southern Turkey) and Gammad (northern Syria?).

[12] " 'Tarshish did business with you because of your great wealth of goods; they exchanged silver, iron, tin and lead for your merchandise.

[13] " 'Greece, Tubal and Meshech traded with you; they exchanged slaves and articles of bronze for your wares.

[14] " 'Men of Beth Togarmah exchanged work horses, war horses and mules for your merchandise.

[15] " 'The men of Rhodes traded with you, and many coastlands were your customers; they paid you with ivory tusks and ebony.

[16] " 'Aram did business with you because of your many products; they exchanged turquoise, purple fabric, embroidered work, fine linen, coral and rubies for your merchandise.

[17] " 'Judah and Israel traded with you; they exchanged wheat from Minnith and confections, honey, oil and balm for your wares.

[18]" 'Damascus, because of your many products and great wealth of goods, did business with you in wine from Helbon and wool from Zahar.

[19]" 'Danites and Greeks from Uzal bought your merchandise; they exchanged wrought iron, cassia and calamus for your wares.

[20]" 'Dedan traded in saddle blankets with you.

[21]" 'Arabia and all the princes of Kedar were your customers; they did business with you in lambs, rams and goats.

[22]" 'The merchants of Sheba and Raamah traded with you; for your merchandise they exchanged the finest of all kinds of spices and precious stones, and gold.

[23]" 'Haran, Canneh and Eden and merchants of Sheba, Asshur and Kilmad traded with you. [24]In your marketplace they traded with you beautiful garments, blue fabric, embroidered work and multicolored rugs with cords twisted and tightly knotted.

This prose description of the vast commerce carried on by Tyre is sandwiched in between two sections of some of the best poetry in the book.

Because of its mountainous geography, Phoenicia had little arable land on which to grow the food needed by its people. One resource it did have in abundance was timber — the cedars of Lebanon, in great demand all over the ancient Near East. When King Solomon had needed timber for the temple in Jerusalem, King Hiram of Tyre was happy to provide it in exchange for thousands of bushels of wheat and thousands of gallons of olive oil each year (1 Kings 5:10,11).

Ezekiel continues the list of Tyre's trading partners (primarily in the Mediterranean basin) and of products traded. Tarshish (Spain or Sardinia), Greece, Tubal (eastern Turkey), Meshech (central Turkey), Beth Togarmah (Armenia), Rhodes (southern Aegean island), Aram (Syria), Judah, Israel, Minnith (Ammonite town east of the Jordan

River), Damascus, Helbon (north of Damascus), Zahar (undetermined), Uzal (Yemen), Dedan (west central Arabia), Kedar (north central Arabia), Sheba and Raaman (southern Arabia), Haran (northwest Iraq), Canneh (east central Syria), Eden, Assur (Iraq) and Kilmad (undetermined) all traded with Tyre. Cassia (verse 19) was either strips of bark or buds of a plant having a cinnamon flavor and aroma. Calamus (verse 19) is a rushlike marsh plant or climbing palm which gave cane for wickerwork.

> 25" 'The ships of Tarshish serve
>   as carriers for your wares.
> You are filled with heavy cargo
>   in the heart of the sea.
> 26Your oarsmen take you
>   out to the high seas.
> But the east wind will break you to pieces
>   in the heart of the sea.
> 27Your wealth, merchandise and wares,
>   your mariners, seamen and shipwrights,
> your merchants and all your soldiers,
>   and everyone else on board
> will sink into the heart of the sea
>   on the day of your shipwreck.
> 28The shorelands will quake
>   when your seamen cry out.
> 29All who handle the oars
>   will abandon their ships;
> the mariners and all the seamen
>   will stand on the shore.
> 30They will raise their voice
>   and cry bitterly over you;
> They will sprinkle dust on their heads
>   and roll in ashes.
> 31They will shave their heads because of you
>   and will put on sackcloth.

They will weep over you with anguish of soul
  and with bitter mourning.
[32]As they wail and mourn over you,
  they will take up a lament concerning you:
  "Who was ever silenced like Tyre,
  surrounded by the sea?"
[33]When your merchandise went out on the seas,
  you satisfied many nations;
  with your great wealth and your wares
  you enriched the kings of the earth.
[34]Now you are shattered by the sea
  in the depths of the waters;
  your wares and all your company
  have gone down with you.
[35]All who live in the coastlands
  are appalled at you;
  their kings shudder with horror
  and their faces are distorted with fear.
[36]The merchants among the nations hiss at you;
  you have come to a horrible end
  and will be no more.' "

Only ocean vessels which were capable of carrying heavy cargo and making the long trip to Spain or Sardinia were classified as ships of Tarshish. The destruction of Tyre, described in chapter 26 as the sea washing over the rock, is here pictured as a heavily laden merchant vessel going down in a storm. Everyone in related industries and commercial ventures throughout the world would mourn the loss of Tyre because the destruction of her commercial empire would also mean loss in trade and prosperity for them. The reference to hissing in the final verse of this section most likely was an expression of dismay and amazement, rather than scorn.

161

A Prophecy Against the King of Tyre

28 The word of the LORD came to me: ²"Son of man, say to the ruler of Tyre, 'This is what the Sovereign LORD says:

" 'In the pride of your heart
   you say, "I am a god;
I sit on the throne of a god
   in the heart of the seas."
But you are a man and not a god,
   though you think you are as wise as a god.
³Are you wiser than Daniel?
   Is no secret hidden from you?
⁴By your wisdom and understanding
   you have gained wealth for yourself
and amassed gold and silver
   in your treasuries.
⁵By your great skill in trading
   you have increased your wealth,
and because of your wealth
   your heart has grown proud.

The ruler of Tyre is addressed more as the representative of the entire nation of Phoenicia, rather than as the particular individual who happened to be on the throne. Because of her "absolutely safe" location, and because of her "absolutely secure" financial standing based on her far-flung commercial ventures, Tyre considered herself to be the god of the sea. She was very proud of what she had accomplished and of her present status. Here we see how God contradicted her thoughts (verse 2), issued some incisive questions (verse 3) and pointed to the problem — pride based on success (verses 4,5).

Pride resulting from success can lead to only one thing, rebellion against God. When we have convinced ourselves that we are totally self-sufficient, self-reliant and secure, there is no room for the Lord who is the giver of all good things. Such an attitude will inevitably lead to a withdrawing from the family of God and a condescending approach to people around us, both of which call down the wrath of God.

⁶" 'Therefore this is what the Sovereign LORD says:
" 'Because you think you are wise,
as wise as a god,
⁷I am going to bring foreigners against you,
the most ruthless of nations;
they will draw their swords against your beauty
and wisdom
and pierce your shining splendor.
⁸They will bring you down to the pit,
and you will die a violent death
in the heart of the seas.
⁹Will you then say, "I am a god,"
in the presence of those who kill you?
You will be but a man, not a god,
in the hands of those who slay you.
¹⁰You will die the death of the uncircumcised
at the hands of foreigners.
I have spoken, declares the Sovereign LORD.' "

Babylon, "the most ruthless of nations," would punish Tyre, destroy her beauty and wisdom and cause her to be totally destroyed. Obviously Tyre's claim to divinity would prove invalid. "Will you then say, 'I am a god'?"

¹¹The word of the LORD came to me: ¹²"Son of man, take up a lament concerning the king of Tyre and say to him: 'This is what the Sovereign LORD says:
" 'You were the model of perfection,
full of wisdom and perfect in beauty.
¹³You were in Eden,
the garden of God;

> every precious stone adorned you:
>> ruby, topaz and emerald,
>> chrysolite, onyx and jasper,
>> sapphire, turquoise and beryl.
> Your settings and mountings were made of gold;
>> on the day you were created they were prepared.
> ¹⁴You were anointed as a guardian cherub,
>> for so I ordained you.
> You were on the holy mount of God;
>> you walked among the fiery stones.
> ¹⁵You were blameless in your ways
>> from the day you were created
>> till wickedness was found in you.
> ¹⁶Through your widespread trade
>> you were filled with violence,
>> and you sinned.
> So I drove you in disgrace from the mount of God,
>> and I expelled you, O guardian cherub,
>> from among the fiery stones.
> ¹⁷Your heart became proud
>> on account of your beauty,
> and you corrupted your wisdom
>> because of your splendor.
> So I threw you to the earth;
>> I made a spectacle of you before kings.
> ¹⁸By your many sins and dishonest trade
>> you have desecrated your sanctuaries.
> So I made a fire come out from you,
>> and it consumed you,
> and I reduced you to ashes on the ground
>> in the sight of all who were watching.
> ¹⁹All the nations who knew you
>> are appalled at you;
> you have come to a horrible end
>> and will be no more.' "

Tyre's beauty and business wisdom had been so perfect she had almost produced another Eden. Her wealth included every possible precious stone imaginable. She had had such fantastic commercial and financial success it seemed as if the wealth had been prepared for her from the beginning of her existence.

The oracle announcing God's judgment on Tyre continues in the form of a poetic lament. To help the reader appreciate that outwardly Tyre was lovely, Ezekiel lets his imagination roam from Paradise to the gem-studded breastpiece of Israel's high priest (verse 13).

Tyre's location was so secure that she could guard herself and all dependent on her like a "guardian cherub." She seemed to be just as safe as if she were situated on the holy mountain of the Lord, protected by "fiery stones" — that is, a wall of fire. Her success in her early history had been due to her fairness and honesty. But that success had led to pride and violence, so God had decided to take away her security. The Lord would use Tyre's sudden downfall as an object lesson to others.

Tyre sounds like a commercial metropolitan society of today. Her sins are contemporary. Materialism is rampant among us as it was in Tyre. The description and warning of these chapters are echoed throughout Scripture. Without God everything we amass in our lives is meaningless (Ecclesiastes 1:2; 2:18-25). Jesus says that "life does not consist in the abundance of possessions" (Luke 12:13-21), even though people spend their lives building bigger barns and checking accounts. We Christians who have died and risen with Christ are to focus our attention on the spiritual side of our lives (Colossians 3:1-11). An overemphasis on material things removes God from his proper position in our lives. Desires to get, to have, to enjoy can so dominate our lives that we make ourselves into our own gods. This disrupts our relationship not only with God, but with all the people around us, since selfishness undermines love and produces friction. Such attitudes still provoke God's anger, just as they did in ancient Tyre.

A Prophecy Against Sidon

²⁰The word of the LORD came to me: ²¹"Son of man, set your face against Sidon; prophesy against her ²²and say: 'This is what the Sovereign LORD says:

" 'I am against you, O Sidon,
    and I will gain glory within you.
They will know that I am the LORD,
    when I inflict punishment on her
    and show myself holy within her.
²³I will send a plague upon her
    and make blood flow in her streets.
The slain will fall within her,
    with the sword against her on every side.
Then they will know that I am the LORD.

Sidon, twenty-five miles up the Mediterranean coast, was at this time dependent on Tyre. What has been said about Tyre is also applicable to Sidon. Perhaps this is the reason the prophecy against Sidon is brief and quite general.

Concluding Statement

²⁴" 'No longer will the people of Israel have malicious neighbors who are painful briers and sharp thorns. Then they will know that I am the Sovereign LORD.

²⁵" 'This is what the Sovereign LORD says: When I gather the people of Israel from the nations where they have been scattered, I will show myself holy among them in the sight of the nations. Then they will live in their own land, which I gave to my servant Jacob. ²⁶They will live there in safety and will build houses and plant vineyards; they will live in safety when I inflict punishment

on all their neighbors who maligned them. Then they will know
that I am the LORD their God.' "

Why did God promise to destroy the countries and city-
states around Judah, including Tyre, Sidon, Ammon,
Moab, Edom and Philistia? God wanted to remove these
people who had made life very difficult for his people so they
could do it no longer. This would make it possible for a
remnant of God's people to return to their land, safe from all
these "malicious neighbors." It would guarantee that the
descendants of Abraham, Isaac and Jacob were in the land
promised to their forefathers. There the Lord could keep his
promise of giving a blessing for all nations through one of
their descendants.

Many scholars have seen in verses 25 and 26 a reference
not only to deliverance from exile but to Christ's deliverance
from sin and the safety of God's people under the rule of
King Messiah.

It is overwhelmingly comforting to note that God, in
the very process of letting his anger burn against people
who insist they don't need him, has the benefit of these
very people in mind! He wants us to be able to live peaceful and quiet lives in all godliness and holiness so we can
"do our thing," namely, bringing others to know the truth
that salvation comes through Jesus Christ. In order to
provide this atmosphere for us he makes use of his appointed cherubs, the guardians of peace and safety, to
punish criminals and to wage war against belligerent nations.

But when the Lord punishes nations, it is not our role to
rejoice as Tyre did over Jerusalem. Rather, it is our role to
thank the Lord for controlling history in our interest and in
the interest of the gospel.

167

A Prophecy Against Egypt
The Prophecy

29 In the tenth year, in the tenth month on the twelfth day, the word of the LORD came to me: ²"Son of man, set your face against Pharaoh king of Egypt and prophesy against him and against all Egypt. ³Speak to him and say: 'This is what the Sovereign LORD says:

" 'I am against you, Pharaoh king of Egypt,
    you great monster lying among your streams.
You say, "The Nile is mine;
    I made it for myself."
⁴But I will put hooks in your jaws
    and make the fish of your streams stick to your scales.
I will pull you out from among your streams,
    with all the fish sticking to your scales.
⁵I will leave you in the desert,
    you and all the fish of your streams.
You will fall on the open field
    and not be gathered or picked up.
I will give you as food
    to the beasts of the earth and the birds of the air.
⁶Then all who live in Egypt will know that I am the LORD.

God's message of judgment on Egypt is announced in seven separate oracles, a fact which makes it the longest of Ezekiel's oracles of judgment against heathen nations.

This first prophecy was made after the siege of Jerusalem had begun (24:1), but before its fall (26:1). Ever since the time of Joseph, there had been constant conflict between Egypt, situated on the Nile, and the world powers located on the Tigris and Euphrates rivers. This put Israel and Judah in the middle. Egypt, therefore, was just as much an antagonist against Israel and Judah as the northern powers were.

Recall the immediate historical context. Egypt's Pharaoh Necho had been defeated by Babylon's Nebuchadnezzar (605 B.C.). Necho's grandson Hophra had unsuccessfully besieged Tyre and Sidon, trying to get them away from under Nebuchadnezzar's influence. Hophra also did whatever he could to stir up rebellion against Nebuchadnezzar in the smaller states in Palestine. King Zedekiah of Judah sought Egyptian help against Babylon in an attempt to withdraw from Nebuchadnezzar's influence. Ezekiel predicted, however, that Egypt would be a poor support in Judah's time of need.

Egypt is called a monster, probably referring to the crocodiles which inhabit the swamps and marshes around the Nile and its delta. God was against Egypt because her pride led her to disregard him. The Pharaohs considered themselves to be gods. They were sure they didn't need any supernatural help for their land, because they had made the irrigation system for the Nile which could keep Egypt's fields green, even without rain from the gods.

The Lord promised to throw the crocodile out of its environment together with all the people and nations dependent on her ("all the fish sticking to your scales"), leaving her to dry out and die in the desert which constitutes 95% of Egypt's land area. Nobody would even bother to bury the body. It would be left to be eaten by the beasts and birds.

Who is the god of our society? Aren't we tempted to believe we are our own gods because we can do almost anything with the wizardry of our technology? When we have convinced ourselves that our own genius provides for us, our technology defends us, and our wisdom preserves us, we have become just like the Pharaohs of ancient Egypt. Then we, too, are inviting God's judgment.

" 'You have been a staff of reed for the house of Israel. ⁷When they grasped you with their hands, you splintered and you tore

open their shoulders; when they leaned on you, you broke and their backs were wrenched.

A staff should support the weight of the person leaning on it. But Egypt would be a staff of reed, the marshgrass along the Nile, which wouldn't support any weight. When Zedekiah would try to lean on Egypt for support against Babylon, Egypt would splinter under the weight and Judah would be injured, to say the very least. Although Pharaoh Hophra did make an effort to help Judah he was unsuccessful (Jeremiah 37:6,7; 44:30). Similar interaction with Egypt had occurred earlier in history (2 Kings 18:21; Isaiah 36:6).

To whom do we turn when twentieth century Nebuchadnezzars stare us in the eyes? We all have tendencies to find Egypts in whom we can trust. But we really don't need to go looking for Egypts when we have the Lord to turn to for help in every circumstance.

8" 'Therefore this is what the Sovereign Lord says: I will bring a sword against you and kill your men and their animals. 9Egypt will become a desolate wasteland. Then they will know that I am the Lord.

" 'Because you said, "The Nile is mine; I made it," 10therefore I am against you and against your streams and I will make the land of Egypt a ruin and a desolate waste from Migdol to Aswan, as far as the border of Cush. 11No foot of man or animal will pass through it; no one will live there for forty years. 12I will make the land of Egypt desolate among devastated lands, and her cities will lie desolate forty years among ruined cities. And I will disperse the Egyptians among the nations and scatter them through the countries.

The usually fertile, watered land of Egypt would become a wasteland. Because her pride was based on her agricultural wealth and independence, which in turn was based on her rivers, especially the Nile, God said he was against her streams. From Migdol in the north to Aswan in the south, from one end of Egypt to the other, there would be a lack of traffic and commerce. The conquest by Nebuchadnezzar (568 B.C.) and the submission to Babylon lasted a full generation, here described as a forty year period. The forty years might have been a specific period or, as the number is sometimes used in the Old Testament, a representative number symbolizing one generation.

Although we have no record of how much destruction Nebuchadnezzar did in Egypt, we do know he took some captives back with him, and many either fled before him, or fled after he had crushed the land.

13" 'Yet this is what the Sovereign LORD says: At the end of forty years I will gather the Egyptians from the nations where they were scattered. 14I will bring them back from captivity and return them to Upper Egypt, the land of their ancestry. There they will be a lowly kingdom. 15It will be the lowliest of kingdoms and will never again exalt itself above the other nations. I will make it so weak that it will never again rule over the nations. 16Egypt will no longer be a source of confidence for the people of Israel but will be a reminder of their sin in turning to her for help. Then they will know that I am the Sovereign LORD.' "

The restoration of Egypt is described here in terms of what the exile and return of Judah would be like. We have no record of a mass exodus and return in Egypt as was the case in Judah. *Upper* Egypt (also known as Pathros), contrary to our usual geographical terminology, is the *southern* part, with Thebes as the ancient capital.

God's judgment on Egypt would be complete. After Nebuchadnezzar's domination, Egypt would never again regain her former glory. Egypt was controlled in succession by ancient Persia, Greece and Rome. Her subsequent history has consisted of repeated conquest and humiliation. For this reason, she could never be of any help to Judah.

[17]In the twenty-seventh year, in the first month on the first day, the word of the LORD came to me: [18]"Son of man, Nebuchadnezzar king of Babylon drove his army in a hard campaign against Tyre; every head was rubbed bare and every shoulder made raw. Yet he and his army got no reward from the campaign he led against Tyre. [19]Therefore this is what the Sovereign LORD says: I am going to give Egypt to Nebuchadnezzar king of Babylon, and he will carry off its wealth. He will loot and plunder the land as pay for his army. [20]I have given him Egypt as a reward for his efforts because he and his army did it for me, declares the Sovereign LORD.

This second oracle of judgment on Egypt was given seventeen years later. During the intervening period, Nebuchadnezzar had besieged Tyre for thirteen years. Many of his men had their heads "rubbed bare" by their helmets while they were working on the ramp out to the island fortress of Tyre. Many had raw shoulders from carrying the fill needed for the massive construction project.

Despite all the effort, there was no major monetary gain for the soldiers after Tyre fell. Perhaps the wealth of Tyre had been spirited away by ship. Nebuchadnezzar couldn't stop such a removal. If he had a navy in the Caspian sea or in the Persian Gulf, it didn't do him much good on the Mediterranean. The Lord promised Nebuchadnezzar Egypt as sort of a consolation prize, since he had been acting as the Lord's executioner against Tyre, and now would be doing the same against Egypt.

[21]"On that day I will make a horn grow for the house of Israel, and I will open your mouth among them. Then they will know that I am the LORD."

The destruction of Egypt's world dominating power had to be beneficial for the strength ("horn") of Israel. With Egypt out of the picture, there would be a much better atmosphere for the exiles when they would return after Cyrus's release edict some years later.

God's statement "I will make a horn grow . . ." again emphasizes his sovereignty over the nations. This gives us the comforting knowledge that the Lord does keep his promises of ruling all things in the interest of his people. And "all things" includes the political rise and fall of world powers.

A Lament for Egypt

30 **The word of the LORD came to me: ²"Son of man, prophesy and say: 'This is what the Sovereign LORD says:**

" 'Wail and say,
   "Alas for that day!"
³for the day is near,
   the day of the LORD is near —
a day of clouds,
   a time of doom for the nations.
⁴A sword will come against Egypt,
   and anguish will come upon Cush.
When the slain fall in Egypt,
   her wealth will be carried away
   and her foundations torn down.

This is God's third oracle of judgment on Egypt. "The day of the LORD," the day in which he visits people with his power and anger, is always a reminder of the final day of God's power and anger. "The day of the LORD is near — a day of clouds." The storm of God's judgment was about to break over Egypt.

⁵Cush and Put, Lydia and all Arabia, Libya and the people of the covenant land will fall by the sword along with Egypt.

173

⁶" 'This is what the LORD says:

" 'The allies of Egypt will fall
    and her proud strength will fail.
From Migdol to Aswan
    they will fall by the sword within her,
                    declares the Sovereign LORD.

⁷" 'They will be desolate
    among desolate lands,
and their cities will lie
    among ruined cities.
⁸Then they will know that I am the LORD,
    when I set fire to Egypt
    and all her helpers are crushed.

⁹" 'On that day messengers will go out from me in ships to frighten Cush out of her complacency. Anguish will take hold of them on the day of Egypt's doom, for it is sure to come.

One of the consequences of Egypt's fall was that her allies would go down with her. Cush (Ethiopia), Put (west of the Nile delta), Lydia (western Turkey), Arabia and Libya, as well as all other allies would suffer the same fate as Egypt. Fugitives would go out in ships warning of what had happened to Egypt, indicating it would spread to these others, too.

¹⁰" 'This is what the Sovereign LORD says:

" 'I will put an end to the hordes of Egypt
    by the hand of Nebuchadnezzar king of Babylon.
¹¹He and his army — the most ruthless of nations —
    will be brought in to destroy the land.
They will draw their swords against Egypt
    and fill the land with the slain.
¹²I will dry up the streams of the Nile
    and sell the land to evil men;
by the hand of foreigners
    I will lay waste the land and everything in it.
I the LORD have spoken.

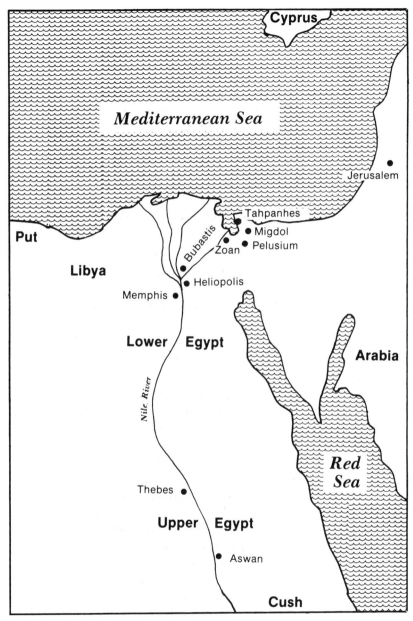

Egypt
(including key cities mentioned in Ezekiel 29-32)

175

Babylon, "the most ruthless of all nations" (32:12), would be God's instrument of judgment. Drying up the streams of the Nile seems to imply some destruction of the canals and irrigation systems, preventing the water from reaching the agricultural fields. Without these streams, the Nile didn't do the farmland any good. The country became a wasteland.

> ¹³" 'This is what the Sovereign LORD says:
>
> > " 'I will destroy the idols
> > and put an end to the images in Memphis.
> > No longer will there be a prince in Egypt,
> > and I will spread fear throughout the land.
> > ¹⁴ I will lay Upper Egypt waste,
> > set fire to Zoan
> > and inflict punishment on Thebes.
> > ¹⁵ I will pour out my wrath on Pelusium,
> > the stronghold of Egypt,
> > and cut off the hordes of Thebes.
> > ¹⁶ I will set fire to Egypt;
> > Pelusium will writhe in agony.
> > Thebes will be taken by storm;
> > Memphis will be in constant distress.
> > ¹⁷ The young men of Heliopolis and Bubastis
> > will fall by the sword,
> > and the cities themselves will go into captivity.
> > ¹⁸ Dark will be the day at Tahpanhes
> > when I break the yoke of Egypt;
> > there her proud strength will come to an end.
> > She will be covered with clouds,
> > and her villages will go into captivity.
> > ¹⁹ So I will inflict punishment on Egypt,
> > and they will know that I am the LORD.' "

A number of Egypt's major cities were singled out for destruction. Each had its own special, personal god. But these idols could not protect the cities against God's vengeance. The cities are mentioned in no specific geographic order, or order of importance. All regions of Egypt are included, however. With no leader in the country, there would be widespread fear of Babylon. Pelusium (verse 15) was considered to be a stronghold because it was surrounded by swamps, marshes and rivers, thus making it very inaccessible to enemy armies.

Egypt's strength would be broken. She would never again be able to subject other nations to her rule for any duration.

20In the eleventh year, in the first month on the seventh day, the word of the LORD came to me: 21"Son of man, I have broken the arm of Pharaoh king of Egypt. It has not been bound up for healing or put in a splint so as to become strong enough to hold a sword. 22Therefore this is what the Sovereign LORD says: I am against Pharaoh king of Egypt. I will break both his arms, the good arm as well as the broken one, and make the sword fall from his hand. 23I will disperse the Egyptians among the nations and scatter them through the countries. 24I will strengthen the arms of the king of Babylon and put my sword in his hand, but I will break the arms of Pharaoh, and he will groan before him like a mortally wounded man. 25I will strengthen the arms of the king of Babylon, but the arms of Pharaoh will fall limp. Then they will know that I am the LORD, when I put my sword into the hand of the king of Babylon and he brandishes it against Egypt. 26I will disperse the Egyptians among the nations and scatter them through the countries. Then they will know that I am the LORD."

This fourth word of judgment against Egypt was given several months before the fall of Jerusalem. The one broken arm of Pharaoh probably is a reference to Pharaoh Hophra's inability to stop the Babylonian siege against Jerusalem (Jeremiah 37:5-11; 2 Kings 24:7). It might also refer to Egypt's major defeat at Carchemish in Syria in 605 B.C.

Egypt never really recovered. The promise of a second broken arm must refer to Nebuchadnezzar's conquest of Egypt in 568 B.C.

A Cedar in Lebanon

31 **In the eleventh year, in the third month on the first day, the word of the LORD came to me: ²"Son of man, say to Pharaoh king of Egypt and to his hordes:**

This fifth oracle against Egypt was spoken just a few months before Jerusalem fell to the Babylonian army. Although it was spoken as a warning to Egypt, as we shall see, all the actual references were to Assyria. The point is that Egypt had dwarfed all of her rivals just as Assyria had done. Assyria had once been the dominant power in the ancient Near East. But three decades earlier it had fallen. What happened to Assyria should have been a warning to Egypt:

> " 'Who can be compared with you in majesty?
> ³Consider Assyria, once a cedar in Lebanon,
>   with beautiful branches overshadowing the forest;
> it towered on high,
>   its top above the thick foliage.
> ⁴The waters nourished it,
>   deep springs made it grow tall;
> their streams flowed
>   all around its base
> and sent their channels
>   to all the trees of the field.
> ⁵So it towered higher
>   than all the trees of the field;
> its boughs increased
>   and its branches grew long,
>   spreading because of abundant waters.
> ⁶All the birds of the air
>   nested in its boughs,

all the beasts of the field
gave birth under its branches;
all the great nations
lived in its shade.
⁷It was majestic in beauty,
with its spreading boughs,
for its roots went down
to abundant waters.
⁸The cedars in the garden of God
could not rival it,
nor could the pine trees
equal its boughs,
nor could the plane trees
compare with its branches —
no tree in the garden of God
could match its beauty.
⁹I made it beautiful
with abundant branches,
the envy of all the trees of Eden
in the garden of God.

Ezekiel compared Assyria to a cedar in Lebanon. Ancient Assyria was located in what is now Iraq, not Lebanon. Nevertheless, Ezekiel used the stately cedar trees for his comparison. The waters of the Tigris and Euphrates rivers nourished Assyria. Beauty, power, leadership, strength, a good support system of dependent countries, and good services rendered to subject peoples — these were the characteristics of Assyria. Everybody else in God's creation ("all the trees of Eden") recognized and envied Assyria's power and prestige.

¹⁰" 'Therefore this is what the Sovereign LORD says: Because it towered on high, lifting its top above the thick foliage, and because it was proud of its height, ¹¹I handed it over to the ruler of

179

the nations, for him to deal with according to its wickedness. I cast it aside, [12]and the most ruthless of foreign nations cut it down and left it. Its boughs fell on the mountains and in all the valleys; its branches lay broken in all the ravines of the land. All the nations of the earth came out from under its shade and left it. [13]All the birds of the air settled on the fallen tree, and all the beasts of the field were among its branches. [14]Therefore no other trees by the waters are ever to tower proudly on high, lifting their tops above the thick foliage. No other trees so well-watered are ever to reach such a height; they are all destined for death, for the earth below, among mortal men, with those who go down to the pit.

[15]" 'This is what the Sovereign LORD says: On the day it was brought down to the grave I covered the deep springs with mourning for it; I held back its streams, and its abundant waters were restrained. Because of it I clothed Lebanon with gloom, and all the trees of the field withered away. [16]I made the nations tremble at the sound of its fall when I brought it down to the grave with those who go down to the pit. Then all the trees of Eden, the choicest and best of Lebanon, all the trees that were well-watered, were consoled in the earth below. [17]Those who lived in its shade, its allies among the nations, had also gone down to the grave with it, joining those killed by the sword.

Because of her pride, God handed Assyria over to the Babylonians. What happened to Assyria should have been a warning to all other nations, a reminder they too were only mortal, destined for death. When this impressive empire collapsed, the whole world trembled, realizing that the same end could overtake them.

[18]" 'Which of the trees of Eden can be compared with you in splendor and majesty? Yet you, too, will be brought down with the trees of Eden to the earth below; you will lie among the uncircumcised, with those killed by the sword.

" 'This is Pharaoh and all his hordes, declares the Sovereign LORD.' "

Ezekiel now drew his conclusion as he applied the solemn story of Assyria to Egypt. Egypt would also be punished and die outside the family of God.

Success is often a bigger temptation to sin than failure is. Leadership is often harder to handle than discipleship. Power is more easily abused than weakness. Beauty can be more easily abused than plainness.

Ezekiel's message applies not only to nations. Not just big, powerful countries need to take heed lest they fall. Successful, influential people can leave God out of their lives. And when that happens, God's judgment may strike more quickly than the time it takes to fell a tree. Mary expressed this truth well when she said: "[God] has scattered those who are proud in their inmost thoughts. He has brought down rulers from their thrones but has lifted up the humble" (Luke 1:51,52).

A Lament for Pharaoh

32 In the twelfth year, in the twelfth month on the first day, the word of the LORD came to me: [2]"Son of man, take up a lament concerning Pharaoh king of Egypt and say to him:

" 'You are like a lion among the nations;
  you are like a monster in the seas
thrashing about in your streams,
  churning the water with your feet
  and muddying the streams.

This lament is dated about a year and a half after the fall of Jerusalem. A lament is usually a mourning song expressing grief over the death of someone. This sixth oracle against Egypt is more like a taunt, rejoicing over Egypt's destruction and mocking the fallen nation and her king. Like a lion or sea monster, Egypt had been the object of fear throughout the ancient world. She had disrupted the tranquil lives of many of the peoples around her and frightened them into submission.

Now those days were past.

³" 'This is what the Sovereign LORD says:

" 'With a great throng of people
I will cast my net over you,
and they will haul you up in my net.
⁴I will throw you on the land
and hurl you on the open field.
I will let all the birds of the air settle on you
and all the beasts of the earth
gorge themselves on you.
⁵I will spread your flesh on the mountains
and fill the valleys with your remains.
⁶I will drench the land with your flowing blood
all the way to the mountains,
and the ravines will be filled with your flesh.
⁷When I snuff you out, I will cover the heavens
and darken their stars;
I will cover the sun with a cloud,
and the moon will not give its light.
⁸All the shining lights in the heavens
I will darken over you;
I will bring darkness over your land,
declares the Sovereign LORD.
⁹I will trouble the hearts of many peoples
when I bring about your destruction
among the nations,
among lands you have not known.
¹⁰I will cause many peoples to be appalled at you,
and their kings will shudder with horror
because of you
when I brandish my sword before them.
On the day of your downfall
each of them will tremble
every moment for his life.

A crocodile won't survive for long if it's forced out of its watery environment. Egypt, forced by God through the Babylonians out of its own home environment, was destroyed. The universe is pictured as mourning over the collapse of this once great civilization. The nations would be horrified, not just because they would lose the benefits of Egypt's commerce and culture, but because this pointed out to them that they also could fall, as mighty Egypt had.

11" 'For this is what the Sovereign LORD says:

" 'The sword of the king of Babylon
will come against you.
12I will cause your hordes to fall
by the swords of mighty men —
the most ruthless of all nations.
They will shatter the pride of Egypt,
and all her hordes will be overthrown.
13I will destroy all her cattle
from beside abundant waters
no longer to be stirred by the foot of man
or muddied by the hoofs of cattle.
14Then I will let her waters settle
and make her streams flow like oil,
declares the Sovereign LORD.
15When I make Egypt desolate
and strip the land of everything in it,
when I strike down all who live there,
then they will know that I am the LORD.'

16"This is the lament they will chant for her. The daughters of the nations will chant it; for Egypt and all her hordes they will chant it, declares the Sovereign LORD."

Because God would take Egypt's power from her, she would no longer be able to make any impact on the nations around her. She would become a placid stream, flowing through the annals of history with hardly a ripple.

17In the twelfth year, on the fifteenth day of the month, the word of the LORD came to me: **18**"Son of man, wail for the hordes of Egypt and consign to the earth below both her and the daughters of mighty nations, with those who go down to the pit. **19**Say to them, 'Are you more favored than others? Go down and be laid among the uncircumcised.' **20**They will fall among those killed by the sword. The sword is drawn; let her be dragged off with all her hordes. **21**From within the grave the mighty leaders will say of Egypt and her allies, 'They have come down and they lie with the uncircumcised, with those killed by the sword.'

Two weeks after Ezekiel announced the previous message of judgment on Egypt, the seventh and final oracle appeared. It was a remarkable prediction. Although Egypt's civilization seemed more favored than anyone else's, she too would end up outside the family of the Lord among the dead people, the has-beens of history whose civilizations had gone down previously.

22"Assyria is there with her whole army; she is surrounded by the graves of all her slain, all who have fallen by the sword. **23**Their graves are in the depths of the pit and her army lies around her grave. All who had spread terror in the land of the living are slain, fallen by the sword.

Before the eye of the prophet the great nations of ancient history passed in review. Assyria was first.

Assyria's capital city of Nineveh had fallen in 612 B.C., about two dozen years before Jerusalem fell and about fifty years before Egypt toppled.

24"Elam is there, with all her hordes around her grave. All of them are slain, fallen by the sword. All who had spread terror in the land of the living went down uncircumcised to the earth below. They bear their shame with those who go down to the pit. **25**A bed is made for her among the slain, with all her hordes around her grave. All of them are uncircumcised, killed by the sword. Because their terror had spread in the land of the living, they bear their shame with those who go down to the pit; they are laid among the slain.

Elam, an ancient nation at the head of the Persian Gulf was destroyed by Nebuchadnezzar (Jeremiah 49:34-38).

[26]"Meshech and Tubal are there, with all their hordes around their graves. All of them are uncircumcised, killed by the sword because they spread their terror in the land of the living. [27]Do they not lie with the other uncircumcised warriors who have fallen, who went down to the grave with their weapons of war, whose swords were placed under their heads? The punishment for their sins rested on their bones, though the terror of these warriors had stalked through the land of the living.

It is hard for us to pinpoint these people, except to say they lived somewhere in present-day Turkey. Ezekiel's first hearers and readers understood that these nations had also passed into death and oblivion.

[28]"You too, O Pharaoh, will be broken and will lie among the uncircumcised, with those killed by the sword.

The history of the rise and fall of nations under God's judgment should have warned Egypt.

[29]"Edom is there, her kings and all her princes; despite their power, they are laid with those killed by the sword. They lie with the uncircumcised, with those who go down to the pit.
[30]"All the princes of the north and all the Sidonians are there; they went down with the slain in disgrace despite the terror caused by their power. They lie uncircumcised with those killed by the sword and bear their shame with those who go down to the pit.

We know what happened to Edom (25:12-14) and to Tyre and Sidon (chapters 26-28) when God permitted Nebuchadnezzar to crush them.

[31]"Pharaoh — he and all his army — will see them and he will be consoled for all his hordes that were killed by the sword, declares the Sovereign LORD. [32]Although I had him spread terror in the land of the living, Pharaoh and all his hordes will be laid among the uncircumcised, with those killed by the sword, declares the Sovereign LORD."

Egypt could take at least a little consolation from knowing she was joining many others in death and obscurity. Ezekiel emphasized that the Lord had used Egypt for his purposes. Now this wicked nation was used up and, like others before her, cast away.

These oracles announcing God's judgment (chapters 25-32) were certainly bad news for the heathen nations around Israel. What effect would these eight chapters have had on Ezekiel's countrymen in exile? The chapters we have just completed taught them that not even world powers like Assyria, Babylonia and Egypt had the final say in Israel's and Judah's destiny.

What value do these chapters have for us today? Are they just interesting museum pieces? Indeed not! They describe the inevitable doom of any person or any nation that tries to block the fulfillment of God's great and good plan. The Lord of nations has the last word in history. A secular student of history will argue that the mighty people and nations rule. A Christian realizes that the ultimate power is in the hands of the Lord.

One final comment on Ezekiel's oracles of judgment on the heathen nations. It might seem strange that in listing these nations, on whom God's judgment was to fall, Ezekiel omitted Babylon. We know from history that God's judgment did in fact strike Babylon fifty years after Jerusalem fell. There might be several reasons for this omission. For one thing, God's people were residents of Babylon, enjoying her protection and, in fact, commanded by God to pray for her peace and prosperity (Jeremiah 29:4-7). Then, too, it was very clear that at this time God was using Babylon as his instrument for doing some work that was necessary and important, even though it was painful for the people of Judah. Yet the implication was clear: someday Babylon could expect to end up as the others.

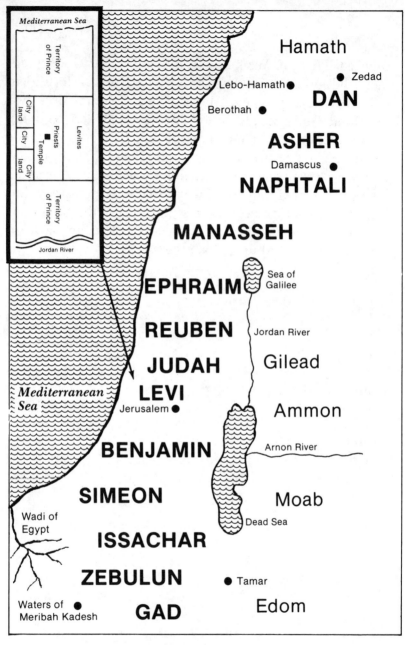

Division of the land
(Ezekiel 45:1-8; 47; 48)

188

PART III

PROMISE OF RESTORATION FOR GOD'S CHASTENED PEOPLE
EZEKIEL 33 — 48

Ezekiel as a Watchman

33 The word of the LORD came to me: [2]"Son of man, speak to your countrymen and say to them: 'When I bring the sword against a land, and the people of the land choose one of their men and make him their watchman, [3]and he sees the sword coming against the land and blows the trumpet to warn the people, [4]then if anyone hears the trumpet but does not take warning and the sword comes and takes his life, his blood will be on his own head. [5]Since he heard the sound of the trumpet but did not take warning, his blood will be on his own head. If he had taken warning, he would have saved himself. [6]But if the watchman sees the sword coming and does not blow the trumpet to warn the people and the sword comes and takes the life of one of them, that man will be taken away because of his sin, but I will hold the watchman accountable for his blood.'**

The past eight chapters of the book of Ezekiel consisted of messages addressed to heathen nations. Now God told Ezekiel: "Speak to your countrymen." The message Ezekiel was to bring them is an expanded version of something the Lord had already told Ezekiel when he commissioned him as a prophet (3:17-21). In an ancient walled city, the watchman played a very important role. In large metropolitan areas, most of the people lived outside the city walls. Even in smaller cities, the people worked in the fields, vineyards, orchards or commercial establishments, most of which were outside the city walls. When danger threatened the city, perhaps from an invading army, the watchman high atop the city walls would see it first. He would then sound the warning trumpet so all within hearing distance could hurry inside the walls. The city gates would be shut and preparation made to repel the attacker. If someone heard the warning, but paid no attention, it was his own fault if something happened to him. But if, on the other hand, the watchman saw the danger and did not warn the citizens, he was held accountable for the lives of those who died.

The Old Testament was very specific about assigning blame and punishment when a human life was lost. The person responsible for the loss of life forfeited his own life, unless he had acted in self-defense or unless a court proved him not responsible. The family avenger was to act (Numbers 35:19) in cases of premeditated murder, but also when a life was taken due to carelessness or accident. The watchman's life would be forfeited because his carelessness caused the loss of life. In Ezekiel's analogy the assumption is made that the person warned by the watchman and caught by the sword of the enemy was being subjected to God's anger because of his sins. This would surely fit the historical context of Jerusalem and Judah in Ezekiel's time. They deserved God's anger over their sins.

Parents, teachers, teachers of the Word and government officials are all in leadership positions. In this sense they are "above" others. God puts some in these positions to watch out for others. Positions of authority are by definition positions of watchmen. Those in positions of authority can see dangers facing children, pupils or constituency which they sometimes don't see for themselves. If the watchmen make no attempt to thwart the temptations and dangers which they observe from their vantage point, the Lord holds them responsible for the lives and souls of those individuals. From God's view, positions of authority are positions of responsibility. They are not positions which give people the right merely to throw their weight around.

7" 'Son of man, I have made you a watchman for the house of Israel; so hear the word I speak and give them warning from me. 8When I say to the wicked, 'O wicked man, you will surely die,' and you do not speak out to dissuade him from his ways, that wicked man will die for his sin, and I will hold you accountable for his blood. 9But if you do warn the wicked man to turn from his ways and he does not do so, he will die for his sin, but you will have saved yourself.

Because Jerusalem had fallen to the Babylonians, the nation of Judah was no longer an independent political entity. Therefore, as a watchman Ezekiel could more easily focus the people's attention on their relationship with God. Their real enemy was no longer Babylon, or Egypt, or anyone else. Their real enemy was sin. The inhabitants had only themselves to blame for what had happened to Jerusalem. When Ezekiel here speaks about dying, he's referring to being separated from God.

Why such a repetitious section? Isn't this the same thing Ezekiel had heard before (3:17-31)? Yes, but the situation had radically changed for God's people. Jerusalem had fallen (26:1), as the exiles were about to be informed (33:21). Before Jerusalem fell most of the transplanted people were too busy becoming comfortable in their new surroundings to be as concerned about the dreadful fall of Jerusalem as Ezekiel was. Besides, the false prophets has assured them

191

Jerusalem would never fall. Now that the city had indeed fallen to the Babylonian army, Ezekiel was the only one who could look ahead with hope. The rest of the exiles were overwhelmed by the disaster.

In such a setting, Ezekiel had to ask himself, "Have I been a failure? I was supposed to call the people to repentance by threatening the fall of Jerusalem. Now it has fallen, but the people didn't repent. What am I supposed to do now?" Chapter 33 marks the beginning of God's answer to such questions. The answer was: "Ezekiel, you are still a watchman. My commission to you hasn't changed. You are a watchman of people's souls whether those people are penitent or not. Now you are to be a watchman of their souls by pointing them to my promise to deliver and restore them, so they don't bury themselves in despair. Even though at the present time there isn't really a Jewish nation, the relationship of these individuals to me is still of primary importance to me. You are still to warn against sin. You are still to proclaim the message of my love for sinners. This message alone can bring people to saving faith. This message will recreate the nation as a viable entity when I will need it to be one."

Looking back from our point in history, we know Ezekiel was successful. His work was largely responsible for accomplishing the seemingly impossible task of keeping a scattered handful of interested people spiritually eager to maintain their national existence. This was what the Lord needed if he was going to carry out his promises of the world's Savior through this nation.

Most of us at some point in our lives have wondered with Ezekiel, "Lord, what am I supposed to do now?" The reason we ask this question may be that some circumstances in our life have changed. We think changed circumstances mean changes in our orders from the Lord. We hear him tell us in his Word, "Continue to witness to me by talking about Jesus the Savior. Continue to witness to me by living your life in a God-pleasing manner. Continue to apply the message of my law when it's needed to point out sin. And continue to apply the message of my love when it's needed to comfort the sinner." And we reply, "But we tried that already." Then the Lord comes to us, as he did to Ezekiel, and says, "You are still a watchman. Circumstances don't change my message, nor do they change your use of it."

Some things change, others never do.

¹⁰"Son of man, say to the house of Israel, 'This is what you are saying: "Our offenses and sins weigh us down, and we are wasting away because of them. How then can we live?"' ¹¹Say to them, 'As surely as I live, declares the Sovereign Lᴏʀᴅ, I take no pleasure in the death of the wicked, but rather that they turn from their ways and live. Turn! Turn from your evil ways! Why will you die, O house of Israel?'

Some of God's people in Babylon had started to despair. Their attitude was: "Why repent? We are being punished for the sins of our fathers and for the sins of those who were left behind in Israel after the first exile. How can we live with a God who punishes in this way? If deliverance from exile is out of the question, how do you expect us to live?" God's answer was simple and direct. He doesn't punish and discipline merely because he likes to. By punishing and disciplining the Lord seeks to turn people from their wicked ways, to turn them back to him. He wants them to shrug off death and live. The implication for the exiles was obvious. When the sins of indifference and rejection would be purged from their lives, then they would be alive again, and God would be delighted. But these things hadn't happened yet.

The person whose circumstances of life are good and whose future looks bright easily glosses over God's promise, "I have no pleasure in the death of the wicked." He doesn't think this promise applies to him. Death is the farthest thing from his mind. On the other hand, to the person whose life is filled with death and destruction, God's promise, "I have no pleasure in the death of the wicked" sounds hollow and accusatory. He is dying. Therefore, he concludes that he must be a wicked one being punished by God.

But this promise is gospel. It is good news. To human beings, all of whom by nature are wicked, God says, "I have no pleasure in your death." He doesn't want us to be cut off from him. Through water and the Word he has called us to be his children, and he wants us in his family. God's attitude, which we usually call his grace, is so comforting to us because it is present in God even though we, the objects of his grace, are wicked.

[12]"Therefore, son of man, say to your countrymen, 'The righteousness of the righteous man will not save him when he disobeys, and the wickedness of the wicked man will not cause him to fall when he turns from it. The righteous man, if he sins, will not be allowed to live because of his former righteousness.' [13]If I tell the righteous man that he will surely live, but then he trusts in his righteousness and does evil, none of the righteous things he has done will be remembered; he will die for the evil he has done. [14]And if I say to the wicked man, 'You will surely die,' but he then turns away from his sin and does what is just and right — [15]if he gives back what he took in pledge for a loan, returns what he has stolen, follows the decrees that give life, and does no evil, he will surely live; he will not die. [16]None of the sins he has committed will be remembered against him. He has done what is just and right; he will surely live.

For background comments, refer to Ezekiel 18:5-29, which is a longer section dealing with the same topic. As in chapter 18, Ezekiel again cites examples of what kind of action is evidence of a penitent heart. According to a passage like this, God obviously considered conversions of lifelong sinners or lapses of lifelong saints to be possible.

[17]"Yet your countrymen say, 'The way of the Lord is not just.' But it is their way that is not just. [18]If a righteous man turns from his righteousness and does evil, he will die for it. [19]And if a wicked man turns away from his wickedness and does what is just and right, he will live by doing so. [20]Yet, O house of Israel, you say, 'The way of the Lord is not just.' But I will judge each of you according to his own ways."

When the Lord permitted Jerusalem to be destroyed and its citizens to be led into captivity, the people judged him to be unfair. God flatly rejected their conclusion and said the problem was their own rebelliousness.

Jerusalem's Fall Explained

[21]In the twelfth year of our exile, in the tenth month on the fifth day, a man who had escaped from Jerusalem came to me and said, "The city has fallen!" [22]Now the evening before the man arrived, the hand of the LORD was upon me, and he opened my mouth before the man came to me in the morning. So my mouth was opened and I was no longer silent.

This is the turning point of Ezekiel's ministry and of his book of prophecy. The long-threatened fall of Jerusalem finally took place. Why it took eighteen months (compare 26:1,2 with 33:21) for a fugitive to travel from Jerusalem to Babylon is a question which Ezekiel doesn't answer. The night before, the Lord himself had given Ezekiel a presentiment of what was about to happen. This occurrence indicated to Ezekiel that he was free from the restrictions God had previously imposed on him (24:27; 3:25-27).

²³Then the word of the LORD came to me: ²⁴"Son of man, the people living in those ruins in the land of Israel are saying, 'Abraham was only one man, yet he possessed the land. But we are many; surely the land has been given to us as our possession.' ²⁵Therefore say to them, 'This is what the Sovereign LORD says: Since you eat meat with the blood still in it and look to your idols and shed blood, should you then possess the land? ²⁶You rely on your sword, you do detestable things, and each of you defiles his neighbor's wife. Should you then possess the land?'

The people left behind after the fall of Jerusalem were just as foolish and brazen as those who had been left behind in Judah after the first deportation to Babylon! (11:14,15) They were brazenly saying, "If God gave this land to Abraham who was only one individual, he will surely give it to us who are many, since we are the only descendants of Abraham left in the promised land."

Ezekiel's answer from the Lord was: "You need to repent." How could God let such impenitent people possess his land, people who refused to follow his will for them? They didn't respect his law regarding idols (Exodus 20:3,4) his dietary law regarding blood (Leviticus 3:16,17) or his moral law regarding the shedding of blood (Exodus 20:13) and adultery (Exodus 20:14). Moreover, they still attempted to get their way by force (2 Kings 25:25, Jeremiah 41:1-3).

One of the easiest things for us to do is to compartmentalize our lives. One area of life is the religious area; and we're tempted to limit that to Sunday mornings. So often people seem to think their relationship to God doesn't need to influence or have any bearing on the rest of their lives. "Can't mix politics and religion," we say. "Can't mix religion and reality (everyday life)," we seem to say. But as God sees it, things don't work that way. We can't claim the blessings of being God's people by faith in Jesus Christ, and at the same time deny by the way we live that we are his people. Our relationship with the Lord is a package deal.

²⁷"Say this to them: 'This is what the Sovereign LORD says: As surely as I live, those who are left in the ruins will fall by the sword, those out in the country I will give to the wild animals to be devoured, and those in strongholds and caves will die of a plague. ²⁸I will make the land a desolate waste, and her proud strength will come to an end, and the mountains of Israel will become desolate so that no one will cross them. ²⁹Then they will know that I am the LORD, when I have made the land a desolate waste because of all the detestable things they have done.'

To those brazen Jerusalemites left behind, the Lord promised complete desolation of the land. According to Jeremiah 52:30, five years after the fall of Jerusalem a small remnant of 745 Jews was taken into exile. The land was left desolate.

³⁰"As for you, son of man, your countrymen are talking together about you by the walls and at the doors of the houses, saying to each other, 'Come and hear the message that has come from the LORD.' ³¹My people come to you, as they usually do, and sit before you to listen to your words, but they do not put them into practice. With their mouths they express devotion, but their hearts are greedy for unjust gain. ³²Indeed, to them you are nothing more than one who sings love songs with a beautiful voice and plays an instrument well, for they hear your words but do not put them into practice.

³³"When all this comes true — and it surely will — then they will know that a prophet has been among them."

Ezekiel's preaching had aroused interest among the exiles. In fact, it seemed as if he had by this time gained a rather large audience. Some invited their neighbors to come to hear him. Some even said his message was coming from the Lord.

But there was still a problem. They didn't put what they heard into practice. They were still concerned only about their own personal gain. To them Ezekiel was just some good entertainment. After his presentations were over, they went home to lives that had not changed. The fulfillment of the prophet's message of doom was the only thing which would convince such people. Then they would realize what he had been saying was from the Lord. It was worth listening to, and worth practicing in their lives.

In today's religious world it is interesting to observe the huge crowds and followings evangelists and crusades seem to get wherever they go. Ezekiel also drew large crowds. Such crowds love the music and the excitement, and in an emotionally charged moment make some religious commitments. Then comes the hard part. Christianity is not a momentary resolution; Christianity is living by faith. The Lord through Ezekiel calls it "putting into practice what we have heard." Recognizing Jesus Christ as the Savior of our souls and acknowledging him as the Lord of our lives — that's what Christianity is.

Shepherds and Sheep

34 The word of the LORD came to me: [2]"Son of man, prophesy against the shepherds of Israel; prophesy and say to them: 'This is what the Sovereign LORD says: Woe to the shepherds of Israel who only take care of themselves! Should not shepherds take care of the flock? [3]You eat the curds, clothe yourselves with the wool and slaughter the choice animals, but you do not take care of the flock. [4]You have not strengthened the weak or healed the sick or bound up the injured. You have not brought back the strays or searched for the lost. You have ruled them harshly and brutally. [5]So they were scattered because there was no shepherd, and when they were scattered they became food for all the wild animals. ⁶My sheep wandered over all the mountains and on every high hill. They were scattered over the whole earth, and no one searched or looked for them.

Shepherds take care of, lead, defend and feed their sheep. The shepherds of Israel were the political and religious leaders — judges, priests, prophets and especially kings. Ezekiel had previously documented their failure (22:25-30; 19:1-14). Israel's leaders, especially her kings, had taken every advantage they could from their positions. They had not shouldered their responsibilities properly, but had ruled just as brutally as the Egyptian taskmasters had done before the exodus under Moses.

Because there had been no spiritual leadership and no godly political leadership, the nation was harassed, robbed and finally scattered. Ezekiel's mention of the sheep wandering "on every high hill" was a stinging remark, since the high hills were the locations on which heathen shrines were erected and gods were worshiped. And yet God called this people "my sheep," although they had been abandoned by their shepherds and scattered by their enemies. His covenant, his solemn contract with them, was still intact, because God cannot go back on his word.

⁷" 'Therefore, you shepherds, hear the word of the LORD: ⁸As surely as I live, declares the Sovereign LORD, because my flock lacks a shepherd and so has been plundered and has become food for all the wild animals, and because my shepherds did not search for my flock but cared for themselves rather than for my flock, ⁹therefore, O shepherds, hear the word of the LORD: ¹⁰This is what the Sovereign LORD says: I am against the shepherds and will hold them accountable for my flock. I will remove them from tending the flock so that the shepherds can no longer feed themselves. I will rescue my flock from their mouths, and it will no longer be food for them.

God continued to call the unfaithful leaders of his people "my shepherds." He had appointed them and he expected them to carry out their duties. God did, however, promise to remove these leaders from their offices so they could no longer take advantage of the people.

God's ideal of a leader has not changed with the years. When God appoints a man as leader — of a congregation or a country — he calls him to serve the needs of people, to safeguard them against the dangers that threaten them. Leaders who take advantage of the people they are called to serve can hardly expect the Lord's blessing on their efforts.

Even if we fail in our role as shepherds, God doesn't change. Nor does his covenant of forgiveness through the Messiah change. He still wants to call us his sheep and shepherds, no matter how much we do to deserve his anger.

[11]" 'For this is what the Sovereign Lord says: I myself will search for my sheep and look after them. [12]As a shepherd looks after his scattered flock when he is with them, so will I look after my sheep. I will rescue them from all the places where they were scattered on a day of clouds and darkness. [13]I will bring them out from the nations and gather them from the countries, and I will bring them into their own land. I will pasture them on the mountains of Israel, in the ravines and in all the settlements in the land. [14]I will tend them in a good pasture, and the mountain heights of Israel will be their grazing land. There they will lie down in good grazing land, and there they will feed in a rich pasture on the mountains of Israel. [15]I myself will tend my sheep and have them lie down, declares the Sovereign Lord. [16]I will search for the lost and bring back the strays. I will bind up the injured and strengthen the weak, but the sleek and the strong I will destroy. I will shepherd the flock with justice.

Since Israel's shepherds weren't doing the job God had called them to do, God here promised to do two things. In the first place he would remove those wicked shepherds who were taking advantage of the flock. And then he would personally provide for the needs of his flock. He would search for the lost, bring back the strays, strengthen the weak, and punish the proud and unrepentant.

In a world where it is increasingly difficult to find Christian leaders in any area of life, it is comforting to know the Lord has promised to get personally involved in caring for the needs of his people when those who should be providing leadership aren't doing their jobs. When you think about it, that's much better anyway. He is a faithful shepherd. It is more comforting to put yourself in his care then in anybody else's.

17" 'As for you, my flock, this is what the Sovereign LORD says: I will judge between one sheep and another, and between rams and goats. 18Is it not enough for you to feed on the good pasture? Must you also trample the rest of your pasture with your feet? Is it not enough for you to drink clear water? Must you also muddy the rest with your feet? 19Must my flock feed on what you have trampled and drink what you have muddied with your feet?

20" 'Therefore this is what the Sovereign LORD says to them: See, I myself will judge between the fat sheep and the lean sheep. 21Because you shove with flank and shoulder, butting all the weak sheep with your horns until you have driven them away, 22I will save my flock, and they will no longer be plundered. I will judge between one sheep and another.

When leaders abuse their high calling, the people begin to abuse one another. Since Israel's shepherds weren't protecting the people, the Lord had to assume the role of judge.

If we fail to be good shepherds in our families, in our country, in our congregations, we can expect our constituency, our family members and the rest of the congregation to start trampling the pasture, muddying the water and shoving and taking advantage of the weak. Sinful human beings do such things, if they are not constantly pointed to the Lord and his way. This is the obligation of those in leadership positions.

²³I will place over them one shepherd, my servant David, and he will tend them; he will tend them and be their shepherd. ²⁴I the LORD will be their God, and my servant David will be prince among them. I the LORD have spoken.

Here is the high point of the chapter. Since Israel's shepherds had not been interested in safeguarding the welfare of God's people, God promised to send a shepherd who would. This shepherd would be the Lord's servant David. Since King David had been dead for more than 400 years, this is a reference to the Messiah who would rise from David's royal line. This new Son of David would bring peace and unity, just as David had done to a land constantly plagued by war and dissent. Under his reign God's people will live securely.

From a New Testament perspective, we know Jesus of Nazareth was from the house and line of David (Luke 3:31). In fact, the angel had indicated to his mother he would occupy the position of David: "The Lord God will give him the throne of his father David, . . . his kingdom will never end" (Luke 1:32,33). Ezekiel's prophecy reminds us of the Good Shepherd, the Spiritual Shepherd, the Savior Jesus who described himself in these terms, "I am the good shepherd. . . " (John 10:11-18). As our Shepherd Jesus gives us spiritual care and nourishment and protection (John 6:32-40). When the people listening to Ezekiel heard these verses, they received the comfort of knowing the Lord had a special Shepherd-Prince who would reign forever (37:25), and who was going to tend them. It became very obvious to them that this promised Shepherd had to be more than just a human being. He had to be God.

Many years later Jesus claimed to be the fulfillment of God's promise here. When he claimed to be the Good Shepherd, his hearers understood clearly that he was claiming to be God. And we are told that when he said this his hearers picked up stones to stone him (John 10:27-31). Death by stoning was the ancient Jewish penalty for blasphemy.

25" 'I will make a covenant of peace with them and rid the land of wild beasts so that they may live in the desert and sleep in the forests in safety. 26I will bless them and the places surrounding my hill. I will send down showers in season; there will be showers of blessing. 27The trees of the field will yield their fruit and the ground will yield its crops; the people will be secure in their land. They will know that I am the LORD, when I break the bars of their yoke and rescue them from the hands of those who enslaved them. 28They will no longer be plundered by the nations, nor will wild animals devour them. They will live in safety, and no one will make them afraid. 29I will provide for them a land renowned for its crops, and they will no longer be victims of famine in the land or bear the scorn of the nations. 30Then they will know that I, the LORD their God, am with them and that they, the house of Israel, are my people, declares the Sovereign LORD. 31You my sheep, the sheep of my pasture, are people, and I am your God, declares the Sovereign LORD.' "

The rule of the Good Shepherd is described in terms of joy and blessing for his flock. This was language easy to understand for ancient people who made their living by farming or raising sheep. For them ideal conditions would include the absence of wild beasts to attack the flocks or shepherds, rain at the proper time so the land would be productive, fields and orchards free from attackers who might destroy and steal, and no domination by foreign powers who would demand the produce of the land.

This description reminds us of the one time when such conditions existed — back in Eden. Adam and Eve and all creation were in communion with God and received all the blessings of such communion.

The rule of the Shepherd-Prince David, the Messiah, would bring people back into a "covenant of peace." It would be a restoration of the people to the position our first parents had in Eden. For most of us who aren't farmers or shepherds the ideal existence in communion with and under all the blessings of the Lord might be described in terms different from those above. But Ezekiel's point is obvious. Under the reign of the Messiah, everything will be restored to perfection.

When Jesus Christ came to our world, people didn't allow him to be their Shepherd-Prince. They rejected him. Their society didn't change because few in it lived close to God in repentance and faith. It is no different today. If all the members of our society would be followers of the Shepherd-King and live lives of loyalty to him, then we might look around us and see a reflection of Eden. But such is not the case. We will have to wait until we are removed from this sin-infested world to experience perfection. There everyone will be following the Shepherd-King-Messiah Jesus perfectly. There will be abundant showers, productive trees and crops. There will be no wild animals to jeopardize our security, no yoke or enslavement to rob us of freedom. Or to put it another way, "there will be no more death or mourning or crying or pain, for the old order of things has passed away" (Revelation 21:4).

A Prophecy Against Edom

35 The word of the Lord came to me: [2]"Son of man, set your face against Mount Seir; prophesy against it [3]and say: 'This is what the Sovereign Lord says: I am against you, Mount Seir, and I will stretch out my hand against you and make you a

desolate waste. ⁴I will turn your towns into ruins and you will be desolate. Then you will know that I am the LORD.

Once again our attention is directed to Edom, Israel's neighbor to the southeast. Mt. Seir and the range of which it is a part are the predominant geographical feature of the country and here stand for the nation of Edom. At first glance this chapter would seem to fit better with chapters 25-32, the prophecies of judgment against the surrounding heathen nations. In fact there already had been a prophecy against Edom (25:12-14). (For a more detailed discussion of the historical interaction between Edom and Israel, see the comments on those verses.) Chapter 35 does, however, serve a purpose at this point. The chapter is not displaced nor is it empty repetition.

After Jerusalem fell and her citizens were deported, neighboring nations moved in. One of those neighbors was Edom. In order for the Lord to carry out his promise to bring his people back to this land, these intruders had to be removed again. This is the Lord's promise in this chapter. The promise fits here because in the very next chapter God will begin to delineate the blessings he had in store for Judah in the future. The blessings promised to Judah in chapter 36 are even more outstanding when contrasted to the destruction promised to Edom in chapter 35. There is also literary parallelism between the two chapters. Chapters 35 and 36 form a connected unit; chapter 36 completes the unit of prophecy begun in chapter 35. (Compare 35:1-3 with 36:1-3 and 35:8 with 36:6-9.) The desolation God promised to send upon Edom was carried out through Babylon, Persia and then John Hyrcanus, one of the Maccabees (125 B.C.). There is no trace of the Edomite people left today.

⁵" 'Because you harbored an ancient hostility and delivered the Israelites over to the sword at the time of their calamity, the time

their punishment reached its climax, ⁶therefore as surely as I live, declares the Sovereign Lᴏʀᴅ, I will give you over to bloodshed and it will pursue you. Since you did not hate bloodshed, bloodshed will pursue you. ⁷I will make Mount Seir a desolate waste and cut off from it all who come and go. ⁸I will fill your mountains with the slain; those killed by the sword will fall on your hills and in your valleys and in all your ravines. ⁹I will make you desolate forever; your towns will not be inhabited. Then you will know that I am the Lᴏʀᴅ.

The hostility between Edom and Israel went all the way back to Jacob and his twin brother Esau. We are told that "Esau held a grudge against Jacob" (Genesis 27:41). This hatred resurfaced when Edom — the descendants of Esau — aided Babylon against Israel — the descendants of Jacob — at the time Jerusalem fell. The blood which Edom shed at the fall of Jerusalem would pursue her. The land of Edom straddled trade routes, so many came and went through Edom. Now because of God's judgment, she would be cut off from the commercial traffic. The ultimate disgrace for ancient people was to be refused proper burial. This, said God, was in store for the people of Edom.

¹⁰" 'Because you have said, "These two nations and countries will be ours and we will take possession of them," even though I the Lᴏʀᴅ was there, ¹¹therefore as surely as I live, declares the Sovereign Lᴏʀᴅ, I will treat you in accordance with the anger and jealousy you showed in your hatred of them and I will make myself known among them when I judge you. ¹²Then you will know that I the Lᴏʀᴅ have heard all the contemptible things you have said against the mountains of Israel. You said, "They have been laid waste and have been given over to us to devour." ¹³You boasted against me and spoke against me without restraint, and I heard it. ¹⁴This is what the Sovereign Lᴏʀᴅ says: While the whole earth rejoices, I will make you desolate. ¹⁵Because you rejoiced

when the inheritance of the house of Israel became desolate, that is how I will treat you. You will be desolate, O Mount Seir, you and all of Edom. Then they will know that I am the LORD.' "

One of Edom's sins for which God would judge her was her desire to take over the Jews' homeland after the fall of Jerusalem. Now that both Israel and Judah were out of the picture as national entities, Edom decided to take possession of the country. Her knowledge of the history of Abraham and Isaac, the father and grandfather of Esau, should have made her aware that this land had been promised to the descendants of Jacob (Genesis 15:18). Earlier as we read Ezekiel 10 and 11 we had observed that the Lord symbolically removed his presence from both the temple and Jerusalem. But to Edom God said he was still there. In chapters 10 and 11 we were dealing with symbols and visions. God's people had, as it were, driven him out spiritually, so you could say he was gone. Yet God couldn't actually abandon the land. It was part of the cluster of promises he had once given to Abraham.

The Lord still identified himself with his nation. God made it clear that when Edom spoke against Judah and Israel, she spoke against him. When the rest of the world would have reason to rejoice, Edom would not because she would be no more. God's promise to Abraham would find fulfillment: "Those who curse you will be cursed" (Genesis 12:3).

We often consider ourselves or others to be victims of historical circumstance. In a sense the nation of Edom was a product of the politics of the ancient Near East. But that didn't relieve her of her responsibility before God for the kind of morality she espoused. In our world, where violence and bloodshed are matter of fact because of ancient hostilities between Protestant and Catholic, between Muslim and

Jew, between believers and unbelievers, the word of the Lord in this chapter is needed more and more. God holds people personally responsible for their actions. This remains true no matter what the political-historical circumstances were or are which provide impetus for their activities.

Prophecy to the Mountains of Israel

36 "Son of man, prophesy to the mountains of Israel and say, 'O mountains of Israel, hear the word of the LORD. ²This is what the Sovereign LORD says: The enemy said of you, "Aha! The ancient heights have become our possession." ' ³Therefore prophesy and say, 'This is what the Sovereign LORD says: Because they ravaged and hounded you from every side so that you became the possession of the rest of the nations and the object of people's malicious talk and slander, ⁴therefore, O mountains of Israel, hear the word of the Sovereign LORD: This is what the Sovereign LORD says to the mountains and hills, to the ravines and valleys, to the desolate ruins and the deserted towns that have been plundered and ridiculed by the rest of the nations around you — ⁵this is what the Sovereign LORD says: In my burning zeal I have spoken against the rest of the nations, and against all Edom, for with glee and with malice in their hearts they made my land their own possession so that they might plunder its pastureland.' ⁶Therefore prophesy concerning the land of Israel and say to the mountains and hills, to the ravines and valleys: 'This is what the Sovereign LORD says: I speak in my jealous wrath because you have suffered the scorn of the nations. ⁷Therefore this is what the Sovereign LORD says: I swear with uplifted hand that the nations around you will also suffer scorn.

The mountains are addressed, but as in the previous chapter the mountains represent the entire land since they are the most prominent features of the landscape. In Israel the mountains also became the locations for the worship of idols, and thus places which deserved to be everlastingly detestable to the Lord. When an enemy took the heights, he not only controlled the most strategic locations in the country, but also the usual places of worship, and by implication the gods who were worshiped there. God had spoken against the enemy nations (chapters 25-32) and promised them the same destruction and scorn which Israel had to undergo.

8" 'But you, O mountains of Israel, will produce branches and fruit for my people Israel, for they will soon come home. ⁹I am concerned for you and will look on you with favor; you will be plowed and sown, ¹⁰and I will multiply the number of people upon you, even the whole house of Israel. The towns will be inhabited and the ruins rebuilt. ¹¹I will increase the number of men and animals upon you, and they will be fruitful and become numerous. I will settle people on you as in the past and will make you prosper more than before. Then you will know that I am the LORD. ¹²I will cause people, my people Israel, to walk upon you. They will possess you, and you will be their inheritance; you will never again deprive them of their children.

When God punished the sins of Israel and Judah by sending their citizens into captivity, the promised land was desolate. The desolation would not, however, last forever. The land would again be productive, so people would have a place to go when they returned from exile in Babylon. Why the promised blessings? God's chastisement, though bitter, would lead many to repent, to look to the Lord for deliverance not only from sin but from exile as well, and to be willing to make the long trip back to their old homeland, trusting that the Lord wanted them there.

Prosperity is a blessing from the Lord. Because covetousness is a sin with which we must all wrestle every day, it is very easy for the child of God to overreact and take a negative attitude toward wealth and prosperity. But if the Lord could say to people, "I will prosper you more than ever before," it should be obvious that wealth is a blessing from God. This realization should take away the stigma under which rich Christians sometimes suffer. Rather than hiding their wealth, they ought to be openly using it for others. The problem is not with the blessings God has given, but with the way we acquire them or use them. The wealthy Christian actually has to carry a heavier responsibility than the poor Christian. Someone has aptly remarked, "It takes a strong back to carry prosperity." God expects the wealthy Christian to be a good manager of his many blessings. This involves greater responsibility.

13" 'This is what the Sovereign LORD says: Because people say to you, "You devour men and deprive your nation of its children," 14therefore you will no longer devour men or make your nation childless, declares the Sovereign LORD. 15No longer will I make you hear the taunts of the nations, and no longer will you suffer the scorn of the peoples or cause your nation to fall, declares the Sovereign LORD.' "

The land of Canaan by this time had acquired a very bad reputation. Every nation that lived there had been devoured. The Amorites, the Canaanites, and now the Israelites had all lost their national identity while living in Canaan. People had begun to say, "If you live in Canaan, something is going to get you. It might be famine, drought, wild beasts, war, or an invasion, but something will get you." Now God promised to take away the bad reputation from the land.

"Your surroundings are going to eat you alive," said the people of Ezekiel's day about Canaan. Not really. Circumstances and surroundings don't cause problems, people do. Judah's rebellion caused her to be taken into exile. The blatant ungodliness of the earlier Canaanite inhabitants led God to have the Israelites dispossess and displace them.

¹⁶Again the word of the LORD came to me: ¹⁷"Son of man, when the people of Israel were living in their own land, they defiled it by their conduct and their actions. Their conduct was like woman's monthly uncleanness in my sight. ¹⁸So I poured out my wrath on them because they had shed blood in the land and because they had defiled it with their idols. ¹⁹I dispersed them among the nations, and they were scattered through the countries; I judged them according to their conduct and their actions. ²⁰And wherever they went among the nations they profaned my holy name, for it was said of them, 'These are the LORD's people, and yet they had to leave his land.' ²¹I had concern for my holy name, which the house of Israel profaned among the nations where they had gone.

According to the Old Testament law, a woman was ceremonially unclean during her monthly period (Leviticus 15:19-24). Because of Israel's idolatry and ungodliness God set her aside from himself as impure and unclean. There was one tragic and very public result from the exile. Other nations came to the conclusion: "Israel's God is unable to protect his people or keep his promises to them. He must be a weak God indeed, not even worth our time or consideration." God was concerned about his reputation. He didn't want to have people misinformed about him. God was correct in saying Israel had profaned his name; their rebellion had caused him to withdraw his protection from them.

Do we profane the name of God in our lives? When people observe us do they get the impression that God is important to us? Or does it appear as if we relegate God to the back shelf of our lives much of the time? If we regard God as insignificant in our lives, aren't we reinforcing others in their opinion that the Lord is not important? And isn't that profaning the name of the Lord? When we act, do we purposefully program the Lord and his will into our actions? Or do we act as if God and his will are irrelevant? If the latter is true, we are reinforcing others in the notion that the Lord has nothing to say to modern man. Is that not profaning the name of the Lord?

God is the most important Being in the universe. Life has no other purpose than to serve and glorify him. Anything we say which detracts from his position of importance and reduces his credibility is profaning his name. What a dreadful misuse of the precious gift of life!

22"Therefore say to the house of Israel, 'This is what the Sovereign LORD says: It is not for your sake, O house of Israel, that I am going to do these things, but for the sake of my holy name, which you have profaned among the nations where you have gone. 23I will show the holiness of my great name, which has been profaned among the nations, the name you have profaned among them. Then the nations will know that I am the LORD, declares the Sovereign LORD, when I show myself holy through you before their eyes.

God promised to do something, not so much for the sake of the exiles as for the sake of those who had been falsely informed about him by the situation of the exiles. God would show he does not lie. He would show that his promises were valid. He would show he was holy by what he would do in the land of Israel. Bringing the exiles back would indicate to the nations that he was a God to be reckoned with, a God who keeps all his promises.

God wasn't and isn't interested only in his people. He is the Savior of all. If others are going to know him and believe in him, his reputation needs to be disseminated. God wants to show everybody out there that he is holy. What a privilege it is to be a tool in the Lord's hand to spread the knowledge of him to others! Not only does he want to be a part of our lives and bless us, but he also wants to offer his benefits to others through us. No wonder we talk about joy in the Holy Spirit. What a tremendous reason to be alive! What a tremendous reason to look forward to tomorrow! God wants to use me. He wants to work through me. He wants to show himself to other people through me. How can life be boring and depressing when we know that?

24"'For I will take you out of the nations: I will gather you from all the countries and bring you back into your own land. 25I will sprinkle clean water on you, and you will be clean; I will cleanse you from all your impurities and from all your idols. 26I will give you a new heart and put a new spirit in you; I will remove from you your heart of stone and give you a heart of flesh. 27And I will put my Spirit in you and move you to follow my decrees and be careful to keep my laws. 28You will live in the land I gave your forefathers; you will be my people, and I will be your God. 29I will save you from all your uncleanness. I will call for the grain and make it plentiful and will not bring famine upon you. 30I will increase the fruit of the trees and the crops of the field, so that you will no longer suffer disgrace among the nations because of famine. 31Then you will remember your evil ways and wicked deeds, and you will loathe yourselves for your sins and detestable practices. 32I want you to know that I am not doing this for your sake, declares the Sovereign LORD. Be ashamed and disgraced for your conduct, O house of Israel!

God would use the very land that had been defiled and devastated to show that he is the holy Lord, ruler of all things. In order to show he is holy and doesn't lie, God would carry out his promise to return the people to the land. Then his promise to Abraham would be fulfilled. In order to be brought back into his family, the people needed to be cleansed of their sins. No longer would a priest in a purification ceremony wash them clean from their sins and idolatry; God would do it: ". . . I will cleanse you from all your impurities. . . ." God would change their hard unbelieving hearts into hearts softened by the Savior's message of love. Together with changed hearts he would also give them a new desire to live according to his will. He would keep the promises first made to their forefather Abraham. He would bless them with all they would need in the land.

All these blessings would lead them to ask, "How could we have ever acted so foolishly as to abandon such a loving, providing God?" But God reminded them once more he wasn't doing it just for them. He was telling them and the entire world what he was really like.

Sometimes the unconditional outpouring of God's blessings into our lives is just as effective a call to repentance as a harsh use of the law. We are driven to our knees and exclaim, "My God is so good to me, and still I act toward him in such a disinterested way!" What ungrateful people we are!

33" 'This is what the Sovereign LORD says: On the day I cleanse you from all your sins, I will resettle your towns, and the ruins will be rebuilt. 34The desolate land will be cultivated instead of lying desolate in the sight of all who pass through it. 35They will say, "This land that was laid waste has become like the garden of Eden; the cities that were lying in ruins, desolate and destroyed, are now fortified and inhabited." 36Then the nations around you that remain will know that I the LORD have rebuilt what was destroyed and have replanted what was desolate. I the LORD have spoken, and I will do it.'

The repopulating and rebuilding of the promised land would lead the nations to say, "A change as drastic as this could have happened only if the Lord was behind it." Things would go so well that one would be tempted to draw a comparison between the resettled land and the garden of

Eden! Thus, God's promises to Abraham were kept and his reputation among the nations was restored.

When we have labored and sweated in order to accomplish something, whether it was building or rebuilding, claiming or reclaiming, it is the natural reaction of others to say, "You certainly have accomplished a lot." When we are open about our faith and express its meaning freely, there is often a slightly different reaction. When we assign our success to the blessing of the Lord, the people who are observing us tend to think and communicate along the same lines. They say, "The Lord has blessed your efforts," instead of, "You did a great job." This is what the Lord wants the nations to learn about him from observing us. Our actions and words will praise him, and they will lead others to do the same. This is the reason God has put us on earth: ". . . that they may see your good deeds and praise your Father in heaven" (Matthew 5:16).

37"This is what the Sovereign Lord says: Once again I will yield to the pleas of the house of Israel and do this for them: I will make their people as numerous as sheep, 38as numerous as the flocks for offerings at Jerusalem during her appointed feasts. So will the ruined cities be filled with flocks of people. Then they will know that I am the Lord."

Previously (14:3, 20:3), the Lord had refused to listen to the people. Now he would listen to their pleas for help and deliverance. The promise here is almost a verbatim repetition of God's promise to Abraham in Genesis 15:5. God repeated it on this occasion as a comfort to the few believing Jews who would return after the exile.

"Once again I will yield to their pleas." What a comfort! In spite of our sins, God hears our prayers. In spite of our failures, he does something about our pleas. He has to. He has promised to. And God does not lie.

215

The valley of dry bones

The Valley of Dry Bones

37 **The hand of the LORD was upon me, and he brought me out by the Spirit of the LORD and set me in the middle of a valley; it was full of bones. ²He led me back and forth among them, and I saw a great many bones on the floor of the valley, bones that were very dry. ³He asked me, "Son of man, can these bones live?"**

I said, "O Sovereign LORD, you alone know."

The faith of the child of God is constantly threatened by two opposite dangers: overconfidence and despair. It was to the second of these dangers that God's message in Ezekiel 37 is addressed. In the previous chapter God had assured his people that the exiles now in Babylon were not forever gone, but that "they will soon come home" (36:8). God's people were so depressed by their situation, however, that they found it difficult to believe God's promise. They said: "Our hope is gone; we are cut off" (37:11). To reassure his people God granted Ezekiel a remarkable vision: the vision of the valley of dry bones.

God's question to Ezekiel — "can these bones live?" — normally would have been answered in the negative. Ezekiel's reply was interesting. He said, "Only the Person who made all those bones could make them alive." Only the God who made man from the dust of the earth could make something living out of that valley full of bones which represented the whole community of exiles.

⁴Then he said to me, "Prophesy to these bones and say to them, 'Dry bones, hear the word of the LORD! ⁵This is what the Sovereign LORD says to these bones: I will make breath enter you, and you will come to life. ⁶I will attach tendons to you and make flesh come upon you and cover you with skin; I will put breath in you, and you will come to life. Then you will know that I am the LORD.' "

217

The Lord promised to do for these bones just what he had done for the dust formed into a body in Eden: "The LORD God formed the man from the dust of the ground and breathed into his nostrils the breath of life, and man became a living being" (Genesis 2:7).

⁷So I prophesied as I was commanded. And as I was prophesying, there was a noise, a rattling sound, and the bones came together, bone to bone. ⁸I looked, and tendons and flesh appeared on them and skin covered them, but there was no breath in them.

⁹Then he said to me, "Prophesy to the breath; prophesy, son of man, and say to it, 'This is what the Sovereign LORD says: Come from the four winds, O breath, and breathe into these slain, that they may live.' " ¹⁰So I prophesied as he commanded me, and breath entered them; they came to life and stood up on their feet — a vast army.

At the Lord's command, Ezekiel prophesied to lifeless bones, and a miracle happened. There was a rattling noise as bone came together to bone. To Ezekiel the valley seemed no longer to be full of disconnected bones but of skeletons. God's miracle continued, "Tendons and flesh appeared on them." Now the valley resembled a battlefield littered with corpses. But God's miracle was still not over. At God's command Ezekiel continued to prophesy, and breath entered that army of corpses, and they came to life and stood up. Through a vision Ezekiel saw how God would re-create his people now apparently hopelessly lost in Babylon.

Ezekiel carried out his orders and the Lord kept his promise. This ought to be a description of our lives: We carried out the Lord's orders and the Lord carried out his promises. Knowledge that we are doing the Lord's will in our lives is what takes away the boredom and drudgery. We are not just working for a paycheck. We are serving God and supporting our families as God expects. We are not just studying. We are using our minds to the maximum capacity because the Lord has called us to be good managers of our intellect. We are not just taking care of the kids. We are shaping the souls of God's own children by letting them learn of Jesus from the way we talk and act. And the Lord keeps his promises, just as he did when Ezekiel preached to those dry bones as he was instructed to.

¹¹Then he said to me: "Son of man, these bones are the whole house of Israel. They say, 'Our bones are dried up and our hope is gone; we are cut off.' ¹²Therefore prophesy and say to them: 'This is what the Sovereign LORD says: O my people, I am going to open your graves and bring you up from them; I will bring you back to the land of Israel. ¹³Then you, my people, will know that I am the LORD, when I open your graves and bring you up from them. ¹⁴I will put my Spirit in you and you will live, and I will settle you in your own land. Then you will know that I the LORD have spoken, and I have done it, declares the LORD.' "

After Jerusalem had fallen and the rest of the nation had joined them in exile, the Jews in Babylon had given up hope. "As a people and a nation we are just as good as dead," they said. To that the Lord replied, "I can change that. I can raise you from the dead! I can return you to your land. *Nothing* is impossible for me."

This vision of the dry bones might have been the basis for the New Testament picture of the spiritual status of all people. St. Paul, for example, wrote, "You were dead in your transgressions and sins" (Ephesians 2:1). By nature everyone is spiritually dead, unable to do anything pleasing to God. But in his might and mercy the Lord has made us "alive with Christ" (Ephesians 2:4). This makes it possible for us who were "foreigners and aliens," exiled from God because of sin, to become "fellow citizens with God's people" (Ephesians 2:11-13,19).

One Nation Under One King

¹⁵The word of the LORD came to me: ¹⁶"Son of man, take a stick of wood and write on it, 'Belonging to Judah and the Israelites associated with him.' Then take another stick of wood, and write on it, 'Ephraim's stick, belonging to Joseph and all the house of Israel associated with him.' ¹⁷Join them together into one stick so that they will become one in your hand.

Here again Ezekiel used a prop as a teaching device. He was to take two pieces of stick in his hand, making it appear as if he was holding a single stick. One stick was labeled Ephraim, the other Judah. Ephraim, named after one of the sons of Joseph, was the most prominent of the ten tribes which had formed the northern kingdom of Israel. As a matter of fact, Ephraim is often a designation for Israel.

¹⁸"When your countrymen ask you, 'Won't you tell us what you mean by this?' ¹⁹say to them, 'This is what the Sovereign LORD says: I am going to take the stick of Joseph — which is in Ephraim's hand — and of the Israelite tribes associated with him, and join it to Judah's stick, making them a single stick of wood, and they will become one in my hand.' ²⁰Hold before their eyes the sticks you have written on ²¹and say to them, 'This is what the Sovereign LORD says: I will take the Israelites out of the nations where they have gone. I will gather them from all around and bring them back into their own land. ²²I will make them one nation in the land, on the mountains of Israel. There will be one king over all of them and they will never again be two nations or be divided into two kingdoms. ²³They will no longer defile themselves with their idols and vile images or with any of their offenses, for I will save them from all their sinful backslid-

ing, and I will cleanse them. They will be my people, and I will be their God.

When the people asked what Ezekiel's symbolic action was to teach, the prophet was to explain that the time was coming when the two kingdoms would no longer be split. They would be rejoined into a national entity. They would have one king who would perfectly assume the role of shepherd. From Ezekiel 34:11-22 we know the king to be the Lord himself.

We know from history that the northern ten tribes never did return from captivity in Assyria. Israel and Judah were never reunited as a political unit in the promised land. What the Lord is describing here is the New Testament church of believers, gathered from all over the world into one invisible body and living under the rulership of King Messiah. Of them God says, "I will cleanse them. They will be my people, and I will be their God."

²⁴" 'My servant David will be king over them, and they will all have one shepherd. They will follow my laws and be careful to keep my decrees. ²⁵They will live in the land I gave to my servant Jacob, the land where your fathers lived. They and their children and their children's children will live there forever, and David my servant will be their prince forever. ²⁶I will make a covenant of peace with them; it will be an everlasting covenant. I will establish them and increase their numbers, and I will put my sanctuary among them forever. ²⁷My dwelling place will be with them; I will be their God, and they will be my people. ²⁸Then the nations will know that I the LORD make Israel holy, when my sanctuary is among them forever.' "

This is a comforting repetition of 34:23. Under the rule of the Messiah-Shepherd, the people would do God's will. They would continue such an existence forever, since the rule of the Messiah-Shepherd would be forever (2 Samuel

7:13,16). Everything about this was intended to be permanent. This would be an everlasting covenant of peace, a solemn contract God made with his people forever.

After reading a section like this, some might wonder, "Why wasn't a permanent earthly kingdom established on the mountains of Israel at the time of Jesus?" The answer is: Because the people who returned from the exile became exactly like the people before the exile. Jesus, the Messiah-Shepherd-King, came, but the people of Jerusalem rejected him. This produced a terrible result; their house was again left "desolate" (Matthew 23:38).

God gave the wonderful promises in chapters 34, 36 and 37 to revive people who had given up hope. The Lord assured them there would be a drastic change from the present evil situation in which they found themselves. He reminded them that he still had a special plan and purpose for them. He wanted those to whom these promises were given to believe them. If the people of Israel had committed themselves to a life of repentance, if they had accepted God's cleansing from their idolatrous practices and turned away from them, and if they had followed the rule of the Messiah-Shepherd-King — then the Lord's blessings would have continued without interruption. In actuality, the people forfeited the fulfillment of these promises.

God would gather his new Israel from all nations, from east to west. This New Testament Israel would enjoy all the blessings Old Testament Israel had forfeited; deliverance and cleansing from sin, and the assurance that God has taken up his dwelling among them.

Another question might arise after reading these chapters. Why did God promise his people physical, material blessings, when the Messiah was interested primarily in the souls of the people under his care? Because these promises were made in terms of things to which God's Old Testament people could relate. The descriptions of the Messiah's rule were given in terms of the past. It was not as if the past would actually happen again, but the past was something with which the people of Israel were familiar and to which they could relate. They knew who David was. They knew what he had been like and what physical blessings they had enjoyed under his rule. They had enjoyed good crops, security, safety, and freedom from foreign oppression. They also knew what spiritual blessings were theirs when in time past they had followed the Lord. The promises of God through Ezekiel, therefore, were put in terms that were familiar to them from their history.

The blessings the Shepherd-King brings — his rule in our world as the triumphant God-Man our Savior and especially his rule in our hearts — are much greater and more comprehensive than the blessings Israel once enjoyed under David. But how could people living centuries before Christ understand them or even get a glimpse of them, if they were not described in terms of something they knew?

We can look at this section and be reminded of Jesus' promise that there would be one fold under one Good Shepherd (John 10:16). In these passages from Ezekiel we can see parallels of our relationship with the Lord as his New Testament people. But when Ezekiel originally spoke to the exiles in their physical situation, his words also had definite physical aspects. It would be incorrect to spiritualize away this aspect of the promises.

Prophecy Against Gog

Chapter 37 pictured a bright future for the restored people of God. God promised to gather his scattered people through the Messiah, to forgive them, to dwell

223

among them and to rule over them forever. Does this mean that the enemies of God and of his people will concede defeat and stop their efforts to destroy God's people? In chapters 38 and 39 God gave Ezekiel a glimpse of the answer. The view is in part a frightening one. Enemy hordes will wage war against the people of God in an attempt to destroy them. But the view God gave Ezekiel is also a reassuring one. God promises to send fiery judgment on those who attack his people.

It seems best not to interpret this next section literally. In the events described in chapters 38 and 39 there is a lack of historical precision and chronological clarity. The characters, descriptions and actions pictured represent general concepts rather than some particular person or thing. The focus is on general statements about God's role in the world, rather than about specific times and events.

Instead of the very precise dating to which we have become accustomed in Ezekiel's message, we now have phrases such as "after many days" (38:8), "in future years" (38:8), "in that day" (38:14), and "in days to come" (38:16). "Seven years" (39:9) and "seven months" (39:12) seem to be stylized representative numbers, perhaps indicating the complete overthrow of God's enemies, rather than a particular period of time.

38 **The word of the Lord came to me: ²"Son of man, set your face against Gog, of the land of Magog, the chief prince of Meshech and Tubal; prophesy against him ³and say: 'This is what the Sovereign Lord says: I am against you, O Gog, chief prince of Meshech and Tubal. ⁴I will turn you around, put hooks in your jaws and bring you out with your whole army — your horses, your horsemen fully armed, and a great horde with large and small shields, all of them brandishing their swords. ⁵Persia, Cush and Put will be with them, all with shields and helmets, ⁶also Gomer with all its troops, and Beth Togarmah from the far north with all its troops — the many nations with you.**

Although many attempts have been made to link the name Gog with some particular ancient ruler, people or city, and although there are other scriptural references to Magog, Meshech, Gomer and Tubal (Genesis 10:2,3), we have already learned from Ezekiel that Meshech and Tubal were destroyed as seats of power long ago (32:26). It seems most likely, therefore, that Ezekiel was referring to something from the distant past, with which the people would have been familiar, in order to emphasize an important truth. Gog here represented any or all forces of evil bent on destroying God's people. Gog was a fitting symbol of these forces because he most likely had been intent on destroying God's people when he actually was on the scene in history.

As the Prophet Ezekiel looked ahead to view the rule of the Messiah, he saw that the forces of evil would continue to attack the Lord and his people as they had done in the past. A rather obvious indication that this is a generalization and not a specific prophecy of what would happen is the combination of nations. They are from the four corners of the known world. Meshech and Tubal were located in northern Asia Minor in the area of the Black Sea; Cush was south of Egypt; Put was the area west of the Egyptian delta; Persia is present-day Iran; and Beth Togarmah is in the region of Armenia. It would have been unlikely even from a geographical standpoint for such a coalition of nations from these scattered areas to have formed. But the idea that opposition to the Lord and his people would come from all four corners of the world is in perfect keeping with the rest of Scripture.

One comforting thought stands out — the Lord is the one who leads the nations by the nose; he puts "hooks in their jaws." This is true even when the nations are hostile to God's people. The Lord is ultimately in control. God was able to bend the Assyrians' and Babylonians' lust for power so that

225

they served his purposes. Throughout history he has continued to do the same for his people, no matter which nations or powers would be involved at any given time.

7" 'Get ready; be prepared, you and all the hordes gathered about you, and take command of them. 8After many days you will be called to arms. In future years you will invade a land that has recovered from war, whose people were gathered from many nations to the mountains of Israel, which had long been desolate. They had been brought out from the nations, and now all of them live in safety. 9You and all your troops and the many nations with you will go up, advancing like a storm; you will be like a cloud covering the land.

The events which would occur "after many days. . . . in future years" must be placed in the indefinite future, after the return from the exile. With the Lord's foreknowledge and with his permission, powerful forces of evil will move against the people of God.

10" 'This is what the Sovereign Lord says: On that day thoughts will come into your mind and you will devise an evil scheme. 11You will say, "I will invade a land of unwalled villages; I will attack a peaceful and unsuspecting people — all of them living without walls and without gates and bars. 12I will plunder and loot and turn my hand against the resettled ruins and the people gathered from the nations, rich in livestock and goods, living at the center of the land." 13Sheba and Dedan and the merchants of Tarshish and all her villages will say to you, "Have you come to plunder? Have you gathered your hordes to loot, to carry off silver and gold, to take away livestock and goods and to seize much plunder?" '

The plans of the forces of evil were plain enough. They wanted to take advantage of the seemingly defenseless people of God. Since God would provide his people with many blessings, these evil schemers would attempt to plunder their livestock and goods. In chapters 36 and 37 Ezekiel had just described the blessings which the Lord would shower upon his people after he had restored them. So the status of God's blessed people in this description is couched in similar terms of restoration and renewed blessing. Merchant and commercial people from all over the world would try to get their share from plundering God's people. You can almost see them greedily rubbing their hands together. Jesus said the people of this world are more shrewd in dealing with their own kind than are the people of the light (Luke 16:8).

[14]"Therefore, son of man, prophesy and say to Gog: 'This is what the Sovereign LORD says: In that day, when my people Israel are living in safety, will you not take notice of it? [15]You will come from your place in the far north, you and many nations with you, all of them riding on horses, a great horde, a mighty army. [16]You will advance against my people Israel like a cloud that covers the land. In days to come, O Gog, I will bring you against my land, so that the nations may know me when I show myself holy through you before their eyes.

God's purpose in allowing these things to happen "in that day" would be the same purpose which he previously explained in chapter 36. God wants the nations to know the truth about him. More than that, he will use both his enemies and his own people to display the truth about himself.

[17]" 'This is what the Sovereign LORD says: Are you not the one I spoke of in former days by my servants the prophets of Israel? At that time they prophesied for years that I would bring you against them. [18]This is what will happen in that day: When Gog attacks the land of Israel, my hot anger will be aroused, declares the Sovereign LORD. [19]In my zeal and fiery wrath I declare that at that time there shall be a great earthquake in the land of Israel. [20]The

fish of the sea, the birds of the air, the beasts of the field, every creature that moves along the ground, and all the people on the face of the earth will tremble at my presence. The mountains will be overturned, the cliffs will crumble and every wall will fall to the ground. [21]I will summon a sword against Gog on all my mountains, declares the Sovereign LORD. Every man's sword will be against his brother. [22]I will execute judgment upon him with plague and bloodshed; I will pour down torrents of rain, hailstones and burning sulfur on him and on his troops and on the many nations with him. [23]And so I will show my greatness and my holiness, and I will make myself known in the sight of many nations. Then they will know that I am the LORD.'

Ezekiel's message was not new. Other prophets had repeatedly predicted that enemies of God's people would constantly attack them. Whenever that happened, however, God's anger would be vented against those enemies. The Almighty would use even the forces of nature to display his power and anger against this opposition. This would cause such terror among them that they would begin to battle each other. Because of this overthrow of the enemies, the nations would know he is the Lord.

It is comforting to know that the God we worship is in control of everything, including the forces of nature. We are not subject to the whims of a cold and impersonal universe.

There is even more comfort for us here. The King of creation actually uses things in nature to prove he is the Lord. Earthquakes, plagues and storms all testify to the Creator's power. He allows events to happen, and even causes them to happen, with the express intent of defeating his and our enemies and proving to all that he is the Lord.

39 "Son of man, prophesy against Gog and say: 'This is what the Sovereign LORD says: I am against you, O Gog, chief prince of Meshech and Tubal. [2]I will turn you around and drag you along. I will bring you from the far north and send you against the mountains of Israel. ³Then I will strike your bow from your left hand and make your arrows drop from your right hand. ⁴On the mountains of Israel you will fall, you and all your troops and the nations with you. I will give you as food to all kinds of carrion birds and to the wild animals. ⁵You will fall in the open field, for I have spoken, declares the Sovereign LORD. ⁶I will send fire on Magog and on those who live in safety in the coastlands, and they will know that I am the LORD.

In this chapter we are given a second look at the battle introduced in chapter 38. Here we receive some additional details about the ongoing conflict between the Lord, his people, and their enemies. The concepts are repeated, but the descriptions of the participants and the results are expanded.

God was the one who promised to allow and even bring opposition against his people: "I will . . . send you against the mountains of Israel." Yet that same Lord has assured us that the very gates of hell will not overcome his church. He will oppose those who rise against his redeemed; he will disarm them; and in the end he will inflict on them a humiliating defeat.

⁷" 'I will make known my holy name among my people Israel. I will no longer let my holy name be profaned, and the nations will know that I the LORD am the Holy One in Israel. ⁸It is coming! It will surely take place, declares the Sovereign LORD. This is the day I have spoken of.

The Lord's conquest of his people's enemies would indicate to everyone that he is not to be mocked. Unbelievers could no longer ridicule his power just because he had allowed his people to be attacked or taken captive.

Although the Lord's victory over Gog is described here as a one-time occurrence, it has in fact been a recurring phenomenon in the history of God's redeemed. At the same time this description of the day of the Lord certainly does point ahead to his final day of justice, the day which our New Testament knowledge has led us to call Judgment Day.

Who of us has not experienced the frustration of witnessing to Jesus Christ in a world that refuses to acknowledge him or even to listen to his message? This unhappy experience has led some Christians to question the validity of the gospel of Christ because of its apparently limited results. If not comforting, it is at least vindicating to remember at the end of the ages the Lord by force of circumstance will be acknowledged by all to be the ruler of all, just as he has claimed to be. The Lord Jesus declares, "For the Son of Man is going to come in his Father's glory with his angels, and then he will reward each person according to what he has done" (Matthew 16:27). When we remember this, we can overcome the desire for visible and measurable results from our gospel witness and get back to our God-given task of faithfully sharing the good news.

9" 'Then those who live in the towns of Israel will go out and use the weapons for fuel and burn them up — the small and large shields, the bows and arrows, the war clubs and spears. For seven years they will use them for fuel. 10They will not need to gather wood from the fields or cut it from the forests, because they will use the weapons for fuel. And they will plunder those who plundered them and loot those who looted them, declares the Sovereign LORD.

In figurative language God gave the prophet and his readers some idea of how numerous the enemy was who had threatened God's people, and how complete was his destruction. His weapons would provide a seven-year supply of firewood for God's people.

230

11" 'On that day I will give Gog a burial place in Israel, in the valley of those who travel east toward the Sea. It will block the way of travelers, because Gog and all his hordes will be buried there. So it will be called the Valley of Hamon Gog.

Down through the centuries of church history those who have risen against God's people and gone down to defeat have been numerous. God here predicts that there will be so many of them that if their corpses were all buried in one valley they would fill the valley and block the traveler's way.

12" 'For seven months the house of Israel will be burying them in order to cleanse the land. 13All the people of the land will bury them, and the day I am glorified will be a memorable day for them, declares the Sovereign LORD.
14" 'Men will be regularly employed to cleanse the land. Some will go throughout the land and, in addition to them, others will bury those that remain on the ground. At the end of the seven months they will begin their search. 15As they go through the land and one of them sees a human bone, he will set up a marker beside it until the gravediggers have buried it in the Valley of Hamon Gog. 16(Also a town called Hamonah will be there.) And so they will cleanse the land.'

There would be so many enemies of the Lord and his people that it would take more than seven months to find all the dead and bury them, in order to rid the land of the ceremonial defilement which unburied dead bodies caused. And even after that time, God's people would still need to search for corpses hidden here and there! As mentioned earlier, Ezekiel's use of seven may be figurative. It may point to the complete outpouring of God's wrath. God's enemies in this world are many. The Lord is aware of this. And he will judge them all.

¹⁷"Son of man, this is what the Sovereign LORD says: Call out to every kind of bird and all the wild animals: 'Assemble and come together from all around to the sacrifice I am preparing for you, the great sacrifice on the mountains of Israel. There you will eat flesh and drink blood. ¹⁸You will eat the flesh of mighty men and drink the blood of the princes of the earth as if they were rams and lambs, goats and bulls — all of them fattened animals from Bashan. ¹⁹At the sacrifice I am preparing for you, you will eat fat till you are glutted and drink blood till you are drunk. ²⁰At my table you will eat your fill of horses and riders, mighty men and soldiers of every kind,' declares the Sovereign LORD.

Instead of dethroning God and annihilating his people, the enemies would end up becoming a sacrificial feast. The animals and birds are called in to rid the earth of the many dead bodies which would result from the slaughter. The picture of sacrifice and eating parts of the sacrifice is taken from Israel's sacrificial worship at the temple in Jerusalem. Bashan was grazing land east of the Sea of Galilee where cattle and sheep were fattened for sale. The language of these verses is stark, a strong picture of God's strong judgment upon unbelievers.

²¹"I will display my glory among the nations, and all the nations will see the punishment I inflict and the hand I lay upon them. ²²From that day forward the house of Israel will know that I am the LORD their God. ²³And the nations will know that the people of Israel went into exile for their sin, because they were unfaithful to me. So I hid my face from them and handed them over to their enemies, and they all fell by the sword. ²⁴I dealt with them according to their uncleanness and their offenses, and I hid my face from them.

After a preview of the dismal future awaiting God's enemies, we are brought back to the reality of the situation of

Ezekiel, the exiles and the Lord. The generalities about God, his people and his enemies are now applied to the hard fact of their present circumstances. The lesson to be gained from the Lord's defeat of his enemies was this: The reason the nation of Judah was exiled to Babylon was not that her God was too weak to handle the foreign powers. She had been exiled because she had been sinful, unfaithful to the Lord her God.

25"Therefore this is what the Sovereign LORD says: I will now bring Jacob back from captivity and will have compassion on all the people of Israel, and I will be zealous for my holy name. 26They will forget their shame and all the unfaithfulness they showed toward me when they lived in safety in their land with no one to make them afraid. 27When I have brought them back from the nations and have gathered them from the countries of their enemies, I will show myself holy through them in the sight of many nations. 28Then they will know that I am the LORD their God, for though I sent them into exile among the nations, I will gather them to their own land, not leaving any behind. 29I will no longer hide my face from them, for I will pour out my Spirit on the house of Israel, declares the Sovereign LORD."

God's shattering defeat of his enemies and his marvelous rescue of his people was not just a pious dream of the faithful. Nor was it something for which they would have to wait. It would begin "now," when the armies of Persian King Cyrus toppled mighty Babylon and freed the Jewish exiles.

Although Cyrus's edict would allow all the Jews to return to their homeland, not all did. Yet when the time came the Lord saw to it that no one was left behind in exile against his or her will. None of his special remnant would be left behind. Verse 29 gives us a one-sentence review of chapter 37; God would smile with favor on those who returned to the land of promise.

If chapters 38 and 39 of Ezekiel — bloodshed — were to be made into a movie, it would very likely get an R rating. It may at first seem strange that a portion of Scripture so filled with violence was given by the Lord to *comfort* his people. But after reading this section, it should not surprise us that the overwhelming majority of people in our world oppose the Lord and his people, because the Lord has already told us it would be like this. What comfort, then, does God intend by telling us these things? He is reminding us that this opposition to him isn't taking place in a world where he has lost control. God knew about it ahead of time and is allowing it. The ultimate comfort in these chapters is the preview he gives us of the complete defeat of the opposition. No matter how many they are, they are no match for our mighty and majestic Lord. After he has used the evil design of his enemies to refine his people, and to make people more eager to leave this sinful world and be with him forever, then God will crush all who oppose him.

It is also comforting to notice how God can prove himself Lord to the very people whom he allows to oppose him. His primary and dominant characteristic is his grace. He wants even those who oppose him and attack his people to know he is the Lord. In the end all will acknowledge the Sovereign Lord — whether they experience his grace or judgment.

Visions of Restoration
The New Temple

We now come to the final section of Ezekiel's prophecy. There was a very practical reason for the Lord to give Ezekiel a vision of a new temple at this time. Ezekiel was confidently expecting a return from exile. He wanted his fellow exiles to understand and believe this. He wanted to help them share the same hope and expectations which he had.

The year was 572 B.C. The once-beautiful temple in Jerusalem had lain in ruins for fourteen years. To many a Jew it began to look like the temple would remain a pile of ruins. At that time God gave Ezekiel a vision, the details of which cover the final nine chapters of his book. In Ezekiel's vision an angel, who had previously led Ezekiel on a tour of the doomed city (chapters 8-11), led him about the new Jerusalem.

These nine chapters confront us with the most difficult problem of interpretation posed by the book of Ezekiel. Some have understood the chapters *literally*. They see in them a blueprint according to which the exiles were to build their temple after returning to Jerusalem.

Luther and the reformers preferred a *symbolic* interpretation of chapters 40-48. According to this view, what God would do for the exiled Israelites in bringing them back from captivity and reestablishing them in their ancient homeland was a pledge of a much greater deliverance God would effect through the promised Savior. In 37:26,27 God had promised: "I will put my sanctuary among them forever. My dwelling place will be with them." This promise received a partial fulfillment when the returning exiles built their sanctuary in Jerusalem. But through Jesus Christ God has truly come to dwell among his people (chapter 43), so that they are restored to communion with him. As a result they can bring sacrifices pleasing to him (chapters 44-46). And assured of his abiding presence (48:35) they will forever live in security. Read Revelation 21 and compare it to Ezekiel 40 and it will be clear that St. John uses some of Ezekiel's pictures to describe God's redeemed people in heaven. For example, John states, "He carried me away in the Spirit to a mountain great and high, and showed me the Holy

City, Jerusalem" (Revelation 21:10). Ezekiel writes, "In visions of God he took me to the land of Israel and set me on a very high mountain, on whose south side were some buildings that looked like a city" (Ezekiel 40:2).

In describing the future covenant which he would make with the world in Jesus Christ, God makes liberal use of the terms of his old covenant once made with ancient Israel at Mt. Sinai:

> the place of worship (chapters 40-43);
> the forms of worship (44-46);
> the locale in the promised land (47,48).

Because of the symbolism, symmetry and futurism in this description, it becomes obvious this is not merely a physical description. Rather, Ezekiel here describes some general principles about the relationship between God and his people. For example, the temple plans indicate that holiness must be separated from unrighteousness; God's designs for people are perfect; the Lord is forever present among his people; he continues to dispense blessings; his people function in an orderly way as they serve him in their worship lives. While such truths are contained in the temple description, we will want to beware of finding exact parallels between every detail recorded here and reality.

The vision of the new temple fits well with the many other visions Ezekiel had seen and recorded in his book. All of them were presented in terms of something which happened in Israel's past and which now was recurring in somewhat changed form. The point is not that the outward form (of priesthood, or sacrifice or whatever) would occur again. The point is that the essential character or circumstances would repeat. Some of the details in the vision give us the unmistakable hint that we are dealing here with an ideal rather than with something literal. The visionary sizes of the temple courts, city and surrounding land are improbable, if not impossible, when compared to the actual land area available in Jerusalem. To cite just a single example. According to 45:1, the sacred district to be set aside for the sanctuary was an area roughly five by seven *miles*. By contrast, at Christ's time the temple area was 500 *yards* square.

Although the exiles built only a small replica of Solomon's temple when they returned, and although they did not build Ezekiel's temple with its ideal dimensions, the temple described in Ezekiel's vision served the same purpose as Solomon's temple had and as the new one would. Ezekiel's building dimensions and worship specifications were visual reminders of God's presence among his people.

The almost exhausting detail given by Ezekiel doesn't contradict the view that this is a presentation of an ideal rather than a physical building. The reader will remember that Ezekiel went into similar detail about Egypt (chapters 29-32), the cooking pot (24), the infant (16) and the sin bearing (18). Those were all word pictures, not historical sequences.

As you read the verses of these chapters, it will be helpful if you compare the text with the diagrams.

The New Temple Area

40 In the twenty-fifth year of our exile, at the beginning of the year, on the tenth of the month, in the fourteenth year after the fall of the city — on that very day the hand of the LORD was upon me and he took me there. ²In visions of God he took me to the land of Israel and set me on a very high mountain, on whose south side were some buildings that looked like a city. ³He took me there, and I saw a man whose appearance was like bronze; he was standing in the gateway with a linen cord and a measuring rod

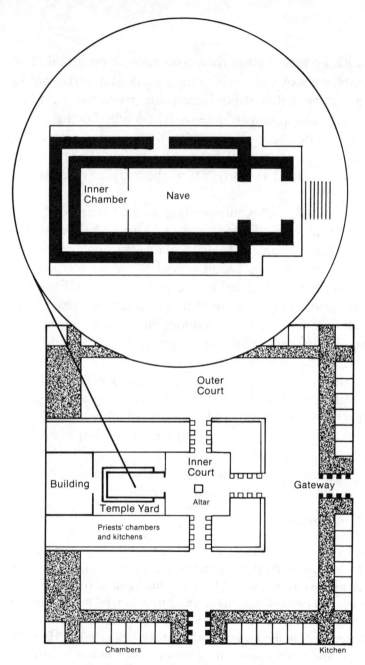

Ezekiel's temple and surrounding area

in his hand. ⁴This man said to me, "Son of man, look with your eyes and hear with your ears and pay attention to everything I am going to show you, for that is why you have been brought here. Tell the house of Israel everything you see."

The year of this vision was 572 B.C. As Ezekiel began his guided tour of the visionary temple, he stated that it looked like a city. The size of the structure reminds us the Lord is a mighty fortress. The bronze in verse 3 might be an indication of the strength of the angelic being leading Ezekiel through the temple. He carried a linen cord, used for measuring longer distances, and a rod for shorter distances.

It's important for us to note what Ezekiel's assignment was. He was not told to build this temple (it was already complete!) but to walk through it, to look, to listen, to pay attention, and then to describe what he saw.

The East Gate to the Outer Court

⁵I saw a wall completely surrounding the temple area. The length of the measuring rod in the man's hand was six long cubits, each of which was a cubit and a handbreadth. He measured the wall; it was one measuring rod thick and one rod high.
⁶Then he went to the gate facing east. He climbed its steps and measured the threshold of the gate; it was one rod deep. ⁷The alcoves for the guards were one rod long and one rod wide, and the projecting walls between the alcoves were five cubits thick. And the threshold of the gate next to the portico facing the temple was one rod deep.
⁸Then he measured the portico of the gateway; ⁹it was eight cubits deep and its jambs were two cubits thick. The portico of the gateway faced the temple.
¹⁰Inside the east gate were three alcoves on each side; the three had the same measurements, and the faces of the projecting walls on each side had the same measurements. ¹¹Then he measured the width of the entrance to the gateway; it was ten cubits and its

length was thirteen cubits. ¹²In front of each alcove was a wall one cubit high, and the alcoves were six cubits square. ¹³Then he measured the gateway from the top of the rear wall of one alcove to the top of the opposite one; the distance was twenty-five cubits from one parapet opening to the opposite one. ¹⁴He measured along the faces of the projecting walls all around the inside of the gateway — sixty cubits. The measurement was up to the portico facing the courtyard. ¹⁵The distance from the entrance of the gateway to the far end of its portico was fifty cubits. ¹⁶The alcoves and the projecting walls inside the gateway were surmounted by narrow parapet openings all around, as was the portico; the openings all around faced inward. The faces of the projecting walls were decorated with palm trees.

Ezekiel's guided tour of the temple area began in the outer court which surrounded the sanctuary; the sanctuary itself will be described in chapter 41. The angel's measuring rod was 10.5 feet long. (The common cubit was about a foot and a half long, the handbreadth about three inches long.) The thickness and height of the wall might indicate the separateness of the Lord from the unholy. The steps raised the outer court above the level of the surrounding land. The height of the platform on which the temple was built made people look up to it and to the Lord. The guards were responsible for keeping order and taking care of the grounds.

The separation between God and what is sinful is not absolute. God himself has provided the gateways through which sinful human beings can approach him. This is true both in the physical sense, going into the temple through the gateways, and in the spiritual sense, going into the Lord's presence through Jesus, the doorway to eternal life. The decorative palm trees were symbols of beauty, fruitfulness, salvation and glory.

The Outer Court

¹⁷Then he brought me into the outer court. There I saw some rooms and a pavement that had been constructed all around the court; there were thirty rooms along the pavement. ¹⁸It abutted the sides of the gateways and was as wide as they were long; this was the lower pavement. ¹⁹Then he measured the distance from the inside of the lower gateway to the outside of the inner court; it was a hundred cubits on the east side as well as on the north.

The North Gate

²⁰Then he measured the length and width of the gate facing north, leading into the outer court. ²¹Its alcoves — three on each side — its projecting walls and its portico had the same measurements as those of the first gateway. It was fifty cubits long and twenty-five cubits wide. ²²Its openings, its portico and its palm tree decorations had the same measurements as those of the gate facing east. Seven steps led up to it, with its portico opposite them. ²³There was a gate to the inner court facing the north gate, just as there was on the east. He measured from one gate to the opposite one; it was a hundred cubits.

The South Gate

²⁴Then he led me to the south side and I saw a gate facing south. He measured its jambs and its portico, and they had the same measurements as the others. ²⁵The gateway and its portico had narrow openings all around, like the openings of the others. It was fifty cubits long and twenty-five cubits wide. ²⁶Seven steps led up to it, with its portico opposite them; it had palm tree decorations on the faces of the projecting walls on each side. ²⁷The inner court also had a gate facing south, and he measured from this gate to the outer gate on the south side; it was a hundred cubits.

Gates to the Inner Court

²⁸Then he brought me into the inner court through the south gate, and he measured the south gate; it had the same measure-

ments as the others. ²⁹Its alcoves, its projecting walls and its portico had the same measurements as the others. The gateway and its portico had openings all around. It was fifty cubits long and twenty-five cubits wide. ³⁰(The porticoes of the gateways around the inner court were twenty-five cubits wide and five cubits deep.) ³¹Its portico faced the outer court; palm trees decorated its jambs and eight steps led up to it.

³²Then he brought me to the inner court on the east side, and he measured the gateway; it had the same measurements as the others. ³³Its alcoves, its projecting walls and its portico had the same measurements as the others. The gateway and its portico had openings all around. It was fifty cubits long and twenty-five cubits wide. ³⁴Its portico faced the outer court; palm trees decorated the jambs on either side, and eight steps led up to it.

³⁵Then he brought me to the north gate and measured it. It had the same measurements as the others, ³⁶as did its alcoves, its projecting walls and its portico, and it had openings all around. It was fifty cubits long and twenty-five cubits wide. ³⁷Its portico faced the outer court; palm trees decorated the jambs on either side, and eight steps led up to it.

The Rooms for Preparing Sacrifices

³⁸A room with a doorway was by the portico in each of the inner gateways, where the burnt offerings were washed. ³⁹In the portico of the gateway were two tables on each side, on which the burnt offerings, sin offerings and guilt offerings were slaughtered. ⁴⁰By the outside wall of the portico of the gateway, near the steps at the entrance to the north gateway were two tables, and on the other side of the steps were two tables. ⁴¹So there were four tables on one side of the gateway and four on the other — eight tables in all — on which the sacrifices were slaughtered. ⁴²There were also four tables of dressed stone for the burnt offerings, each a cubit and a half long, a cubit and a half wide and a cubit high. On them were placed the utensils for slaughtering the burnt offerings and the other sacrifices. ⁴³And double-pronged hooks, each a hand-

breadth long, were attached to the wall all around. The tables were for the flesh of the offerings.

The burnt offering was by far the most frequently offered blood sacrifice in ancient Israel. It was the only sacrifice in which the entire animal was offered up on the altar. As such it symbolized the worshiper's total dedication to God. The Apostle Paul alluded to this when he wrote, "I urge you . . . to offer your bodies as living sacrifices"(Romans 12:1). The special emphasis of the sin offering (Leviticus 4) was confession and absolution. The special emphasis of the guilt offering (Leviticus 5:14ff) was restitution to the one whom the worshiper had wronged.

Rooms for the Priests

⁴⁴Outside the inner gate, within the inner court, were two rooms, one at the side of the north gate and facing south, and another at the side of the south gate and facing north. ⁴⁵He said to me, "The room facing south is for the priests who have charge of the temple, ⁴⁶and the room facing north is for the priests who have charge of the altar. These are the sons of Zadok, who are the only Levites who may draw near to the LORD to minister before him."
⁴⁷Then he measured the court: It was square — a hundred cubits long and a hundred cubits wide. And the altar was in front of the temple.

Zadok, mentioned in verse 46, was the priest who had remained faithful to David (2 Samuel 15:24). These were the preparation rooms for the priests.

The Temple

⁴⁸He brought me to the portico of the temple and measured the jambs of the portico; they were five cubits wide on either side. The width of the entrance was fourteen cubits and its projecting walls

were three cubits wide on either side. ⁴⁹The portico was twenty cubits wide, and twelve cubits from front to back. It was reached by a flight of stairs, and there were pillars on each side of the jambs.

41 Then the man brought me to the outer sanctuary and measured the jambs; the width of the jambs was six cubits on each side. ²The entrance was ten cubits wide, and the projecting walls on each side of it were five cubits wide. He also measured the outer sanctuary; it was forty cubits long and twenty cubits wide.

³Then he went into the inner sanctuary and measured the jambs of the entrance; each was two cubits wide. The entrance was six cubits wide, and the projecting walls on each side of it were seven cubits wide. ⁴And he measured the length of the inner sanctuary; it was twenty cubits, and its width was twenty cubits across the end of the outer sanctuary. He said to me, "This is the Most Holy Place."

⁵Then he measured the wall of the temple; it was six cubits thick, and each side room around the temple was four cubits wide. ⁶The side rooms were on three levels, one above another, thirty on each level. There were ledges all around the wall of the temple to serve as supports for the side rooms, so that the supports were not inserted into the wall of the temple. ⁷The side rooms all around the temple were wider at each successive level. The structure surrounding the temple was built in ascending stages, so that the rooms widened as one went upward. A stairway went up from the lowest floor to the top floor through the middle floor.

⁸I saw that the temple had a raised base all around it, forming the foundation of the side rooms. It was the length of the rod, six long cubits. ⁹The outer wall of the side rooms was five cubits thick. The open area between the side rooms of the temple ¹⁰and the ⌊priests'⌋ rooms was twenty cubits wide all around the temple. ¹¹There were entrances to the side rooms from the open area, one on the north and another on the south; and the base adjoining the open area was five cubits wide all around.

¹²The building facing the temple courtyard on the west side was seventy cubits wide. The wall of the building was five cubits thick all around, and its length was ninety cubits.

¹³Then he measured the temple; it was a hundred cubits long, and the temple courtyard and the building with its walls were also a hundred cubits long. ¹⁴The width of the temple courtyard on the east, including the front of the temple, was a hundred cubits.

¹⁵Then he measured the length of the building facing the courtyard at the rear of the temple, including its galleries on each side; it was a hundred cubits.

The outer sanctuary, the inner sanctuary and the portico facing the court, ¹⁶as well as the thresholds and the narrow windows and galleries around the three of them — everything beyond and including the threshold was covered with wood. The floor, the wall up to the windows, and the windows were covered. ¹⁷In the space above the outside of the entrance to the inner sanctuary and on the walls at regular intervals all around the inner and outer sanctuary ¹⁸were carved cherubim and palm trees. Palm trees alternated with cherubim. Each cherub had two faces: ¹⁹the face of a man toward the palm tree on one side and the face of a lion toward the palm tree on the other. They were carved all around the whole temple. ²⁰From the floor to the area above the entrance, cherubim and palm trees were carved on the wall of the outer sanctuary.

²¹The outer sanctuary had a rectangular doorframe, and the one at the front of the Most Holy Place was similar. ²²There was a wooden altar three cubits high and two cubits square; its corners, its base and its sides were of wood. The man said to me, "This is the table that is before the LORD." ²³Both the outer sanctuary and the Most Holy Place had double doors. ²⁴Each door had two leaves — two hinged leaves for each door. ²⁵And on the doors of the outer sanctuary were carved cherubim and palm trees like those carved on the walls, and there was a wooden overhang on the front of the portico. ²⁶On the sidewalls of the portico were narrow windows with palm trees carved on each side. The side rooms of the temple also had overhangs.

The side rooms were probably depositories for gifts and for garments of the priests. Because the walls were two-dimensional, these cherubim (verse 18) did not have four faces as did those in chapter 1. The measurements of the temple (verses 13-15) exhibit a perfect symmetry.

From the outer courtyard Ezekiel's angelic guide led him to the outer sanctuary (verse 1), which we have come to know as the Holy Place. Ezekiel noted that the width of the jambs was nine feet, indicating an immense structure. When they came to the inner sanctuary (verse 3) known in the Old Testament as the Most Holy Place, only Ezekiel's guide entered. In Ezekiel's vision no mention is made of the ark of the covenant, presumably destroyed or deported to Babylon when Jerusalem fell.

Rooms for the Priests

42 Then the man led me northward into the outer court and brought me to the rooms opposite the temple courtyard and opposite the outer wall on the north side. ²The building whose door faced north was a hundred cubits long and fifty cubits wide. ³Both in the section twenty cubits from the inner court and in the section opposite the pavement of the outer court, gallery faced gallery at the three levels. ⁴In front of the rooms was an inner passageway ten cubits wide and a hundred cubits long. Their doors were on the north. ⁵Now the upper rooms were narrower, for the galleries took more space from them than from the rooms on the lower and middle floors of the building. ⁶The rooms on the third floor had no pillars, as the courts had; so they were smaller in floor space than those on the lower and middle floors. ⁷There was an outer wall parallel to the rooms and the outer court; it extended in front of the rooms for fifty cubits. ⁸While the row of rooms on the side next to the outer court was fifty cubits long, the row on the side nearest the sanctuary was a hundred cubits long. ⁹The lower rooms had an entrance on the east side as one enters them from the outer court.

¹⁰On the south side along the length of the wall of the outer court, adjoining the temple courtyard and opposite the outer wall, were rooms ¹¹with a passageway in front of them. These were like the rooms on the north; they had the same length and width, with similar exits and dimensions. Similar to the doorways on the north ¹²were the doorways of the rooms on the south. There was a doorway at the beginning of the passageway that was parallel to the corresponding wall extending eastward, by which one enters the rooms.

¹³Then he said to me, "The north and south rooms facing the temple courtyard are the priests' rooms, where the priests who approach the LORD will eat the most holy offerings. There they will put the most holy offerings — the grain offerings, the sin offerings and the guilt offerings — for the place is holy. ¹⁴Once the priests enter the holy precincts, they are not to go into the outer court until they leave behind the garments in which they minister, for these are holy. They are to put on other clothes before they go near the places that are for the people."

¹⁵When he had finished measuring what was inside the temple area, he led me out by the east gate and measured the area all around: ¹⁶He measured the east side with the measuring rod; it was five hundred cubits. ¹⁷He measured the north side; it was five hundred cubits by the measuring rod. ¹⁸He measured the south side; it was five hundred cubits by the measuring rod. ¹⁹Then he turned to the west side and measured; it was five hundred cubits by the measuring rod. ²⁰So he measured the area on all four sides. It had a wall around it, five hundred cubits long and five hundred cubits wide, to separate the holy from the common.

After viewing the sanctuary, Ezekiel was again led outside for one final survey of the temple area.

Inside the walled enclosure, facing the temple yard, was a series of rooms built in three stories. These rooms were for the priests who officiated at the altar. Here they would "eat the most holy offerings," those portions of the sacrificial animals which the officiating priest and his family were allowed to eat. In these rooms the priests would also remove the garments in which they had approached the altar and would put on street clothes. The action of changing clothes (verses 13,14) is another obvious symbol of the difference between the holy God and sinful men.

The sanctuary proper which Ezekiel saw in his vision was 100 cubits (150 feet) square. The entire temple area also formed a perfect square 500 cubits (750 feet) on a side. Again we scc perfect symmetry, not by accident but by divine design.

The Glory Returns to the Temple

43 **Then the man brought me to the gate facing east, ²and I saw the glory of the God of Israel coming from the east. His voice was like the roar of rushing waters, and the land was radiant with his glory. ³The vision I saw was like the vision I had seen when he came to destroy the city and like the visions I had seen by the Kebar River, and I fell facedown. ⁴The glory of the Lord entered the temple through the gate facing east. ⁵Then the Spirit lifted me up and brought me into the inner court, and the glory of the Lord filled the temple.**

This chapter marks the high point of chapters 40-48. The temple Ezekiel had witnessed and described had been prepared for this event: the return of "the glory of the Lord."

On two previous occasions the glory of the Lord had appeared to Ezekiel. He had seen it the first time when he was called (1:1-28; 3:23). He saw it again when God abandoned and destroyed the city of Jerusalem (8:4; 10:18-22; 11:22-24). The sound (2) was the same, "like the roar of rushing waters" (1:24). The appearance was also the same (1:4). The glory of the Lord was even returning from the east, the direction to which it had previously departed (11:23). This visible appearance of God's glory reentered through the east gate because it was directly in line with the temple entrance.

To Ezekiel all this repetition was a reminder of God's unchangeableness. In spite of all that had happened to the Jewish nation, in spite of all the changes in the political structures of the world powers, the same Lord was still in charge who had given Ezekiel the original vision twenty years earlier. This time the vision reminded Ezekiel that the Lord had never lost his desire to be among his people. He had never lost sight of the goal of again being more obviously among his people.

The fact that we abandon the Lord doesn't mean that he automatically turns off his grace. He still wants to be our God and wants us to be his people. Just because he must chastise us for our sins, he doesn't wish evil upon us. Unless he disciplines us, he might not turn us around. And then he wouldn't be able to take up residence in our hearts and lives. After God's discipline has done its work and we have been led to repentance, we again are enveloped in the glory of God's grace. Sometimes it seems God has changed from an angry judge to a gracious God. We need to realize he doesn't change. Rather he changes us.

6While the man was standing beside me, I heard someone speaking to me from inside the temple. 7He said: "Son of man, this is the place of my throne and the place for the soles of my feet. This is where I will live among the Israelites forever. The house of Israel will never again defile my holy name — neither they nor their kings — by their prostitution and the lifeless idols of their kings at their high places. 8When they placed their threshold next to my threshold and their doorposts beside my doorposts, with only a wall between me and them, they defiled my holy name by their detestable practices. So I destroyed them in my anger. 9Now let them put away from me their prostitution and the lifeless idols of their kings, and I will live among them forever.

¹⁰"Son of man, describe the temple to the people of Israel, that they may be ashamed of their sins. Let them consider the plan, ¹¹and if they are ashamed of all they have done, make known to them the design of the temple — its arrangement, its exits and entrances — its whole design and all its regulations and laws. Write these down before them so that they may be faithful to its design and follow all its regulations.

¹²"This is the law of the temple: All the surrounding area on top of the mountain will be most holy. Such is the law of the temple.

The Lord personally dedicated this ideal temple. In the past the temple had been defiled by the religious prostitution that was allowed in the land (1 Kings 14:24) and by the idolatry which the kings had often introduced and led (1 Kings 21:25,26). Such actions had caused the Lord to send his people into exile. God wanted these practices to be abandoned, so he could take up residence with these people forever.

The perfection of the temple described in both the previous and the succeeding chapters was to serve two purposes. It should have reminded them of their sins, their failure to properly worship their perfect Lord. It should also have led them to keep this ideal picture of worship before them as a goal toward which to strive in the future. Then they might not fall away again from the Lord. And he would not have to depart from them again. The Lord who inhabited the temple was holy. Everything related to the temple was perfect. The ideal for the worshipers was perfection, too.

Did this vision of the perfect temple call Israel to repentance and motivate them to strive for perfection? During the bitter years of the exile, the spiritual life of the remnant of believers reached a high point. Since they had no temple, it was impossible for them in their worship to focus their attention on an earthly place of worship. The emphasis had to be on the personal relationship between redeemed sinners and their gracious God. This should always have been the focus, even when there was a physical temple. But it had been, and it would be, so easy to zero in on the outward temple and the activities connected with it.

When their political situation changed and the exiles were allowed to return, those who did return took back a revitalized spirituality as well as a desire to institute a purified worship life. They had listened to Ezekiel. But after some time back home with a rebuilt temple, once again outward, meaningless worship activity took over. This was the situation at the time of Jesus. The house again was left desolate. God couldn't remain a permanent resident among them even though that was his wish expressed through Ezekiel's vision.

God's perfection has two sides in its application to us. It serves as a mirror. When we compare our performance with his ideal, we are led to acknowledge our sinfulness. This is necessary. We need to acknowledge our sinfulness, be ashamed of our selfishness, and recognize our wretched position under God's anger. Only then can we be led to repent and turn to the Lord for help and forgiveness.

The Lord's perfection does more than condemn. It also is our guide. When we are looking for a way to thank the Lord for all his blessings, we turn to his perfection as our ideal. We ask him to strengthen us so that we might live more and more according to his ideal. We ask his strength to make our lives into more and more perfect worship of him. When every word, action and thought worships him, when we give glory to him as we eat and drink and in whatever else we do, we are striving after the perfection which is our goal. Even with his help we couldn't strive after perfection, unless he first described this goal to us.

The Altar

¹³"These are the measurements of the altar in long cubits, that cubit being a cubit and a handbreadth: Its gutter is a cubit deep and a cubit wide, with a rim of one span around the edge. And this is the height of the altar: ¹⁴From the gutter on the ground up to the lower ledge it is two cubits high and a cubit wide, and from the smaller ledge up to the larger ledge it is four cubits high and a cubit wide. ¹⁵The altar hearth is four cubits high, and four horns project upward from the hearth. ¹⁶The altar hearth is square, twelve cubits long and twelve cubits wide. ¹⁷The upper ledge also is square, fourteen cubits long and fourteen cubits wide, with a rim of half a cubit and a gutter of a cubit all around. The steps of the altar face east."

The altar, which stood at the geometric center of the temple area, seems to have been the most prominent article in this temple, most likely because the ark of the covenant had been lost in the destruction of Jerusalem. No longer could the ark be regarded as the personal seat of the Lord. It wasn't there anymore. A replacement would be no good. The horns of the altar were probably symbols of God's power as it is directed to all four corners of the earth. The "span" mentioned in verse 13 was a measurement of about nine inches.

The primary piece of symbolism in our houses of worship is also a place of sacrifice. The cross, so prominent in church architecture, hangs or rests in front of our worship locations as a constant reminder of the sacrifice of Jesus which took away the guilt and punishment of our sins. It is a reminder that the Lord demanded a life to pay for our sins. That was also the purpose of the altar and the sacrifices in the Old Testament temples. The altar reminded Old Testament worshipers of the need for a sacrifice of a life for sin. In their case it pointed to a special life to be sacrificed.

In our case the cross points to a special, holy life which has been sacrificed.

Sometimes we miss the picturesque teaching functions of much of the symbolism around us in our churches because we don't bother with it. That is our loss. Even the horns on the altar had a meaning for the Old Testament worshiper.

18Then he said to me, "Son of man, this is what the Sovereign LORD says: These will be the regulations for sacrificing burnt offerings and sprinkling blood upon the altar when it is built: 19You are to give a young bull as a sin offering to the priests, who are Levites, of the family of Zadok, who come near to minister before me, declares the Sovereign LORD. 20You are to take some of its blood and put it on the four horns of the altar and on the four corners of the upper ledge and all around the rim, and so purify the altar and make atonement for it. 21You are to take the bull for the sin offering and burn it in the designated part of the temple area outside the sanctuary.

The altar had to be purified with blood so it might be acceptable to God. This was a reminder to the worshipers that sin had polluted everything in the world. Everything needed to be bought back with a life so it might be pleasing to God. The blood was a symbol of the life sacrificed. Putting blood on the altar symbolized that this altar was now set apart for use in the worship of the Lord.

Only the descendants of Zadok were allowed to function at the altar. The rest of the descendants of the priestly tribe were forbidden to be involved in this work because of their past idolatrous practices (44:10-14), although they were allowed to function as helpers in the temple. Here we see another indication that the goal of this idealized worship was perfection.

Sadly, in our New Testament freedom and our easy-does-it approach to worship, we can easily lose sight of the tremendous cost Christ paid to make our relationship with God possible. It wasn't quite as easy for the Old Testament worshiper to forget. Everywhere he looked there was a reminder that a life had to be given to keep him in his position as a child of God. Our worship services should also remind us, "The only reason you can be talking to God as your dear Father is that a life was given for you." Such reminders lead us to appreciate what God has done for us in Christ. Our New Testament freedom to approach God in Christ is a source of joy which we never want to de-emphasize. Yet the danger for Christians is to forget about all the barriers which Christ had to remove so we can enjoy direct access to the heart and to the home of the heavenly Father. The danger of taking our spiritual blessings for granted is always present.

22"On the second day you are to offer a male goat without defect for a sin offering, and the altar is to be purified as it was purified with the bull. 23When you have finished purifying it, you are to offer a young bull and a ram from the flock, both without defect. 24You are to offer them before the LORD, and the priests are to sprinkle salt on them and sacrifice them as a burnt offering to the LORD.

In addition to the sin offering, a burnt offering (Leviticus 1:6-9) was to be given. Again the emphasis was on the necessary perfection of the offering; the sacrificial animal could have no defects. The burnt offering was the only one in which the entire animal was burned. This offering was more of a gift to the Lord than any of the others, since nothing from it was eaten by the worshipers or the priests. With this offering the worshiper said, "Lord, we want to give our entire lives to you just as we are burning this entire animal which has no defect. In the same way we want to give you lives of perfect worship. We want our lives to be one continuous act of worship to you, just as this burnt offering is being continually burned before you."

The addition of some salt to the sacrifice was an additional emphasis. Salt enabled food to resist decay, so it would not spoil. The addition of salt to the Israelites' sacrifice indicated that the commitment of the people to the Lord needed to have the strength to overcome impurity of life, hypocrisy of practice, and anything else which might make them or their worship unacceptable in the eyes of the Lord.

We sometimes feel sorry for the Old Testament worshipers because they had to rest their faith on promises, whereas we have the reality of the fulfillment of those promises in the life and death of Jesus Christ. But because of our focus on the realities, we have lost much of the picturesque. Dealing with the abstractions of faith and spirituality, we tend to miss much because the picturesque has been removed. The Israelite could wander into the temple at any time of the day and see a visual expression of his relationship to the Lord and a reminder of his commitment to the Lord being carried out in front of his eyes. We can't do that. As we salt our food we aren't reminded, as he was, of the strength we need to remain in God's family. If the Old Testament worshiper would observe our colorless, symbol-less, and often sterile approach to life and worship, he might very well feel just as sorry for us as we often feel for him.

25"For seven days you are to provide a male goat daily for a sin offering; you are also to provide a young bull and a ram from the flock, both without defect. 26For seven days they are to make atonement for the altar and cleanse it; thus they will dedicate it. 27At the end of these days, from the eighth day on, the priests are to present your burnt offerings and fellowship offerings on the altar. Then I will accept you, declares the Sovereign LORD."

After the altar was dedicated, the burnt and fellowship offerings could be sacrificed on a regular basis. The fellowship offering (Leviticus 7:11-21) had a slightly different connotation from the others. After the fat parts of the animal were burned, the breast and the right thigh were given to the priest's family. The remaining meat was roasted and eaten by the offerers in a festival banquet together with the priest as God's representative. This expressed the happy fellowship between the Lord and the offerers. Part of the animal was eaten by the Lord in fire, part by the family of the priest, and part by the worshipers at the meal. They were all joining in a family meal together.

Any reminder in our lives that God is sharing our lives with us is doing what the fellowship offering and meal did for the Old Testament worshiper. The closeness with our Lord which we have in Christ needs to be nurtured and strengthened constantly, as the fellowship meal did for the Old Testament believer. Unless the bond between us and the Savior is tightened, Satan will see to it that it loosens.

Worship and Service

The Prince, the Levites, the Priests

44 **Then the man brought me back to the outer gate of the sanctuary, the one facing east, and it was shut. ²The LORD said to me, "This gate is to remain shut. It must not be opened; no one may enter through it. It is to remain shut because the LORD, the God of Israel, has entered through it. ³The prince himself is the only one who may sit inside the gateway to eat in the presence of the LORD. He is to enter by way of the portico of the gateway and go out the same way."**

After the Lord had returned through the east gate (43:4), it was closed as a sign of reverence. The closed door made two other statements. First, the Lord would not again leave his people and, second, the Lord is the only one who can open the door of access to himself. Any sinner who tries to gain access to God on his own terms is doomed to eternal disappointment. Although the prince was given the special privilege of eating the fellowship meal inside the gate, he would not have any priestly function.

⁴Then the man brought me by way of the north gate to the front of the temple. I looked and saw the glory of the LORD filling the temple of the LORD, and I fell facedown.

⁵The LORD said to me, "Son of man, look carefully, listen closely and give attention to everything I tell you concerning all the regulations regarding the temple of the LORD. Give attention to the entrance of the temple and all the exits of the sanctuary. ⁶Say to the rebellious house of Israel, 'This is what the Sovereign LORD says: Enough of your detestable practices, O house of Israel! ⁷In addition to all your other detestable practices, you brought foreigners uncircumcised in heart and flesh into my sanctuary, desecrating my temple while you offered me food, fat and blood and you broke my covenant. ⁸Instead of carrying out your duty in regard to my holy things, you put others in charge of my sanctuary. ⁹This is what the Sovereign LORD says: No foreigner uncircumcised in heart and flesh is to enter my sanctuary, not even the foreigners who live among the Israelites.

Verse 4 seems to be a reminder of the occurrence recorded in 43:1-5. Apparently Israel's officials had turned over to hired people the hard work of chopping and stacking wood for the sacrifices, cleaning ashes from the altar, and carrying sides of beef. Instead of looking upon these temple activities as a privilege, an expression of their covenant relationship with the Lord, the priests didn't want to bother themselves. But the Lord wanted only those who were part of his covenant to lead in the outward expression of the covenant relationship, the worship at the temple. The "uncircumcised in heart and flesh," those spiritually unfit, were not to approach the altar.

In our congregational life, which focuses to a large degree on our public worship, there are aspects which are pretty ordinary and perhaps even menial. Maintaining the worship facility, preparing materials for education and worship, reciting and teaching truths we want children to learn are activities that don't seem all that glamorous. We tend to want other people to do these supposedly menial, support tasks. Personally we prefer to be in leadership roles, doing exciting things for the Lord. But every task we do for the Lord in our congregational life and in our personal life is our side of the covenant relationship. There is nothing menial about *any* service done to the Lord. Roles differ, but the importance of the service to the Lord doesn't. When we realize that, we won't be looking for someone else to hire to do the Lord's work. It will be a privilege to chop and stack the wood. Cleaning out yesterday's ashes and carrying sides of beef to the Lord's altar will have a glow and a glamor all their own.

[10] 'The Levites who went far from me when Israel went astray and who wandered from me after their idols must bear the consequences of their sin. [11] They may serve in my sanctuary, having charge of the gates of the temple and serving in it; they may slaughter the burnt offerings and sacrifices for the people and stand before the people and serve them. [12] But because they served them in the presence of their idols and made the house of Israel fall into sin, therefore I have sworn with uplifted hand that they must bear the consequences of their sin, declares the Sovereign LORD. [13] They are not to come near to serve me as priests or come near any of my holy things or my most holy offerings; they must bear the shame of their detestable practices. [14] Yet I will put them in charge of the duties of the temple and all the work that is to be done in it.

15" 'But the priests, who are Levites and descendants of Zadok and who faithfully carried out the duties of my sanctuary when the Israelites went astray from me, are to come near to minister before me; they are to stand before me to offer sacrifices of fat and blood, declares the Sovereign LORD. 16They alone are to enter my sanctuary; they alone are to come near my table to minister before me and perform my service.

God wanted the priests to be men who hadn't abandoned him and worshiped other gods. Those who had abandoned him could still serve him, but not in the roles they had filled before. God wants only those in leadership roles who have stood firm in the past and are willing to stand firm again.

One of the primary characteristics God stresses for his leaders of every age if faithfulness. Faithfulness to his Word very often demands standing firm against opposition. People who choose leaders often consider other characteristics more important than faithfulness. But charisma, eloquence, productivity, tact and all the others on the list are really worthless for a leader of God's people if he isn't faithful to the Lord and his Word.

17" 'When they enter the gates of the inner court, they are to wear linen clothes; they must not wear any woolen garment while ministering at the gates of the inner court or inside the temple. 18They are to wear linen turbans on their heads and linen undergarments around their waists. They must not wear anything that makes them perspire. 19When they go out into the outer court where the people are, they are to take off the clothes they have been ministering in and are to leave them in the sacred rooms, and put on other clothes, so that they do not consecrate the people by means of their garments.

Only what was clean could enter the inner court surrounding the sanctuary. A perspiring priest was considered unclean, so he was to wear lightweight linen garments to prevent that. The removal of priestly clothes before contact with the people was another indication of the distinction God wanted to make between the holy and the common.

In congregations of Christians where ceremony is at a minimum, the danger is always present of handling things dedicated to the Lord with little or no respect. We know, of course, that symbols of the Lord are only symbols. But when a person's attitude toward things dedicated to the worship of the Lord doesn't seem to be respectful, he will be tempted to transfer that lack of respect to the Lord himself.

20" 'They must not shave their heads or let their hair grow long, but they are to keep the hair of their heads trimmed. 21No priest is to drink wine when he enters the inner court. 22They must not marry widows or divorced women; they may marry only virgins of Israelite descent or widows of priests. 23They are to teach my people the difference between the holy and the common and show them how to distinguish between the unclean and the clean.

The regulation about hair must have been a reaction to a pagan custom. Moderation is urged. There was no place for drunken or even slightly "high" priests in the service of the Lord. The priests were to remain married to people of their own nation. Their personal lives were to be pictures of what the Lord considered to be pure and holy.

Pastors and congregational leaders today are not under the regulations described by Ezekiel. For example, they are free to marry widows. Nevertheless, they and their families realize that their positions put them into glass houses. God wants them to be models for the rest of his people, to practice moderation, not swinging from one extreme to the other. They are to be examples of what is holy and statements against what is not. This is a very heavy responsibility, and no one perfectly fulfills it. Yet it is also a tremendous privilege. Our actions are the best teaching device we have.

24" 'In any dispute, the priests are to serve as judges and decide it according to my ordinances. They are to keep my laws and my decrees for all my appointed feasts, and they are to keep my Sabbaths holy.

The priests were to be the teachers and the judges. Since they knew God's ordinances they were to apply their knowledge to the daily life of the people.

Christians who have a working knowledge of God's will can well serve as resource people for the difficulties of others. The Lord grants wisdom regarding his will, because he wants us to use it to help others through their problems.

25" 'A priest must not defile himself by going near a dead person; however, if the dead person was his father or mother, son or daughter, brother or unmarried sister, then he may defile himself. ²⁶After he is cleansed, he must wait seven days. ²⁷On the day he goes into the inner court of the sanctuary to minister in the sanctuary, he is to offer a sin offering for himself, declares the Sovereign LORD.

In the Old Testament scheme of things contact with the dead always made a person ceremonially unclean. Death came into the world because of sin; it was a violent intrusion into the world. Sin makes a person unacceptable to God. A cleansing ceremony was needed. This emphasis and even reinforcement of the concept reminds us in yet another way that God wanted the clean and holy to be separate from the unclean and unholy.

28" 'I am to be the only inheritance the priests have. You are to give them no possession in Israel; I will be their possession. ²⁹They

261

will eat the grain offerings, the sin offerings and the guilt offerings; and everything in Israel devoted to the LORD will belong to them. [30]The best of all the firstfruits and of all your special gifts will belong to the priests. You are to give them the first portion of your ground meal so that a blessing may rest on your household. [31]The priests must not eat anything, bird or animal, found dead or torn by wild animals.

The support for the priest would come from the people. The priests were not to be tied to land and inheritance, but to the Lord. Moreover, the priests were to respect God's will about clean and unclean animals.

Back in Bible times some men of God like the Apostle Paul supported themselves from outside work; Paul was a tentmaker (Acts 18:3). And certain religious groups today seem to be financially more capable of reaching out to the world because they do not have paid clergy. Yet there is precedent in the Scriptures for supporting our spiritual leaders and enabling them to carry out this work as their full-time occupation. This portion of Ezekiel reminds us that God's ancient people supported the priesthood while it carried out its duties at the temple. St. Paul indicated he was an exception rather than the rule: "Don't you know that those who work in the temple get their food from the temple, and those who serve at the altar share in what is offered on the altar? In the same way, the Lord has commanded that those who preach the gospel should receive their living from the gospel" (1 Corinthians 9:13,14). Jesus himself spoke in similar terms. When he sent out seventy-two disciples to preach, he told them, "When you enter a town and are welcomed, eat what is set before you" (Luke 10:8).

Division of the Land

45 " 'When you allot the land as an inheritance, you are to present to the LORD a portion of the land as a sacred district,

25,000 cubits long and 20,000 cubits wide; the entire area will be holy. [2]Of this, a section 500 cubits square is to be for the sanctuary, with 50 cubits around it for open land. [3]In the sacred district, measure off a section 25,000 cubits long and 10,000 cubits wide. In it will be the sanctuary, the Most Holy Place. [4]It will be the sacred portion of the land for the priests, who minister in the sanctuary and who draw near to minister before the LORD. It will be a place for their houses as well as a holy place for the sanctuary. [5]An area 25,000 cubits long and 10,000 cubits wide will belong to the Levites, who serve in the temple, as their possession for towns to live in.

In Jesus' day the temple area in Jerusalem was rather small — perhaps 500 yards square. By contrast, the area allocated for sacred purposes in Ezekiel's vision was immense — 25,000 cubits by 20,000 cubits, something like six by seven miles. This roughly square area was to be divided into three parallel strips. (See map inset on page 188.) In the center of the middle strip of land stood the sanctuary. By locating his house in the center, God seems to be indicating that man's central business is the worship of God.

Around this central section was a portion of land reserved for the priests, the ones who conducted the services, offering the blood sacrifices to mediate between sinful people and a holy God. The northernmost of the three strips of land was to belong to the Levites, those who assisted the priests in the worship services. In this new idealized arrangement the Lord wanted a section set aside for those who served him in public worship, so they could live near their place of work. The 50 cubits around the sanctuary were an open area indicating the separation of the holy from the ordinary.

Ezekiel's stylized use of numbers underscores the fact that we are dealing with a symbolic representation of an ideal goal to which the prophet was pointing the people as a focus for their hopes and dreams. This was intended to comfort them in their situation. "Think of what it would be like if we were back there and things were like this," Ezekiel was saying. He was trying to get the people to think, "We want to get back home." For some of them, dreaming of this ideal produced the desire.

Since every believer is a priest of God (1 Peter 2:9), we all actively take part in our New Testament worship. It not only gives us an opportunity to thank God for what he has done for us, but it also gives us an opportunity to publicly proclaim his gospel. In Ezekiel's idealized temple setting those serving the Lord were given land close to the sanctuary, to enable them to function more easily. In our world, God's priests (that is, all his people) are not always so privileged, but have to move here and there at the whim of the company which employs them. A question God's priests may want to ask when contemplating a move is: "Will this move be a help or a detriment to my worship and my witness as a priest of God?"

⁶" 'You are to give the city as its property an area 5,000 cubits wide and 25,000 cubits long, adjoining the sacred portion; it will belong to the whole house of Israel.

The strip of land to the south of the sanctuary was to be occupied by "the city." The old city of Jerusalem which the exiles remembered as their home contained within its city limits the temple area. The new Jerusalem envisioned by Ezekiel would be adjacent to the temple, in an area belonging not to one tribe, but to the entire nation.

The sanctuary, the dwelling place of the Lord, was to be separate from the rest of the city, where the secular ruler dwelled. Although this seems normal enough to us, to the

Old Testament person the idea of the temple in a portion outside the capital city of Jerusalem would have been unknown and not understood.

Again the picturesque and symbolic must have been the reason for this arrangement. The separation of the city from the location of the temple reinforced the idea that the relationship between the people and their God was basically spiritual, not dependent on a particular location of worship or a particular building in a particular city. It also guaranteed that the worship of God could be conducted with as little disturbance and interruption as possible.

⁷" 'The prince will have the land bordering each side of the area formed by the sacred district and the property of the city. It will extend westward from the west side and eastward from the east side, running lengthwise from the western to the eastern border parallel to one of the tribal portions. ⁸This land will be his possession in Israel. And my princes will no longer oppress my people but will allow the house of Israel to possess the land according to their tribes.

⁹" 'This is what the Sovereign LORD says: You have gone far enough, O princes of Israel! Give up your violence and oppression and do what is just and right. Stop dispossessing my people, declares the Sovereign LORD. ¹⁰You are to use accurate scales, an accurate ephah and an accurate bath. ¹¹The ephah and the bath are to be the same size, the bath containing a tenth of a homer and the ephah a tenth of a homer; the homer is to be the standard measure for both. ¹²The shekel is to consist of twenty gerahs. Twenty shekels plus twenty-five shekels plus fifteen shekels equal one mina.

To the east and the west of the sacred square were areas of land assigned to the prince, land from which the king and his court would be supported. The split between the spiritual function of the priests and the secular function of the kings is apparent. Since this generous allotment of land to the secu-

265

lar rulers would have supported them, there would be no reason for them to appropriate land as Ahab did from Naboth (1 Kings 21:1-16). God's hand of responsibility still was there. He referred to the secular leaders of this people as "my princes" because he still considered secular government authority to be a blessing from him, even if the people at the head of the government were corrupt.

God did, however, warn against the kind of corruption which had occurred in the past. Ezekiel mentioned a number of ancient weights and measures. Some were rather large, such as the homer which was fifty gallons; others were small, such as the shekel which was a weight of less than half an ounce. Whether dealing with big or little quantities God looks for accuracy and honesty.

Since God has given to government the special function of protecting its citizens and to his church the special function of transmitting his message, it is a distinct and uncommon blessing to be living in a society where these two institutions are clearly separated from one another. When a government is fulfilling its assignment, God's people are able to worship and witness in a society of peace and order. And when God's people fulfill their assignment, society is better off because of the lives God's people lead. But when government gets entangled in the work of the people of God, the message of the Lord is being handled by those who are not qualified. The purity of God's message has to suffer. And when the church tries to get involved in running the government, it often tries to impose godly standards on people who have blocked the Lord out of their lives, people who are not motivated by the gospel of Christ. God's law doesn't work as a guide in that case. In the process, God's law is not allowed to function as a curb to society as it should.

266

Offerings and Holy Days

¹³" 'This is the special gift you are to offer: a sixth of an ephah from each homer of wheat and a sixth of an ephah from each homer of barley. ¹⁴The prescribed portion of oil, measured by the bath, is a tenth of a bath from each cor (which consists of ten baths or one homer, for ten baths are equivalent to a homer). ¹⁵Also one sheep is to be taken from every flock of two hundred from the well-watered pastures of Israel. These will be used for the grain offerings, burnt offerings and fellowship offerings to make atonement for the people, declares the Sovereign LORD. ¹⁶All the people of the land will participate in this special gift for the use of the prince in Israel. ¹⁷It will be the duty of the prince to provide the burnt offerings, grain offerings and drink offerings at the festivals, the New Moons and the Sabbaths — at all the appointed feasts of the house of Israel. He will provide the sin offerings, grain offerings, burnt offerings and fellowship offerings to make atonement for the house of Israel.

After describing the location of the new sanctuary, God now gave Ezekiel a series of ordinances for regulating the worship there. The offerings for the worship were to be provided by the people. The amount was to be based on their income — about 2% of the grain; 1% of the olive oil; ½ of 1% of their flocks. For a discussion of the various types of offerings see chapter 43:18-27. In the new Jerusalem the prince was to be the provider of the items of worship. The people would give him portions of their income, and he would use these offerings in providing the sacrificial animals. The drink offering was the wine poured out over the sacrifice in token of the worshiper's gratitude to God.

¹⁸" 'This is what the Sovereign LORD says: In the first month on the first day you are to take a young bull without defect and purify the sanctuary. ¹⁹The priest is to take some of the blood of the sin offering and put it on the doorposts of the temple, on the four

267

corners of the upper ledge of the altar and on the gateposts of the inner court. ²⁰You are to do the same on the seventh day of the month for anyone who sins unintentionally or through ignorance; so you are to make atonement for the temple.

²¹" 'In the first month on the fourteenth day you are to observe the Passover, a feast lasting seven days, during which you shall eat bread made without yeast. ²²On that day the prince is to provide a bull as a sin offering for himself and for all the people of the land. ²³Every day during the seven days of the Feast he is to provide seven bulls and seven rams without defect as a burnt offering to the LORD, and a male goat for a sin offering. ²⁴He is to provide as a grain offering an ephah for each bull and an ephah for each ram, along with a hin of oil for each ephah.

²⁵" 'During the seven days of the Feast, which begins in the seventh month on the fifteenth day, he is to make the same provision for sin offerings, burnt offerings, grain offerings and oil.

Here the Lord mentions three of the most familiar Jewish feasts: New Year, Passover and Tabernacles (verse 25). Why the other Old Testament festivals were not included we are not told. The fact that God specified worship times, locations and procedures may seem restrictive, but it made things easier in another way. The Old Testament believers didn't have to make decisions as to whether or not to worship in a particular way, at a particular place, at a particular time. God had told them specifically how and when and where and what.

Our New Testament freedom places on us the responsibility for deciding the frequency, time, location and mode of worship. For us worship celebrations at festival times are not mandated by the Lord, but done by popular demand. The abuse of our freedom occurs when we fail to use opportunities to worship God, whenever or wherever those opportunities are offered.

46 " 'This is what the Sovereign LORD says: The gate of the inner court facing east is to be shut on the six working days, but on the Sabbath day and on the day of the New Moon it is to be opened. ²The prince is to enter from the outside through the portico of the gateway and stand by the gatepost. The priests are to sacrifice his burnt offering and his fellowship offerings. He is to worship at the threshold of the gateway and then go out, but the gate will not be shut until evening. ³On the Sabbaths and New Moons the people of the land are to worship in the presence of the LORD at the entrance to that gateway. ⁴The burnt offering the prince brings to the LORD on the Sabbath day is to be six male lambs and a ram, all without defect. ⁵The grain offering given with the ram is to be an ephah, and the grain offering with the lambs is to be as much as he pleases, along with a hin of oil for each ephah. ⁶On the day of the New Moon he is to offer a young bull, six lambs and a ram, all without defect. ⁷He is to provide as a grain offering one ephah with the bull, one ephah with the ram, and with the lambs as much as he wants to give, along with a hin of oil with each ephah. ⁸When the prince enters, he is to go in through the portico of the gateway, and he is to come out the same way.

The inner east gate was closed out of reverence for the Lord who had entered there (44:1-3). Although the prince did not act as a worship leader, he was the only one who had the privilege of observing the priest at this proximity. This indicated the privileged state he had as the head of the secular society and as the channel of God's blessings to the restored people of God. Because of his position of responsibility, he was given the opportunity for a special expression of his relationship with the God of his people.

An ephah was five gallons and a hin about four quarts. These measurements were used in the various offerings. Each of the offerings expressed a different facet of the people's relation to God. The burnt offering symbolized complete surrender to God. The fellowship offering indicated a willingness to be part of God's family. And the grain offering was an acknowledgment of God's goodness and providence.

⁹" 'When the people of the land come before the LORD at the appointed feasts, whoever enters by the north gate to worship is to go out the south gate; and whoever enters by the south gate is to go out the north gate. No one is to return through the gate by which he entered, but each is to go out the opposite gate. ¹⁰The prince is to be among them, going in when they go in and going out when they go out.

Ezekiel's vision supplied some crowd control measures for the worshipers who would fill the temple on festival days. Public worship needs some direction and order so it doesn't become a disorganized, mass activity which has no meaning because of the confusion caused by the large numbers of people. Although ritual and procedure can get in the way of spiritual worship, a lack of procedure and pattern can cause confusion, and the atmosphere of worship and reverence suffers.

At festival times when everybody worshiped, the prince was to be just another worshiper. Before God all people are equal. All are sinful and in need of forgiveness. All believers are equally acceptable to God in Christ.

¹¹" 'At the festivals and the appointed feasts, the grain offering is to be an ephah with a bull, an ephah with a ram, and with the lambs as much as one pleases, along with a hin of oil for each ephah. ¹²When the prince provides a freewill offering to the LORD — whether a burnt offering or fellowship offerings — the gate facing east is to be opened for him. He shall offer his burnt offering or his fellowship offerings as he does on the Sabbath day. Then he shall go out, and after he has gone out, the gate will be shut.

270

¹³" 'Every day you are to provide a year-old lamb without defect for a burnt offering to the LORD; morning by morning you shall provide it. ¹⁴You are also to provide with it morning by morning a grain offering, consisting of a sixth of an ephah with a third of a hin of oil to moisten the flour. The presenting of this grain offering to the LORD is a lasting ordinance. ¹⁵So the lamb and the grain offering and the oil shall be provided morning by morning for a regular burnt offering.

The limitations on the prince's entrances and exits were lifted when he came to bring a freewill offering. This was a voluntary offering above and beyond what God required.

No explanations are given for the fact that the evening sacrifice (Exodus 29:38-41) is omitted here.

¹⁶" 'This is what the Sovereign LORD says: If the prince makes a gift from his inheritance to one of his sons, it will also belong to his descendants; it is to be their property by inheritance. ¹⁷If, however, he makes a gift from his inheritance to one of his servants, the servant may keep it until the year of freedom; then it will revert to the prince. His inheritance belongs to his sons only; it is theirs. ¹⁸The prince must not take any of the inheritance of the people, driving them off their property. He is to give his sons their inheritance out of his own property, so that none of my people will be separated from his property.' "

The stipulations about land ownership implemented in the Year of Jubilee (Leviticus 25) were to apply to the prince also. Every fiftieth year land went back to the family that originally owned it. The prince would, therefore, have no reason to appropriate land from any of his subjects.

God's laws regarding property are still for our benefit. He doesn't give us the Seventh Commandment — "You shall not steal" — because he doesn't want us to have things. But God does expect us to obtain and use material possessions properly. We are to use them for the needs of our families, to help others in need, to support the government and to support the work of preaching the gospel. If we give away or waste what we need to carry out those activities, it is not pleasing to God. If we take away from somebody else what he needs to carry out those activities, it is a sin against him and against God. God's love and wisdom are always the source of his commandments. He knows what we need and what is best for us.

[19] Then the man brought me through the entrance at the side of the gate to the sacred rooms facing north, which belonged to the priests, and showed me a place at the western end. [20] He said to me, "This is the place where the priests will cook the guilt offering and the sin offering and bake the grain offering, to avoid bringing them into the outer court and consecrating the people."
[21] He then brought me to the outer court and led me around to its four corners, and I saw in each corner another court. [22] In the four corners of the outer court were enclosed courts, forty cubits long and thirty cubits wide; each of the courts in the four corners was the same size. [23] Around the inside of each of the four courts was a ledge of stone, with places for fire built all around under the ledge. [24] He said to me, "These are the kitchens where those who minister at the temple will cook the sacrifices of the people."

After listing the sacrificial offerings, the holy days of the new festival cycle and the laws governing worship, Ezekiel's angelic guide showed him the kitchens in the inner court, where the offerings were to be cooked and baked. Everything had its proper place. The preparation for the sacrificial worship was done in specific locations so that the worship service could be conducted properly, God's people edified, and God glorified. Once again the thought was expressed that if the priests mingled with the people as they carried out their sacred acts, it would obliterate the distinction between the sacred and the ordinary (also 44:19). This could only result in loss of respect for the priests and their sacred functions.

Holy Land and City
The River from the Temple

47 The man brought me back to the entrance of the temple, and I saw water coming out from the threshold of the temple toward the east (for the temple faced east). The water was coming down from under the south side of the temple, south of the altar. ²He then brought me out through the north gate and led me around the outside to the outer gate facing east, and the water was flowing from the south side.

³As the man went eastward with a measuring line in his hand, he measured off a thousand cubits and then led me through the water that was ankle-deep. ⁴He measured off another thousand cubits and led me through water that was knee-deep. He measured off another thousand and led me through water that was up to the waist. ⁵He measured off another thousand, but now it was a river that I could not cross, because the water had risen and was deep enough to swim in — a river that no one could cross. ⁶He asked me, "Son of man, do you see this?"

The angelic guide brought Ezekiel's tour of the new temple to an end by again leading him into the inner court. When we read the description of what he saw, the symbolism of this entire presentation of the ideal temple, the ideal division of the land, and the ideal worship becomes very apparent here. Ezekiel described a river flowing out from the temple to which the God of grace had returned (43:2-5). The river represented the blessings which flow forth from the Lord. God's blessings flow out into the world and multiply as they are transmitted by his people. The blessings get deeper and more abundant. Psalm 46:4 makes

273

use of similar imagery as it depicts the city of God and its river: "There is a river whose streams make glad the city of God, the holy place where the Most High dwells."

For the exiles looking ahead and wishing they were back home, this vision said, "At that time the Lord's blessings will again be able to flow out from among you. These blessings will become deeper and deeper as the Lord will again work more and more obviously among you his people." What a blessed state to look forward to! What an incentive to keep alive the desire to go home! No wonder the Lord had Ezekiel transmit this vision of perfection to the exiles.

Then he led me back to the bank of the river. ⁷When I arrived there, I saw a great number of trees on each side of the river. ⁸He said to me, "This water flows toward the eastern region and goes down into the Arabah, where it enters the Sea. When it empties into the Sea, the water there becomes fresh. ⁹Swarms of living creatures will live wherever the river flows. There will be large numbers of fish, because this water flows there and makes the salt water fresh; so where the river flows everything will live. ¹⁰Fishermen will stand along the shore; from En Gedi to En Eglaim there will be places for spreading nets. The fish will be of many kinds — like the fish of the Great Sea. ¹¹But the swamps and marshes will not become fresh; they will be left for salt. ¹²Fruit trees of all kinds will grow on both banks of the river. Their leaves will not wither, nor will their fruit fail. Every month they will bear, because the water from the sanctuary flows to them. Their fruit will serve for food and their leaves for healing."

In the natural order of things, when fresh water empties into salt water, the salty contaminates the fresh and the entire body of water becomes salty. Here the exact opposite happened — obviously the result of a miracle of the Lord. The "Sea" is the Dead Sea; the "Great Sea" is the Mediterranean. The Arabah is the Jordan Valley and its continuation south. En Eglaim and En Gedi are villages on the western shore of the Dead Sea. The swamps and marshes, where the life-giving water did not penetrate, remained sterile.

The blessings of God produce miracles. He showers love on people and they change. His blessings produce life, both physical and spiritual. He can turn the most salt-encrusted, nonproductive people into new, alive, loving, productive, persevering witnesses to Jesus Christ by blessing them with the gospel, just as he could change the salt sea into a fresh lake. The same almighty power enables him to do both.

The Boundaries of the Land

¹³This is what the Sovereign Lord says: "These are the boundaries by which you are to divide the land for an inheritance among the twelve tribes of Israel, with two portions for Joseph. ¹⁴You are to divide it equally among them. Because I swore with uplifted hand to give it to your forefathers, this land will become your inheritance.

But would God's people always have access to the blessings flowing from the new temple, the dwelling place of their reconciled Father? Here Ezekiel is assured that God has established the borders of his people's promised land, in which they will forever live securely.

In the Old Testament, when the nation of Israel conquered and occupied the promised land of Canaan, the land was apportioned among the twelve tribes of Israel, and only among them. No non-Israelite shared in that allotment. It's different with the distribution described by Ezekiel. In the Messianic era all believers, non-Jews as well as Jews, will share equally in the blessings God distributes to his redeemed:

¹⁵"This is to be the boundary of the land:

"On the north side it will run from the Great Sea by the Hethlon road past Lebo Hamath to Zedad, ¹⁶Berothah and Sibraim (which lies on the border between Damascus and Hamath), as far as Hazer Hatticon, which is on the border of Hauran. ¹⁷The boundary will extend from the sea to Hazar Enan, along the northern border of Damascus, with the border of Hamath to the north. This will be the north boundary.

¹⁸"On the east side the boundary will run between Hauran and Damascus, along the Jordan between Gilead and the land of Israel, to the eastern sea and as far as Tamar. This will be the east boundary.

¹⁹"On the south side it will run from Tamar as far as the waters of Meribah Kadesh, then along the Wadi ⌊of Egypt⌋ to the Great Sea. This will be the south boundary.

²⁰"On the west side, the Great Sea will be the boundary to a point opposite Lebo Hamath. This will be the west boundary.

²¹"You are to distribute this land among yourselves according to the tribes of Israel. ²²You are to allot it as an inheritance for yourselves and for the aliens who have settled among you and who have children. You are to consider them as native-born Israelites; along with you they are to be allotted an inheritance among the tribes of Israel. ²³In whatever tribe the alien settles, there you are to give him his inheritance," declares the Sovereign LORD.

In God's redeemed, restored church all share equally in the privileges. One of the plagues afflicting Christian congregations today is that some members consider themselves superior to others and dare to treat others as outsiders. People who are new to the congregation are not always made to feel welcome. And why not? Perhaps because they're different from the majority of members, perhaps because they're from another part of the world, or because they're of a different race or social class from the majority of the membership. God makes it clear that he wants his message of love and forgiveness to be channeled by us to all people without prejudice or preference.

The Division of the Land

48 "These are the tribes, listed by name: At the northern frontier, Dan will have one portion; it will follow the Hethlon road to Lebo Hamath; Hazar Enan and the northern border of Damascus next to Hamath will be part of its border from the east side to the west side.

²"Asher will have one portion; it will border the territory of Dan from east to west.

³"Naphtali will have one portion; it will border the territory of Asher from east to west.

⁴"Manasseh will have one portion; it will border the territory of Naphtali from east to west.

⁵"Ephraim will have one portion; it will border the territory of Manasseh from east to west.

⁶"Reuben will have one portion; it will border the territory of Ephraim from east to west.

⁷"Judah will have one portion; it will border the territory of Reuben from east to west.

⁸"Bordering the territory of Judah from east to west will be the portion you are to present as a special gift. It will be 25,000 cubits wide, and its length from east to west will equal one of the tribal portions; the sanctuary will be in the center of it.

⁹"The special portion you are to offer to the LORD will be 25,000 cubits long and 10,000 cubits wide. ¹⁰This will be the sacred portion for the priests. It will be 25,000 cubits long on the north side, 10,000 cubits wide on the west side, 10,000 cubits wide on the east side and 25,000 cubits long on the south side. In the center of it will be the sanctuary of the LORD. ¹¹This will be for the consecrated priests, the Zadokites, who were faithful in serving me and did not go astray as the Levites did when the Israelites went astray. ¹²It will be a special gift to them from the

sacred portion of the land, a most holy portion, bordering the territory of the Levites.

¹³"Alongside the territory of the priests, the Levites will have an allotment 25,000 cubits long and 10,000 cubits wide. Its total length will be 25,000 cubits and its width 10,000 cubits. ¹⁴They must not sell or exchange any of it. This is the best of the land and must not pass into other hands, because it is holy to the LORD.

¹⁵"The remaining area, 5,000 cubits wide and 25,000 long, will be for the common use of the city, for houses and for pastureland. The city will be in the center of it ¹⁶and will have these measurements: the north side 4,500 cubits, the south side 4,500 cubits, the east side 4,500 cubits, and the west side 4,500 cubits. ¹⁷The pastureland for the city will be 250 cubits on the north, 250 cubits on the south, 250 cubits on the east, and 250 cubits on the west. ¹⁸What remains of the area, bordering on the sacred portion and running the length of it, will be 10,000 cubits on the east side and 10,000 cubits on the west side. Its produce will supply food for the workers of the city. ¹⁹The workers from the city who farm it will come from all the tribes of Israel. ²⁰The entire portion will be a square, 25,000 cubits on each side. As a special gift you will set aside the sacred portion, along with the property of the city.

²¹"What remains on both sides of the area formed by the sacred portion and the city property will belong to the prince. It will extend eastward from the 25,000 cubits of the sacred portion to the eastern border, and westward from the 25,000 cubits to the western border. Both these areas running the length of the tribal portions will belong to the prince, and the sacred portion with the temple sanctuary will be in the center of them. ²²So the property of the Levites and the property of the city will lie in the center of the area that belongs to the prince. The area belonging to the prince will lie between the border of Judah and the border of Benjamin.

²³"As for the rest of the tribes: Benjamin will have one portion; it will extend from the east side to the west side.

²⁴"Simeon will have one portion; it will border the territory of Benjamin from east to west.

²⁵"Issachar will have one portion; it will border the territory of Simeon from east to west.

²⁶"Zebulun will have one portion; it will border the territory of Issachar from east to west.

²⁷"Gad will have one portion; it will border the territory of Zebulun from east to west.

²⁸"The southern boundary of Gad will run south from Tamar to the waters of Meribah Kadesh, then along the Wadi⌊of Egypt⌋ to the Great Sea.

²⁹"This is the land you are to allot as an inheritance to the tribes of Israel, and these will be their portions," declares the Sovereign LORD.

As the description of the miraculous river in chapter 47 was symbolic of the Messianic era, so we have here a symbolic description of the new division of the promised land.

The undefined strips of land, seemingly all of the same configuration and of the same size for each tribe regardless of the numbers of people in the tribe or geophysical difficulties in divisions, again point to the symbolic nature of this whole presentation. (See map on page 188.) The point is that in the Messianic era all of God's people will have a portion under God. All — non-Jews as well as Jews — will share equal privileges, blessings and obligations under God in the new Jerusalem.

The Gates of the City

³⁰"These will be the exits of the city: Beginning on the north side, which is 4,500 cubits long, ³¹the gates of the city will be named after the tribes of Israel. The three gates on the north side will be the gate of Reuben, the gate of Judah and the gate of Levi.

³²"On the east side, which is 4,500 cubits long, will be three gates: the gate of Joseph, the gate of Benjamin and the gate of Dan.

³³"On the south side, which measures 4,500 cubits, will be three gates: the gate of Simeon, the gate of Issachar and the gate of Zebulun.

³⁴"On the west side, which is 4,500 cubits long, will be three gates: the gate of Gad, the gate of Asher and the gate of Naphtali.

³⁵"The distance all around will be 18,000 cubits.

"And the name of the city from that time on will be:

THE LORD IS THERE."

All of God's people will have equal access (gates) to the city. That is, all can enter the presence of God.

John's visions in the book of Revelation are based to a large degree on the prophecy of Ezekiel. John knew the Old Testament. The Lord must have used John's knowledge as he transmitted to him the visions regarded as the last book of the Bible. The vision of the new Jerusalem and the river of life (Revelation 21 and 22) have obvious parallels to Ezekiel's visions. But John could add the details about the Messiah whom he had known and loved, about the New Testament church whose growth he had observed, and about the perfection of all this symbolism in eternity, aspects which Ezekiel could see only dimly.

With chapter 48 Ezekiel's message has come full circle. Jerusalem had once been the dwelling place of the Lord. But because of the unfaithfulness of his people God had withdrawn his gracious presence. He had appeared to Ezekiel in Babylon to explain what all of this meant. Then God had promised restoration and renewal. Ezekiel was given a vision in which the Lord returned to be among his people. The Lord would again be among his people — forever. But it was still a vision.

In one sense we can say the vision has been fulfilled. THE LORD IS THERE was actually physically fulfilled in the person of the Messiah, Jesus of Nazareth. God incarnate came and lived among his people. Yet we know that none of the perfection of the worship, temple or land in the vision was actually attained. Why not? The sinfulness and selfishness and unfaithfulness of men ruined it again and again.

So in another sense we are in a position no different from that of Ezekiel. We are waiting for a time when we can say, "THE LORD IS THERE" in a very apparent, observable way. There will come a time when our worship of the Lord will be perfect. That was the perspective of the Apostle John when he received and recorded the Revelation. He had personally seen the fulfillment of the promises of the Messiah among the people. He could have said, "THE LORD IS THERE." But John didn't see perfection during his lifetime. So with the Lord's help he looked ahead and said exactly what Ezekiel was saying about a future time: "I saw the Holy City, the new Jerusalem, coming down out of heaven from God. . . . And I heard a voice from the throne saying, 'Now the dwelling of God is with men, and he will live with them. They will be his people, and God himself will be with them and be their God' " (Revelation 21:2,3).

It is to that ultimate fulfillment of all God's promises that we look as Christians. As we struggle with sin and the consequences of sin in this world, we look forward to the time when our worship and service will be perfect. We take courage knowing that even now Christ is with us as he has promised, "Surely I am with you always" (Matthew 28:20). At the same time we anticipate a full view of the glory of the Lord. When he returns on Judgment Day all people will bow before him and acknowledge him as Lord. "You will know that I am the LORD," he declares.

And so we wait for the Messiah-Shepherd to come and take us, his sheep, to be with him forever. It will be our endless source of joy to know that he will never leave us. We can always be confident that

THE LORD IS THERE.